# CROSSFIRE

## Witness in the Clinton Investigation

By

# L.D. BROWN

*BLACK FOREST PRESS*
*San Diego, California*
*April, 1999*
*First Edition*

L.D. Brown has been a witness to almost all the alleged offenses circling around Bill Clinton in Arkansas: misuse of state funds for sexual liasons, Whitewater, illegal campaign fundraising and bribery, as well as cocaine use and cocaine smuggling. And through his ultimate cooperation with prosecutors and congressional investigators, Brown has learned the inside story on Robert Fiske's and Kenneth Starr's operations and on congressional hearings. But most of all, L.D. Brown can tell the story of the methods used by the Clinton White House to control potentially damaging witnesses.

Most of what is written in this book has been told under penalty of perjury to investigators for Congress and the Office of Independent Counsel. Documentation for many events has been included in an appendix. However incredible some details may seem, they are backed up by evidence.

When the investigation of President Clinton started, Brown came under fire from both sides: from the Clintonistas who wanted him to keep his mouth shut and from the "Vast Right-Wing Conspiracy" who wanted him to say what they wanted to hear. With this book he returns the fire—in both directions.

*This book will answer the questions:*

- What did the C. I. A. know about cocaine smuggling at Mena, Arkansas, and when did it know it?
- What did Bill Clinton know about cocaine smuggling at Mena, Arkansas?
- Who was Brown sent to assassinate in Mexico?
- What is the secret relationship between Bill Clinton and George Bush?
- What is the relationship between Mike Wallace and the C. I. A.?
- What Democrat U.S. Senator overheard the President threatening to "sick the I.R.S." on L.D. Brown?
- What Republican U.S. Senator promised L.D. Brown a job in return for cooperation?
- What clandestine operation of the White House National Security Council was aimed at diverting revenues from food aid to support the Irish Republican Army?
- What two specific intelligence jobs was L.D. Brown offered by the White House in return for his silence?
- Who asked Brown to collaborate with James Carville and for what purpose?
- From whom did Brown collect money as Bill Clinton's "bag man"?
- How did Brown end up receiving money from the "Vast Right-Wing Conspiracy"?
- What White House employee, other than Monica Lewinsky, was transferred to the Pentagon when her affair with the President was revealed in court?

# CROSSFIRE

Witness in the Clinton Investigation

BY

# L.D. BROWN

PUBLISHED IN THE UNITED STATES OF AMERICA
BY
BLACK FOREST PRESS
539 TELEGRAPH CANYON ROAD
BOX 521
CHULA VISTA, CA 91910
(619) 656-8048

Disclaimer

This document is an original work of the author. It may include reference to information commonly known or freely available to the general public. Any
resemblance to other published information is purely coincidental.
The author has in no way attempted to use material not of his own
origination. Black Forest Press disclaims any association with or
responsibility for the ideas, opinions or facts as expressed by the
author of this book.

Printed in the United States of America
Library of Congress
Cataloging-in-Publication

ISBN:1-58275-003-3

# CONTENTS

**CHAPTER**

"For Becky"

# PREFACE

"L. D., you're a smart guy. Do *you* consider oral sex adultery?" Bill Clinton's first intimate conversation with me was indeed a curious one. Before I reveal how I answered that, let me explain how two men from such similar yet in many ways diverse backgrounds became close enough to one another to ask each other questions such as that.

Fifteen years, two independent counsels, grand juries and congressional committees later my wife and I regret the first day we ever met Bill and Hillary Clinton. My wife of fourteen years, the former Becky McCoy, was Chelsea Clinton's nanny when we met at the Governor's Mansion in 1983. I was in the middle of what I thought, at the time, were the best years of my life. Little did I know those coalitions my wife and I would build, the deep friendships we would share, might cause our family severe pain and hardship when they would be dissolved. We are not victims, not in any sense. Although we were young and impressionable during the years we were close to the Clintons, we knew full well something was deeply wrong in the way they lived their lives, both personally and politically. Most shocking of all was how they used their friends as tools for their personal gain. When they were through with them, they chewed them up and spit them out, discarded as useless and never to be considered again. When the flavor of the relationship was gone, the Clintons would leave you in their wake.

*i*

I saw it happen many times—but I never thought it would happen to me.

✱    ✱    ✱

Though several years my senior, Bill and I share a common bond in coming from somewhat disrupted childhoods, a detail of which Bill would later try and use against me. My family was not all 'Leave it to Beaver.' This characteristic we shared would cause us to have the commitment of developing close relationships with our children. He too came from a violently broken home. We shared the reluctance to confront our private demons and treated them with a sort of obsessive, compulsive behavior that extended to our malfeasance in marriage and lust for political power.

With all the disregard for our personal and political integrity, we loved our young daughters. We were committed to making their lives free of the torment we had both faced growing up. His love of Chelsea would transcend all the personal and political hell he felt and was tortured by in his life. I knew the feeling and we talked about it often. As I will reveal, Bill has a terrific capacity for compassion, especially for people with whom he empathizes. Bill Clinton is a very complex man. His emotions can run wild ranging from deep compassion while at the next minute he is angry, frustrated and childish. His politics have always been the same. The Bill Clinton I have known and watched for fifteen years has always been running for President of the United States. Every note and speech he made, every political contribution he received and friendship he cultivated from his very first political campaign has been part of his carefully orchestrated presidential campaign.

The circumstances of my coming forward not only to write this book but to openly speak out about the Clintons involved a bit of happenstance. After the Clintons were elected to the White House, two Arkansas State troopers came forward in late 1993 and told what they knew about Bill and Hillary, mostly all of which was negative.  Larry Patterson and Roger Perry had been featured in the *American Spectator* magazine in an article by investigative journalist David Brock.  The pair detailed Bill's liaisons with women, Hillary's tirades and other shenanigans they witnessed while being assigned to the Governor's Security Detail.  The two worked at the Mansion after I did and did not have any first-hand knowledge of the Whitewater scandals but nevertheless their revelations sparked a media frenzy.

During the course of their debriefings, Patterson particularly told Brock and writer Bill Rempel of the *Los Angeles Times* of damaging information he knew I possessed about the Clintons.  Larry had worked with me when I served as President of the State Police union where we shared stories of the Clintons we knew from our service at the Mansion.  Soon after Larry and Roger went public, I received a telephone call at the state police from Danny Wattenberg of the *American Spectator*—he had done his homework.

At this point in my career, I was assigned to the elite special investigations squad in the Director's Office at the state police.  A unit consisting of only three investigators, we investigated public officials and elected officials for crimes allegedly committed during the course of their public service.  I was in the throes of a sensitive investigation involving the possible misappropriation of state school funds, which pitted me against Clinton's successor in Arkansas, Governor Jim Guy Tucker.  Tucker wanted me, ironically enough, to place blame on the previous Clinton administrations for the mishandling of the funds.  My job as a criminal investigator was not to place political blame but to find the facts, if any, that may lead to criminal prosecutions.  I refused Tucker's demands to politicize the case.

I was already in a precarious predicament with the current governor and I didn't need the former one, who was now president, going after me.  But Wattenberg and Rempel had compiled corroborating information on what they by then knew I possessed of damaging information on the Clintons. Wattenberg had gained access to a woman from Plano, Texas named Joyce Miller who told him I had approached her while working for Clinton and asked her where she was staying in Little Rock. The young school teacher was in the city for a dance which Bill and I attended and was giving her account for the record in response to the news stories the troopers had given. Wattenberg was going to write the story with or without my comments.

During this time frame the Whitewater investigation was in its infancy. My partner, Danny Harkins, and I were sitting in our office at the Arkansas State Police headquarters in west Little Rock on Valentine's Day, 1994. I had been talking off the record with Wattenberg and had met with Rempel at the Excelsior Hotel in Little Rock. Rempel had assured me the Clintons were trying to destroy me with slanderous remarks. He said when he asked the White House about a comment actually made by someone other than me, Betsey Wright returned his phone call. The first words out of her mouth according to Rempel were, "L. D. Brown's a goddamned liar!"

As we sat at our desks, Danny and I reminisced about how, several months earlier, we had sat in the same office and read the account of David Hale and the beginnings of what would later become known under the collective title of 'Whitewater.' Hale claimed to have been pressured by then-Governor Bill Clinton to lend money from his federally funded institution to Susan McDougal. As I lowered the paper that day I told Danny, "I'm going to be subpoenaed over this." I went on to tell Danny that I was present with Bill one day at the state capitol as he admonished Hale with words to the effect of, "We need to raise some money. You've got to help us out." Little did I know at the time that this seemingly innocuous conversation would be so important to jump-starting the Whitewater investigation that is still ongoing today.

Danny and I had turned to other matters when the telephone rang from the secretary's office. As I answered line two, I heard a familiar voice in that of Warner Calhoun, an F.B.I. agent who had been called in to work with then-Independent Counsel Robert Fiske. "L. D., we need you to come over to the office. We want you to talk to us about David Hale, Dan Lasater and Clinton."

I would eventually talk with the Independent Counsel and Congress, but only after threats, offers of bribes and intimidation had taken their toll. But first, how I got to that point.

# CHAPTER ONE
## Shared Humble Beginnings

I grew up in Pine Bluff, Arkansas, a city somewhat larger than Bill's native Hot Springs. Hot Springs was a resort city my family would visit when I was a child for vacation when we could afford it. I was born in Greenville, Mississippi while my father was working a job there. My brother Dwayne, three years my senior, grew up with as keen an interest in politics as I did. We all grieved with my mother at the loss of John Kennedy. I would not know until many years later how that same event had affected Bill's life. Our many conversations, recounted later in this book, revealed his quest to emulate his idol.

In an environment of white and black bathrooms and seg-regated schools, I took up journalism in high school and became the editor of my school newspaper—ultimately winning a high school press association award at a conference in Hot Springs for an editorial on race relations.

But it was an incident that occurred when I was sixteen years old that would change my life forever and years later serve as the basis for forging a common bond between Bill and me. My parents never really got along well. My father, Bobby Brown, who worked at the local paper mill, did not make much money but we lived what I thought at the time was a middle class life. We had a modest two-bedroom frame home in a neighborhood built for the soldiers of World War II and my mother Joann worked at home. But she had too much time on her hands as she watched the soap operas every day while we were at school. When I would come home at the end of the day, I would hear her telling someone on the telephone that "Jenny was killed today" or "Debbie was having John's baby and they weren't even married." I wouldn't learn until hours later that she was discussing fictional characters she watched every day on television.

My mom was a worrier as well. It was at the middle of the Vietnam War and my brother Dwayne was draft age. Even though he had been accepted into Arkansas State University, my mother was constantly worried he may somehow be drafted. Our family would watch Walter Cronkite every night on the evening news and see and hear the death tolls of American boys. My cousin's husband had been blown to pieces in Vietnam and we all attended the funeral in rural south Arkansas. My uncle was never the same after he had to identify what was left of his son-in-law. Boys just one year older than my brother were being killed every day and my mother thought he may be next. Bill and I, in later years, would talk of how we had been affected by the war. One day at the Governor's Mansion, he would give me a book later titled *The Handbook of the Conscientious Objector*, a well worn one at that.

In many ways Dwayne was the exact opposite of me. My Dad and I had hunted ever since I was old enough to hold a gun but Dwayne never did. He would be lost in the military and my mother knew it.

Dwayne left for the university in the fall of 1971, leaving me alone with my parents who increasingly disagreed on just about everything. There was never a drop of beer or liquor in our home to aggravate the situation, they just didn't get along and I never quite knew why. I knew they dearly loved each other. They had first met at a sorghum mill while they were both just children. They both were children of the Depression and lived in rural southern Arkansas.

Pearl Harbor Day would be the mental image I would have to this day of the tragedy that occurred in my home on that night in 1971. It was not a particular matter that my parents were upset about, but this time the argument escalated. I would later as a policeman witness many such altercations between spouses. I tried to intervene when one of them pulled an old shotgun from a gun rack on the wall. As I stepped in between the two of them, the gun fired. Events like these happen in slow motion just like in the movies. The sound of the blast was deafening inside our small home. The smoke was intense and I felt a burning sensation down my arm.

When it was over my mother was gone. Bill would later almost cry himself every time I would mention my mother and her untimely death that night. Even though I had not told him directly of the incident, we would talk in depth of how we both overcome the hardships that we had suffered in our early years. Bill, too, had lost a parent. He lost his father even before he could know him. When we talked of it I knew it was as traumatic to him as my loss was to me. That made it the more disgusting when he turned the events of that night around in an effort to discredit me during the Whitewater investigation. More on that incredible event later.

My father and I went to live with his parents until I finished high school and went off to college at the University of Arkansas at Fayetteville, where Dwayne had transferred the year before. We maintained contact with my father who, understandably, was never quite the same. We didn't hunt together anymore. It was as if I had lost both parents that night.

But at least my dad was still there. Bill envied me that I had a father while growing up. He missed the words of wisdom that a father would give his son and I would share the few nuggets my father had given to me. Bill more than anything admired my father from afar since he had fought in a war—a

'decent war' other than Vietnam. My father had fought in the
Korean War and had won a medal for heroism that I wore while
playing army as a kid. I wore to tatters the medal and the news
clipping from his hometown newspaper that told of how he had
saved his comrade's life as the Communist Chinese overran
their position on the Yalu River on Thanksgiving Day, 1950.
He carried the man for miles, pursued by the Chinese, before
reaching an aid station. I finally lost the medal since I would
carry it everywhere.

One of the stories my Dad told me concerned race relations.
I had already given Bill the copy of my High School Press
Association award winning editorial on race relations which I
wrote during a time in Pine Bluff, Arkansas in which it was not
popular to do so. I got to that point through an experience and
the resultant advice my Dad gave me.

Bill would have me tell the story to a group of black ministers once and indeed he used the story himself while speaking
of matters such as racial reconciliation.

The event occurred when I was in ninth grade and attending
schools that had just been integrated. The integration broke the
color barriers in south Arkansas that had existed forever. I was
used to the white and black segregated drinking fountains and
rest rooms. When we went to the movie downtown, blacks sat
in the balcony, whites downstairs. At the time the schools were
integrated, we had hardly interacted with blacks at all.

The plan in my school district called for busing white
children to formerly all black Townsend Park Junior High
School. My mother would not have me ride a school bus so
she took me to school every day. The first day of school was
an eventful one for me. A black boy in my class that sat behind
me was an obvious troublemaker. I had a lot of pens and
pencils in a bag and he obviously wanted them. He tried to
take them while I wasn't looking and I told the teacher. He
was furious and said he was going to get even with me. When
the bell rang, I stepped out into the hallway and felt someone
pull my shirt with a force that whirled me around. The boy
tagged me in the right eye. I never saw it coming.

As the school rules required, we were both sent home. I waited anxiously as my Dad came home from work that day not knowing whether or not I would be in trouble. I was outraged that I had had to leave school when I hadn't done anything wrong. I was still mad when I finally told my Dad, "A nigger hit me in the eye, for nothing." Now, my Dad had never used that word and he had never heard me say it either. He didn't scold me or tell me not to say it again. Instead he took me aside and explained the sin of race discrimination in a way I could understand, in a way that would impact me forever.

As I would later share with Bill and those black preachers, my Dad told me the story of the Yalu River in Korea. I thought it strange he was finally talking to me about the war, a subject he had preferred to avoid until now. He told me of the Chinese clanging cymbals and riding horses across the river. It was clear to him and his buddy, who were forward observers in a heavy mortar company, that these people were about to attack. When they relayed word back to the rear, the officers in charge assured that these guys wouldn't dare attack, they were Chinese, not North Koreans.

Later, hundreds of thousands poured over the river and overran the 1st Cavalry position and the entire Eighth Army was in jeopardy. He went on to tell me of seeing some of his buddies being captured or killed. His partner was wounded and he told me how he carried the man many miles before he could receive medical attention. "Douglass," he said with a degree of emotion that I had to yet to see in the man, yet "That man was a colored man." He went on to tell me that when they arrived back at the aid station later, he saw a group of North Korean prisoners, their guns secured in a bundle with wire. "I heard someone yell at me to watch out," he said, his voice still charged with emotion as if the incident happened just yesterday. He turned around to see one of the prisoners charging him with one of the guns tipped with a bayonet. He partially deflected the bayonet but it cut into his left leg leaving a scar he would show me many times. If it were not for one of his buddies shooting the North Korean, I would not be here today. "That man who saved my life, Doug," he said calmly, "was a black man."

My dad idolized Douglas McArthur and his ideas of taking on the Communist Chinese by pursuing them directly across the Yalu River back into China. He had seen so many of his friends captured or killed after the Chinese had overrun their positions that November in 1950. It didn't make any sense to him that the Communists had safe haven in China but could attack across the river into North Korea at will. My dad has never been politically active but he vehemently disagreed with Bill's admiration of Harry Truman. My dad was a McArthur fan so much that he would name me, his second son, after his hero.

I took the lesson of the injustice of racial bigotry from that day with me as I served my twenty-three years in the criminal justice system. I would also pass it on to Bill Clinton who had me retell my lesson and would often use the story himself. He even helped my dad get a job with the Arkansas Revenue Department. I had to remind my dad when I introduced him to Bill not to bring up Harry Truman.

Bill had already completed his higher education and was in Fayetteville, Arkansas in 1973 at the law school when I arrived as an undergraduate. My high school sweetheart, Leslie, and I had decided to get married before we went off to college. At such an early age it was tough working at the work study foreign language lab and attending school full time. I chose to also work at the off-campus liberal newspaper, *The Grapevine*, as Bill prepared for his first race against incumbent Congressman John Paul Hammerschmidt. But his path and mine would converge in Little Rock some ten years later and many miles down the road. At that point, we would swap artifacts of that time in Fayetteville—mine a copy of that editorial and him giving me his copy of Ben Franklin's Autobiography signed 'Bill Clinton—Fayetteville, 1975.' Years later we would be returning to Fayetteville as friends to enjoy the ball games and roam the same streets we once did in another time.

# CHAPTER TWO

## The Road to the Mansion

While Bill was making his way to the governor's office, I was laboring as a state employee. One day I ran into a friend of mine whom I had known from high school. He told me he was working at the state penitentiary near Pine Bluff. He was only one year older than me and I asked him how he got the job. He said they were desperately looking for people and that he just went down and applied. I had transferred from the university at Fayetteville to Pine Bluff and needed a job while attending college at night. To my surprise, they hired me.

The Tucker Prison Unit was located halfway between Little Rock and Pine Bluff by way of the back roads and was about a thirty minute drive from my home. The prison is recognizable to Burt Reynolds fans as the opening scenes of the movie *White Lightning* were shot there. Many of my friends who were guards there were used as extras in the film. I bet I've seen the movie 100 times. It was shown about every Saturday night at the prison.

While first serving as a guard on the tower security and later as an inside guard in the state's corrupt prison system, I developed a more sympathetic attitude towards inmates than most of the prison guards. Many would without cause strike inmates or throw them in solitary confinement on a diet of a bread cake and water. In those days the inmates received regular meals while in the 'hole' only once every three days. The cells were on the old death row and opened into a common hallway with windows that did not even have screens. In the hot summers of Arkansas the mosquitoes from the rice fields surrounding the penitentiary would swarm into the open cages in which the young men were imprisoned. The more incorrigible ones were stripped of their mattresses making their torture that much worse. I eventually moved up to the job of 'Field Sergeant' which required riding a horse ten hours a day, carrying a pistol on my side and supervising some twenty inmates in the soybean fields. It was an awful job for many, but I was excited about it at first. I loved horses and liked being outdoors—and would get my fill of both.

In Arkansas there can be a 100-degree temperature change from the middle of winter to the worst stages of summer. There were many times when the inmates worked in sub-freezing temperatures and more when the sun beat down so hard even we couldn't bear it—and we were on horseback and getting all the water we wanted. The horses were literally one step out of the glue factory. They were bought at auction with the most serious consideration being given to price. Each 'line rider,' as we were called, had two horses to ride on an alternating schedule. Many died due to the heat and overwork and not all were completely broken. Bill later enjoyed the horse stories and told me of how he loved horses when he was a kid. I even took up rodeos on the side since it wasn't much different from the work at the prison and there was some money to be made as well.

One story I told Bill brought out the compassion for the downtrodden that stirred within him. Our hoe squads, or young men who carried hoes and worked in the fields cutting weeds from soybean fields in the fall or cleaning ditch banks in the summer, were made up of mostly younger offenders in an age from 15 years old to their mid-twenties. For the most part, they were just kids—like me. These were the incorrigibles from the larger counties mixed with the first-time offenders from the more rural areas of Arkansas where the court system sentenced a larger percentage of felons to prison. Many times a young man who had committed his first burglary in a small county would get as much prison time as a habitual offender from Little Rock. Make no mistake, they were all convicted felons serving time for rape, murder and the like. One of the men I used to supervise was recently executed for a crime he committed after leaving the Tucker Prison. For many of the young men back then, prison was a training ground on which they honed their criminal skills for a lifetime of crime. That's the way the system worked (or didn't work) back then.

Many of the men had seen hard labor before, but most had never worked a day in their life and that was partially the reason they were there. Preferring thievery to work, many were the castoffs of small town Arkansas, not much to work with when it came time to get them to do hard labor.

There were the inmates who did not respect authority as well. They thought of themselves as 'players' who had somebody else do their work for them on 'the street,' or in other words while they weren't in jail. They quickly learned they weren't so slick, after all they were in the Arkansas State Penitentiary.

Bill listened as if hearing tales of some seventeenth century slave ship as I would later tell him how we would make the stronger, more seasoned inmates do the work of the 'slackers,' the ones who didn't pull their fair share of the work. I explained the inmates had to pull the new guy's work as well as his own would soon 'persuade' the slacker it would be in his best interests to do what we said. The inmates took care of the slackers by administering 'attitude adjustments' in the dormitories at night. A preferred treatment was to put a footlocker lock in a sock and twist the end making for an easily and quickly fashioned deadly weapon. A few pops of the sock to the slacker while he was asleep or not looking, was followed by an admonishment to do his own work the next day. The next day, the slacker would be out with a spring in his step and would at least try to do the tiresome and sometimes dangerous work we had assigned to him.

In those days we 'hoe squad riders,' or as the James Darren song immortalized us, 'long line riders,' had help from armed inmate 'trusties.' Whenever we would need to relieve ourselves, we would call over one of the 'trusties,' unsnap our gun and hand it to him while we got off our horse. The trusty would stay on his horse and watch our inmates for us making sure none came near us. The hoes the inmates carried were razor-sharp as they were continually being filed by an inmate hoe-filer to allow them to cut more efficiently. Some of the inmates were doing two life terms for murder and wouldn't hesitate to try to escape if you gave them a chance. We did have many that tried, but none stayed away for long. If we didn't get them, a farmer would. The miserable weather was also a factor and many who crawled over the fences gave up after spending the first night in the snake infected swamps that surrounded the prison.

Bill thought that the experience was like something out of the old west, a Louie L'Amor story. He loved to hear how, when we called an inmate up to our horse, we made them lay their hoe down and walk up to us on our non-gun side. As an added precaution we would take our pistol out and keep it in our hand while draping it over the saddle horn just in case an inmate tried to jerk us off our horse.

It also amazed Bill that we had two inmates on the perimeter towers around the prison itself armed with high-powered rifles.

They were actually more prone to shooting someone than a free-world guard—in part due to the threat that if they allowed someone to escape, they would have to do the escapee's time as well as their own. It wasn't true, but it was a good bluff.

Bill was fascinated that I trusted convicted murderers with my gun. I told him the lifers were the ones we chose to be trusties since they had the most to prove about being loyal. We used them to staff the dog kennel and to lead the tracking dogs when we had an escape. He was particularly amazed that at the close of every day, as the free-world tower guards watched, I would hand my loaded pistol to an inmate as would every other line rider. He would put them all in an old flour sack and take the guns on his horse to the armory at the front of the prison. To add to Bill's astonishment, that trusty would then give the sack of guns to an inmate who staffed the armory. He would clean the dust of the day from the pistols so we would have them ready for the next trip to the fields.

It was easy for Bill to verify and follow up on my stories since one of my former trusties from the prison worked in a prison detail at the Governor's Mansion while I was there. Gary Clark, a black man, who worked the towers at Tucker Prison during my three years there, later served as the assistant to Ms. Liza, the cook at the Mansion. There was a crew of inmates assigned to the Mansion to cook, clean and maintain the grounds of the Mansion. Gary was a good hand at the Mansion as well as at the prison . Bill and Hillary took to him so well that Hillary once took him to the state capitol to serve cookies to legislators, an event not unnoticed by the media.

Gary, a convicted murderer, later had his life sentence commuted by Bill allowing him to be paroled. This happened even though Bill had stated publicly that first-degree murderers' sentences would not be commuted by him during his term as governor.

\*       \*       \*

The inmates at the prison worked five days a week no matter how cold or hot. There were no 'lay-ins' as the inmates of today's Arkansas prison system get to take for insufferably cold or hot weather . Many of them would just quit. After having to break ice to drain water from the idle rice fields in the winter (many inmates did not have any coats), some just laid down their hoes and said, "Take me in Boss." They preferred the 'hole' and loss of good time they would earn by working to suffering the hard labor. The story that shook Bill was the sad tale of one boy who gave up.

I'll leave the boy's name out of this since his family has suffered enough. The young man was one of the 'slackers,' men that wouldn't work and preferred not to address the hoe squad riders as 'sir,' Mr. Brown, or just 'Boss.' He didn't work for me but for the rider just down from my hoe squad. He was not built for the penitentiary in body or mind. Frail, with glasses that wouldn't stay on as he had to bend over constantly all day, the young man laid down his hoe one day and called it quits. He knew what that meant.

Bill sat riveted as I could see he was vividly recreating the events in his mind like he was reading one of his Le Carré novels. Our boss 'The Captain,' who drove a truck to the fields, handcuffed the man who was clearly defeated mentally and physically. He had given up and was ready for the 'hole.'

I paused and Bill was ready for the next event in the chronology eagerly urging me not to stop with the story just as Chelsea would prod him to continue a child's book after the last page had been turned. He sensed I was still impacted by the incident as I told him how we wondered if the man would come back out the next day. Many inmates would take a day in the 'hole' and come back the next, preferring the open fields and fresh air to the decay of the isolation cells. I noticed the man was not in the squad next to me the following morning as we lined up the inmates to go to the fields. I asked his hoe squad rider if he was still in the 'hole.' "Nope," he replied casually. "Hung himself with his long johns. Won't have to deal with him anymore."

Bill was ashamed of this Arkansas he knew and was fascinated by the first hand accounts of it that I could give him. He was also amazed that I experienced the tragic events of Tucker Penitentiary at such a young age. I was equally amazed that as Governor, he never lifted a finger to reform that system while he had the chance. When he left office, the same corrupt prison officials were in power, officials on which I would eventually work a criminal case involving corruption in office. They were summarily removed from office after I had shown they were involved in self-dealing and other forms of corruption. I was sure that while at Yale as he was singing the praises of the huge watermelons for which Arkansas was famous to Hillary Bill did not, at the same time, share the dark side of a corrupt political system in which the prisons were allowed to fester. A political system he was to embrace. A prison system that is still under investigation for selling tainted blood to Canada and other foreign countries.

The story of how prisoners at the state prison system would sell their blood for money, and how the Arkansas officials looked the other way when the HIV problem came to light, has yet to be told. I will tell my small part here for the first time.

As a state prison guard in the early 1970s, I witnessed inmates being almost forced to get on a bus to travel the one hour trip to the Cummins Unit of the Arkansas Department of Corrections to give blood. As an Arkansas State Police investigator, I investigated the incestuous relationships of state prison officials who urged inmates to give blood in the 1980's, the time frame under investigation now[1].

In actuality, an investigation has not really begun as yet. Royal Canadian Mounted Police Forces have been begging the United States Congress to assist them in their investigations. A focus is on the Arkansas prison system under Bill Clinton. As part of my investigation into the corruption of the system I studied the ties of the then-Director of the prison system, Art Lockhart, and his son who ran the blood donor program. A state grand jury was empaneled, an unusual occurrence in

Arkansas since charges are usually filed directly. Nothing happened and a federal grand jury subsequently indicted Lockhart and others on corruption charges which did not include the blood scandal. I have been contacted by numerous sources already regarding the blood program as it existed under Clinton's regime, but none from United States law enforcement. It remains to be seen if Bill Clinton will be investigated for this as well or if he again gets a pass on what he's 'done for Arkansas.'

I ended up as a narcotics investigator working undercover throughout Arkansas with the Arkansas State Police. I was still married to Leslie at that time and we had a daughter, Jan. I lived in an apartment in Forrest City near Memphis while they stayed in Pine Bluff. I would never have moved them around the state as you never knew when you would be transferred in my line of work.

I looked like the grungy 'Serpico' as narcotics investigators of that era were committed to wearing long hair and beards while sporting ragged army coats in efforts of buying drugs undercover. Many times Bill would ask me to show a friend of his my state police identification card with the photograph of me in the undercover getup. In some of the photos I saw of him when he worked for McGovern in 1972, I saw that he actually chose that sort of look at one time in his life. My experiences would provide the fodder for the many anecdotes I would share with Bill in seeking to satisfy his desire to be included as 'one of the boys.'

Bill particularly enjoyed the stories of undercover work that showed a certain recklessness on my part, stupidity I called it. He enjoyed one story I told him that involved a certain flaunting of authority. My partner in Eastern Arkansas, Jerry Howard, and I were working in the small town of Wynne, Arkansas near Memphis. We had been buying marijuana undercover from a young man and were ready to bust him. With an arrest warrant in hand, we told the local police chief that we would be arriving at the suspect's mobile home to effect the arrest. We requested that he be available outside. The way Jerry and I looked, it may look like a couple of thugs trying to rob someone.

Bill particularly loved this story since I was pushing the edge of the envelope of good sense in my actions, something he has done himself with a vengeance lately. The suspect in this case was a former inmate of Tucker Prison while I was working there as a hoe squad rider. I looked so much different now with the long hair and beard that he never recognized me. Bill sensed a climactic arrest and he was right.

Jerry and I always tried to get the suspects to show us the drugs they might have in their house before we arrested them. This saved us from having to get a search warrant and search the house. We accomplished this by telling the suspect when we arrived that we were there to buy everything he had to sell. The guy retreated into the back of his mobile home and came back with some more marijuana. Jerry and I decided we would spice up the deal by using a new and 'fun' technique to tell the guy we were the police and he was under arrest.

Jerry and I both had undercover Arkansas drivers' licenses. Mine was in the name of Spencer Langley and that was the name this guy knew me by. "Anything else Spence?" the guy asked me after he had so nicely cleaned out his house of all the drugs he had. "Well, just one more thing," I replied as I produced my identification case which had my state police photo card bearing my real name along with my badge. "My name's Investigator L. D. Brown with the Arkansas State Police and you're under arrest." The poor guy was startled at best and just stared at the badge and identification. Jerry and I (and now Bill) howled in laughter when the guy, while staring at the badge and identification asked, "Damned Spence, can you get me one of these?" It took us ten minutes to convince this guy we were the police. We eventually had to bring in the old police chief from outside to do it.

The storytelling Bill reciprocated with would be much more revealing and ominous in light of current controversies and investigations.

*     *     *

The first thing I noticed about Bill Clinton, especially after having observed him from afar as the state's attorney general and one-term governor, was his physical appearance. Bill Clinton was much taller than I expected him to be. The first thing I noticed about Hillary was, well, allow me to set the stage first.

I was already intimidated by the circumstances of our first meeting. I had been working in the security detail at the Governor's Mansion for only five months for Governor Frank White when Clinton challenged the Republican to a rematch. White had ousted Bill and Hillary after Clinton's first term, a loss from which Bill would learn a never-forgotten lesson. The White family was as congenial a group of people as one could meet. Free of the expected pretenses, put-ons and demands one may expect from a governor and first lady, I had become fast friends with the family. This was especially true with their twelve-year-old son Kyle who became a sort of mascot in the trooper's guard house, an outbuilding of the governor's Mansion.

In contrast to the violations of public trust I would witness at the Mansion, during my years with the Clintons, the worst thing I ever saw Frank White do happened during the election that brought Bill and Hillary back into the governor's office. Frank, his wife Gay, and I would travel around Little Rock and place yard signs bearing the 'Frank White for Governor' logo. Once, when we were out on a Sunday afternoon, Frank saw a Clinton 'lollipop' sign, as he called them due to the appearance of the round Clinton sign on top of the stick, and said, "hey, L. D., let's pull up that lollipop and put up a real sign." There I was with the governor of Arkansas pulling up a Bill Clinton yard sign like a couple of teenagers on Halloween night. That's the worst thing I ever saw the man say or do. They were really good people.

Frank was a little prone to making a public mistake or two that would cause him some embarrassment. Once we were in my home town of Pine Bluff at a concert that was a fund raiser of some sort. I knew the convention center where the concert was to be held very well. Between the penitentiary job and the state police I was a narcotics officer with the Pine Bluff Police. I would be hired as back stage security for the many concert acts that were held there since I fit in with the bands with my long hair and beard. I got to meet people like Kris Kristofferson, Willie Nelson and rock groups such as KISS and the Doobie Brothers.

Bill got a real kick out of a story I told him about a fellow dope-smoker, Willie Nelson. Willie Nelson was the most eventful guy I ever served as bodyguard for. He almost didn't come out for the show. The coordinator of the event had me go out to his tour bus and see where he was. The people in the bus knew I was the cop (despite my long hair and beard) that had been assigned to keep track of Willie, so they opened the door. I was met with what I knew to be marijuana smoke that would have choked a horse. I yelled inside and saw Willie coming down the aisle. He was wasted. I thought the show would never go on but he strode through the fans who had back stage passes and put on what had to be one the best shows I've ever seen.

Governor White and I had met with the sponsor of the show, Mr. Sam Walton, founder of the Wal-Mart discount store chain. A remarkable man who was as friendly a billionaire as you would want to meet, Sam, Frank and I greeted the musicians who were to perform that day. Country music stars Charlie Daniels and the Oak Ridge Boys were the headliners and all talked with us before it was time to go up on the stage. I followed Governor White and Mr. Walton and stood toward the back of the stage as Frank began to address the crowd while the

Wal-Mart tycoon looked on.  Frank welcomed the fans who had packed into the arena, which is quite large for Pine Bluff. He then turned to Mr. Walton and said, "And ladies and gentleman, I would like to thank all the *K-Mart* people who sponsored the event today." I could have crawled under the stage as a roar of laughter rose up in the crowd at Frank's monumental gaffe by referring to the sponsorship as coming from K-Mart instead of Wal-Mart.  Sam Walton just laughed and the show went on.

When I later worked for Bill, I told him about the incident and he just laughed.  Hillary, however, howled and spoke of the Whites like they were trash under her feet.  She was always jealous that everyone liked the Whites, especially Frank's wife Gay.  She knew she could never match Gay's good-natured personality.  She called Frank 'goofy' and made fun of his weight. It was pitiful the way her insecurity manifested itself.

Several troopers who had worked for Bill and Hillary in their first term prepped me with wild stories of Bill's trysts and Hillary's man-eating tirades.  It was with much trepidation that I met Bill and Hillary when they began moving into the Mansion shortly after the Christmas holidays of 1982.

Barry Spivey, one of the troopers who suffered the Clintons' first term, witnessed my somewhat rude and unexpected introduction to 'Ms. Hillary Rodham' as Barry called her.  It was an experience mirrored by the Secret Service presidential protection detail's miserable introduction to the lamp-breaking Hillary years later in the first days at the White House.  On moving-in-day at the Mansion, I was unfortunate enough to draw the duty for the weekend day assignment providing security as the newly elected couple transferred their personal effects to their regained throne.  Security was not the order of the day. All electronic alarms securing the doors and windows were disabled to allow continued access to the building.

As Barry and I sat and reminisced about the fun times of cooking steaks on Sundays with the White family and about how much we would miss their son Kyle, the direct telephone line from inside the Mansion rang. Barry snatched it from its base and snapped, "Yeah, Barry here!" You see, Barry had already made up his mind. He was not going to hang around and endure one more day—much less another gubernatorial term—of being bashed by the Clintons. As he hung up, he said we were wanted inside. Having as yet not met either one of the new residents, and because Barry was the senior man, I was appointed to go inside and see what was going on.

As I entered what we called the back door—actually the kitchen entrance—I saw no one and proceeded to the breakfast room, a small dining area off the kitchen where the family took most of their meals. I immediately saw two women, one rather small with dark hair, the other with 'coke-bottle' thick glasses, no makeup, and an awful fright-wig of a mop matched by a stinky scowl that shot bullets right my way. Matching her words with an acerbic tone she shouted, "And this door here was open too, and by God I want to know why!" Thinking my days were numbered and convinced this wasn't going to be my second home any more, I was surely not going to be talked to in that way by any of the Clinton gang. I answered with equal force and indignation, "Lady, they're just now moving in today. *All* the doors and windows are open so the movers can get their stuff in!" With that I turned on my heel and walked directly back to the guard house determined not to go back in the Mansion until I received what I expected to be final orders to report back to narcotics duty.

When I reached Barry, he asked what they had wanted. I responded with another question, "Barry, who the hell is that bitch with the thick glasses in the breakfast room?" I nearly called 911 as Barry rolled in the floor laughing at my ignorance until he finally told me, "L. D., you have just met Ms. Hillary Rodham!"

Not long after that eventful meeting I was informed, to my surprise, by my supervisor, Lieutenant Doug Stephens that I could continue on at the Governor's Mansion if I cared to. Needless to say, that came as a shock to me.  It was now time to meet the newly elected governor.  Having moved into the building, Bill, Hillary and Chelsea were already being provided with state police security.  Even during the campaign, the family had state police escorts due to a threat made by an individual to harm Clinton.  I had not completely decided whether or not I wanted to stay on, given what Barry and the other first-termers had told me, but I was willing to give it a try.  I was still concerned about the most inauspicious first meeting with Hillary.

The occasion of Bill and my first meeting came on a night when he was about to leave for a function outside the Mansion. It was before inauguration day, and I was not scheduled to drive him. I did see him come out of the back door by way of a security camera installed there (a camera which would provide some very interesting shots of extracurricular activities later on).  After my leaving the guard house, and him leaving the back door, we met halfway on the sidewalk.  After adjusting the ever-present coffee cup, he grabbed my hand.  Almost shouting, he said, "L. D., I'm really glad to meet you.  I understand we have a lot in common."  That was not exactly what I expected to hear from a man whose wife and first lady I had just essentially told to mind her own business.  In the encounter with Clinton, however brief, I sensed a spark that would ignite a friendship that would be rewarding to both of us.  I also sensed a man that needed to be liked and befriended.  That's exactly what I did.

# CHAPTER THREE

## Arkansas Women.

Inauguration day came and preparations were made to pick up the staff members and dignitaries for the ceremonies to be held at the state capitol in downtown Little Rock. Being one of the more junior members of the security detail, I was assigned to stay at the Mansion and work the radio, an assignment away from the action and very, very boring. The senior and more 'seasoned' troopers were assigned to drive the family. They were less likely to screw up the route, get them there late or just generally do something to get the detail off on the wrong foot. Before the Clintons ever left the Mansion, one of the assigned troopers had forgotten to send a car for one of Clinton's new top staff members. Thinking that the world had come to an end, all hell was raised by the lieutenant until a car was dispatched. The offending trooper was benched at the Mansion in my place and I was assigned to accompany the couple to the inaugural event. Robert Felcher, another veteran of the Clintons' first term, drove the Lincoln Town Car first to another function and then to the state capitol for the swearing-in ceremony inside the state House of Representatives chamber. I walked Clinton down the steps with Bruce Lindsey, a man who is still

at Clinton's side refusing to speak to the independent counsel
and grand juries, to an eager crowd. From there, Clinton gave
a speech outside on the Capitol steps. The Arkansas Capitol, a
granite and marble structure built around the turn of the century
was modeled after the nation's Capitol in Washington, DC.
Under a beautiful sky that day Clinton delivered what was to be
the first of the many inspiring speeches I would witness him
give throughout our association.

It was a nostalgic day for me as well. I ran into a woman
who had shaped my life immeasurably that day. Her name was
Ann McClaren and she was my government teacher in high
school. She strengthened my interest in politics and introduced
me to Dale Bumpers who was then Arkansas governor. She
was at the inaugural that day and we talked briefly. She
seemed proud that I was now protecting one of her favorite
politicians, Bill Clinton. She was always a Democrat and made
every student in her class read the newspaper from cover to
cover at the beginning of each class.

Videos of those moments of Clinton, Lindsey and me along
with still photographs are still being used by researchers
seeking to chronicle some of the events of that time. After Bill
was elected President, I was in a local tavern in Little Rock
when two officials from the Little Rock Convention and
Visitors Bureau came in and sat down at the bar. They didn't
know me and began a conversation among themselves about
how Little Rock was going to be a boom town now that Bill
had been elected. They were obviously proud of a pamphlet
they had designed. It was apparently hot off the press. They
were thumbing through it and just had to ask my opinion. I
took the pamphlet. I was curious to see just what they had
come up with. Would they show the murder capital of
America's crack houses just blocks from the Governor's
Mansion? As I turned the first page to the inside, I just started
laughing. They looked at each other wondering if they had
made some sort of major typo error. "What's wrong?" they
asked jointly. "Don't you think it looks good?" they wondered

as I handed it back to them.  I told them that it was a slick looking professional job and that it was impressive.  I asked them if they had the permission of the people in the first photograph prominently displayed on page one.  They eagerly opened their brochure and examined the photo of Bill and Hillary being escorted down the state House of Representatives steps after their inaugural in Little Rock.  They could see nothing wrong with it until they saw I was the person doing the escorting.  The pamphlet is prominently displayed today at all the hotels and visitor information sites in Little Rock.

Bill Clinton and I read the same books, mostly political, occasionally the errant *Playboy* (for the great articles of course), certainly *Foreign Affairs* and all the national magazines and newspapers.  It was a chore to try and keep up with him since he would read while I would drive.  The first indication of our shared interests came when he picked up my copy of *Foreign Affairs* lying in the front seat of my police car one day as I drove him to the Capitol office.  *"Foreign Affairs*, eh, L. D.?"  As he proceeded to consume the articles one by one, speed-reading through the 'light stuff,' he then placed the book in his briefcase.  Bill is the most absent-minded person I have ever met.  New rules applied to this relationship. (1) Never lend him a book you want to see again. (2) Never lend him any money you need back . . . You get the idea.

I did manage to get that book back and I'm glad I did.  In it, a friend of Bill's, whom he had mentioned he knew in England, had written an article.  His name was Robert Reich and Bill would introduce him to me later at a National Governor's conference in Portland, Maine.  Reich would later become President Clinton's Secretary of Labor.  Reich and I talked in Maine about his newest book, *The Next American Frontier*.  I remember that Reich was clearly surprised I had read the book and his article on free trade in *Foreign Affairs*, being a lowly state trooper from Arkansas.

❋     ❋     ❋

As Bill warmed up to me he became very casual in his demeanor, not all of which was very pretty. He had an awful habit of, well, of picking his nose and wiping it on my seat. I took care to make sure my unmarked police car was kept clean since Bill and Hillary would be riding in it. I never knew quite what to say to get him to stop. It was kind of like what Kathleen Wiley said, "I don't think you can slap the president." He did that with everyone and that wasn't all.

Even when female staffers would be in the car with us traveling to an event, Bill would read and treat them like they weren't there. If the nose-picking wasn't bad enough, he would let what could only be described as elephant farts right there in the front seat. I would crack the window and the staffer would just cringe. The eruption would sort of wake him from his reading trance and he would mumble something like, "What was that?"

Soon Bill realized I actually liked attending the events that were political in nature, meeting the politicians and talking with them about current events. I even knew on which side of the plate the knife and fork went. The other guys at the Mansion were bored with it all and would rather stay at the Mansion and buy a six-pack of beer. They preferred to limit their involvement in the inner workings of politics to making sure Bill had his briefing notes in hand for every function to which they drove him. I had to keep those packets of briefing materials in hand as well. He was always losing his briefcase, so I held onto the paperwork which was essential to making sense of where and when we should be somewhere and what the event was all about. In the morning we might be at a Catholic Church for an Italian festival, in the afternoon at a Rotary Club speaking engagement. The night would be spent at the Excelsior hotel (for business or other purposes). But those briefing notes were all-important. I personally read them before each event in case Bill would catch one of his 'cat naps' where he would sleep for ten minutes and wake up completely rejuvenated. Many times we would arrive at an event after one such nap and Bill would say, "What's this all about L. D.?" I'd tell him he was about to give an award to a state employee of the year or some other, in his mind, innocuous deed. Winging it all the way he would contemporaneously compose himself in mind and body and deliver another trademark rendition of the caring, thinking, feeling governor. I did have one rather nasty habit about those notes, though. I tended to keep some of them (see appendix).

One interesting thing I kept was a speech I had Bill sign for me. Scribbled at the top are the words "To L. D. Brown with thanks for your help and friendship," signed 'Bill Clinton.' The occasion of the speech and its significance was the Democrat National Convention in San Francisco in 1984. I really wanted to make that trip but couldn't. The speech beseeches the participants at the convention and Democrats all across America to remember the words Harry Truman spoke while he was president. Truman was one of Bill's heroes and he loved to quote him. By the second paragraph in the speech, Bill was observing that, "We live in a time which rewards glamour and charisma." No, he wasn't speaking of his rewarding Hollywood friends like Linda and Harry Thomasson but was instead scolding America in 1984. He continued his advice to his fellow Democrats with, "We live in a time when politicians often hedge their bets in language that leaves their options open. He (Truman) spoke plainly and he meant what he said." With his questions today about what *is* is, clearly Bill has forgotten the admonishments he made to the conventioneers. If anything, Bill has made Harry Truman turn over in his grave.

I would ask Bill to sign many things for me and I would keep others he offered to me as souvenirs. One was his paperback copy of *Ben Franklin: the autobiography and other writings*. The book in inscribed 'Bill Clinton, Fayetteville (Arkansas) 1975'. I find it ironic he studied Ben Franklin's words of wisdom that have endured these many years. The chapters on the 'Way to Wealth' and 'Essays to Do Good' stand in sharp contrast to Clinton's political and private behavior.

Another book Bill gave me was *Political and Civil Rights in the United States* by Norman Dorsen and Kent Greenwalt. It was a text book he used at Yale Law School and it is signed 'W J Clinton, Yale' on the first blank page. In it Bill underlined several passages. Several such markings were made in the text of an opinion written and delivered by former Chief Justice of the United States Supreme Court Earl Warren. On page nine of the book Bill underlined the passage, "We do not believe that this settled principle of law was abolished by §1983, which makes liable 'every person' who under color of law deprives another person of his civil rights." I wonder sometimes if he remembers those words as he conducts his day to day slander of people who tell the truth about him.

Perhaps most prophetic of all the memorabilia Bill gave me were bar exam notes made in the margin of the *Nacrelli Bar Review School* book. I am convinced Hillary made most of the notes in preparation for the bar exam when she was licensed to practice law before working for the Watergate Committee in 1974. I know Bill used the book, however, and there are many entries in longhand made throughout the approximately 300 pages of text. The most telling entries are found in the sections on criminal law and taxation. In the definition of treason, the passage concerning treason requiring an <u>overt</u> act as well as involving <u>two witnesses</u> are underlined.

Special treatment is also given by underlining the definition of 'irresistible impulse,' or 'impulsive insanity' which the book defines as the mental condition of a mind that is 'powerless to control' (also underlined).

The sections on 'bribery,' 'conspiracy' and 'false pretenses' receive the same treatment. The book reads like a primer for Bill and Hillary's public life. On page seven of the criminal law section, in the definition of adultery, the following passage is treated as follows, "Adultery was <u>not</u> a crime at common law." The word 'not' is actually double-underlined in red ink.

I bet Bill wishes he had this book back so he could now hold it up to Kenneth Starr and say, "See, it says it right here!"

In the same book, I have to think of the McDougals and Bill and Hillary's partnership with them in the Whitewater land deals as I read the section under 'partnership.' On page one of the section, the words defining a partnership as being 'not a legal entity' are underlined. Later on, in the same paragraph, the words 'a partnership is a legal entity' are underlined in red ink as used in the legal powers of the partnership to own property, to sue and be sued and to go into bankruptcy. Concerning crimes committed by the partnership, the section on liability is particularly relevant to the Whitewater scandal. The words, "The mutual agency of partners is not sufficient to make the other partners liable for a crime committed by a partner within the scope of the partnership business..." These are all underlined in red ink. The following passage, "unless they participate in the crime either as principals or accessories," has the word 'participate' underlined. It stands to reason that the focus on Hillary and Bill's 'participation' in the now-convicted Susan and the late Jim McDougal's Whitewater adventures is the key to the prosecution of the Clintons. With the Clintonites' claim that Hillary is such a sharp lawyer, we now see she studied well.

The 'Taxation' section gets the most treatment in the book by Hillary's handwritten notes in the margins and on the blank face pages. She writes extensively of the 'deductibility' of certain items. Becky and I think of all Bill's used underwear Hillary would have Becky take out to the guard shack at the Mansion to give to the Salvation Army. Hillary's subsequent high valuation attached to the gubernatorial underwear would attract a lot of attention and ridicule in the years to come.

Perhaps the most telling of the passages in the book concerns what Bill has had to undergo recently, swearing to tell the truth under oath. The text states, "As a general rule, no person can be compelled to be a witness against himself." The entire passage is underlined in red ink with the words 'general rule' bracketed for added emphasis. Quite appropriately I think is the fact that the only section in the book where there is not one mark, not one word underlined or note taken is in the section on—legal ethics.

*    *    *

Campobello Island off the northern coast of Maine is a beautiful place. Best known as the summertime retreat of Franklin Roosevelt, it is nevertheless cursed with notoriously dramatic tides. A lighthouse on one end of the island is accessible by foot only during low tide. Being back at a high tide is definitely a priority since the footpath is totally submerged then. I would later take my family there in 1989 when the land had been wrested from the control of the Clinton friends that owned it.

I became interested in the island not only through the film "Sunrise at Campobello" and from my reading on Roosevelt but through one of Bill's more curious friends, Jim McDougal. McDougal was a frequent 'hanger on' of Bill's, who I believe actually pictured himself a sort of reincarnated FDR. A former politico of a United States Senator and an active Clinton supporter, McDougal was now a banker having renovated a building in the formerly decrepit south Main Street area of downtown Little Rock. The now infamous Madison Guaranty would be a haunt for Bill that I would frequently visit with him in his many escapades. It was with 'McDougal of Madison,' as I would call him, that I would first associate Bill and Hillary with the Campobello project. Although Bill has always denied any association with that project which has been included in the overall 'Whitewater' investigation, I know better. It's those pesky briefing notes (included in the appendix).

I would also pick up Bill at Madison many times. In my grand jury testimony I have detailed how I would pick up Bill at Madison on one of his 'jogging' trips. I also told the Office of Independent Counsel how Hillary couldn't stand Jim and

Susan McDougal. She was always griping at how the land deal was not making any money. This fits with Hillary being placed on a $2,000 per month retainer by McDougal and with Bill's frequent trips to the savings and loan.

"L. D. she looks good in those riding pants doesn't she? Tell you what, she looks even better out of them!" Bill said as he was introducing me to Jim McDougal's wife Susan who sometimes pitched one of the McDougals' real estate ventures on horseback in a television commercial. Bill would brag many times about the victories on the sexual playing field and Susan was one of the first in a long line of them. I sometimes wonder just exactly what it is that Susan has gotten in return for her silence sitting in jail while her former self-professed paramour squirms in his own cell at the White House. Clinton would always make comments about poor Jim since he didn't see what Susan saw in him. "He's one goofy son-of-a-bitch" Bill would say about his now-deceased old 'friend,' "but he sure is a cash cow!"

After all McDougal not only thought he was FDR, at times he dressed like him, monocle, cigarette holder and all. I do know that during the time of the Campobello real estate venture, Susan called the governor's office at the state capitol about an upcoming event concerning the Campobello 'investors.' Bill's scheduling secretary at the time, Judy Gaddy, would always place the briefing notes regarding every event in the packet of material to be delivered to the Governor's Mansion the day before the event was to be held. One day I received a packet from Judy telling us that Susan had telephoned her with news of an upcoming Campobello investors' party to be held at the Excelsior Hotel. Judy noted in her memorandum that Susan had said Bill wanted to be notified of the next such event. As Bill usually did (much to his now Nixonian chagrin) he scribbled "let's do this; I want to give Jim the bust of FDR." He also wanted to give something else to Susan that night and according to him he did. All I really cared about was hearing more about the Campobello project. I came away satisfied and eventually took my family there. Bill has denied knowing anything about Campobello, about what Jim and Susan knew or of any hanky-panky that may be investigated. But I sure hung onto those briefing notes—or at least a copy before I turned them over under subpoena from the independent counsel years later. Funny the things you keep.

Bill having taken me into his confidence about his proclivity for women, which mirrored my own, it was natural for him to allow me to work in concert with him in order to successfully complete his sexual missions. On at least one occasion, I delivered him to a condominium where he told me he was going to see Susan. Bill had told me that Susan was living apart from Jim at the time. Bill was a tactical genius in this arena of gamesmanship. While mostly living apart from my then-wife, I did not have the problem of a hawk such as Hillary watching his every move. You see, Hillary received a copy of that schedule too. She pretty much knew where and when Bill would be and for what reason. I knew he envied my freedom and I tried to help him out at every turn. We used many ruses to allow the 'mouse to play' even while the cat wasn't away— some of which have come back to haunt us both now.

The Excelsior Hotel is now a landmark in downtown Little Rock. Noted more for the site of the alleged Paula Jones encounter than for anything else, it was a rendezvous site even then. Bill was an avid 'jogger.' He could jog just about the eighteen blocks to the Excelsior before he would telephone me back at the Governor's Mansion to tell me when to pick him up. Free rooms at the inn were easy. He and I had one there on standby at all times just for the asking. About thirty minutes after the first call, Bill would ring me back—always asking as the first question, "Has Hillary called?" or "Is Hillary back yet?" If the answer was yes, I would make a mad dash down to the Excelsior to pick up an obviously freshly-showered Bill standing out in front. "Do I look like I've been running L. D.?" Giving a deserved stupid answer to a stupid question, "Sure Bill, don't worry about it!" That was easy for me to say since I didn't have to face the wrath of Hillary. At this point, it is important to stress that Hillary tolerated extramarital sex with one partner and one partner only. Hillary would not tolerate what I coined as 'extra-extra-marital sex' like the Excelsior jogging sport sex. If Bill even looked like he was interested in that type of affair, there would be hell to pay—an unrelenting tongue-lashing from Hillary.

Bill would miss out one night at the Excelsior because of one of his political and sexual competitors, Steve Clark, the Arkansas Attorney General. Bill and I attended some sort of fund raiser at Barton Coliseum, a huge indoor stadium that was home to basketball games as well as rodeos and such. The cast of Hee Haw and Leslie Nielson were the celebrity guests, and Bill was having a field day with the ladies.

One was named Elizabeth. Bill clearly had his sights set on her. She was a gorgeous woman and Bill wanted to know where the celebrities were staying. I quickly found out the entire crew was at the good old Excelsior. Hillary was in town and this would be a tough one to pull off.

We left the Coliseum and headed for the Mansion. Bill's mind was working trying to figure out how he could get down to the Excelsior without being castrated by Hillary. You could almost see the light go off as he said, "L. D. I've got it! You go down to the Excelsior and check it out. Call me back and I'll try to figure out some sort of excuse to get out of the house." I knew he had his heart set on the Hee Haw girl and we were in for a good time that night.

I dropped Bill off in the circle drive at the Mansion and headed for the Excelsior. Elizabeth had given me the suite number where the group was to be and I made it on up to the room. A big guy named Kenny, who played the guitar on 'Hee Haw,'answered the door and let me into the living room portion of the suite only to find that Bill's cousin, Marie Clinton was there. She was sitting next to Leslie Nielson on the couch and the drinks were already flowing. Much to my (and later Bill's) chagrin the Hee Haw girl was already taken by the venerable Attorney General of Arkansas, Steve Clark. Clark has been since convicted of a felony, an affliction not uncommon to Arkansas politicians, and is no longer in office. He was on a roll that night, dancing on top of a glass table and losing his shirt (literally) very quickly. I knew that Bill had no hope.

I excused myself and got to a telephone to give Bill the bad news. I rang the Mansion and told the trooper to put me through to Bill. "*Who* is there?" he screamed with obvious disbelief and anger. "That son-of-a-bitch!" he said at the realization Clark had beaten him this time. After all, he was the governor and Steve was only the attorney general. It just didn't sit right with him but I wasn't going to let that spoil my fun. "Guv, I think I'm going to stick this one out and hang around," I told him, probing if he had any problems with my move. "Sure, let me know what happens," he said as he slammed down the phone.

I immediately telephoned Becky at her house on the Mansion grounds and told her to come on down. She did, and we had the time of our lives as Leslie Nielson pulled his whoopie cushion routine on us until I cried laughing. Clinton's cousin Marie would take some great photos of the event which I still have and which Bill never forgot. Bill didn't always get what he wanted. This was the one that got away.

# CHAPTER FOUR

## Bill and Mrs. Jones

I don't believe that what Paula Jones said happened at the Excelsior Hotel that day is totally accurate, even as she has settled her lawsuit. That may disappoint some of the Clinton critics, but as you can see from our escapades, it doesn't exactly fit his method of operation. Unless he just lost his mind after he and I stopped traveling in the same circles of women, I find it hard to believe that the man exposed himself with the 'kiss it' demand unless there was some sort of provocation, complicity, or other variables we don't know about.

I told this to Paula Jones's lawyers, David Pyke and Robert Rader, when they came to see me in 1997 about what I knew. They had done their homework and had read the news accounts of interviews I had given to the *American Spectator* to set the record straight some time ago. They also had been told many things they thought I knew which were not so accurate. I agreed to help them, off the record, but had to tell them I thought they had a flawed conceptual argument in the method of operation Jones said Bill used. I agreed Bill certainly liked to fool around with other women but the way Jones tells this story as an unsolicited sexually harassing encounter was not credible to me.

I did let them in on one detail that might have been of some of significance about Bill's reportedly 'distinguishing characteristics' in the genital area[2]. I told them that on many occasions, when Bill would come into the guard shack at the Mansion, he would go back to the restroom in the back. While leaving the door open, he would start to urinate when all of a sudden the 'lid' would fall and he would yell, "Damned L. D., I just ah, well ah I just spilled water on myself!" I remember thinking 'what's up with that?' and never did figure it out. When he walked back into the room he would be wiping the fluid from his pants and asking me if you could still see the stain.

I asked Paula Jones' lawyers not to subpoena me in efforts of keeping my name out of the suit. My family had been damaged enough, I was trying to establish a business, and dragging the womanizing by Bill and me up again at this time would not be in my best interest. They promised they would do the best they could but I didn't have much hope of staying out of the fray. As I will relate later, the final deposition would be eventful.

I knew when they left my office that I would be subpoenaed anyway. I did give them one parting shot. I told them that if and when Bill's attorney Bob Bennett asked me if I thought that Bill would drop his pants unsolicited and ask for oral sex, I would have to answer truthfully and say no. They countered with the fact that if I wasn't there, how would I know. I left them with the same rationale: if I wasn't at the Excelsior that day, don't call me as a witness. You can't have it both ways.

I received the subpoena on October 28, 1997. It was delivered just like you had ordered it up like a pizza. The private investigator who delivered it knew me, and said that it was regarding the Paula Jones matter. My brother Dwayne was there at my office in downtown Little Rock and shared my concern that by being drug into the fray again our family would suffer renewed attacks from the Clinton camp. The accusations and condemnations would fly and we would be defending ourselves to potential clients, clients that didn't want to have the stigma of having done business with L. D. Brown who was at odds with the President of the United States. Again, then as now, the Little Rock legal and business culture is dominated by Clintonites who worship the ground upon which his Presidential Library will be built. I decided to fight the subpoena.

Little Rock has a law school and a pretty good one. It's ranked in the second tier of law schools in the United States by U. S. News and World Report. It also has a fine law library. I looked up the federal rules for the Eastern District of Arkansas where the Paula Jones case was going to be tried. The 'Motion to Quash' the subpoena wasn't that hard to draft. I included the rationale that I wasn't there the day Paula Jones said that Bill made the unwanted advances toward her. I also stated in the motion that I did not know of a 'pattern' of Bill using sex to get women jobs or more importantly to deny women jobs because of their refusals to submit to his sexual demands. I had until the date of my deposition but I needed to get the motion filed with the court and faxed to all of the parties well in advance. I also asked for a hearing on the matter.

On October 31, 1997 I filed the motion with the clerk of the Federal Court for the Eastern District of Arkansas. It was filed under seal like all the rest of the filings at that time, meaning the media did not have access to it. According to the rules of the court, I had to immediately fax a copy to the parties involved, which meant Bill's attorney Bob Bennett and Trooper Danny Ferguson's lawyer Bill Bristow in Jonesboro, Arkansas. I didn't know how to get in touch with Bennett since he was with one of those Washington, DC law firms with about ten names in the title, none of which was Bennett. I telephoned Bill Bristow in Jonesboro, since I knew I could get his number from directory assistance. I asked him for his fax number. He gave it to me and he also had the fax number of Bennett. I already had Bob Rader and David Pyke's numbers in Dallas so I went to work.

I faxed all three of the law firms one after the other. The motion would reach all of them that day as required by the rules. I was surprised by the response from one of the parties. Not long after I had faxed the motion, I received a telephone call from Bob Rader, one of Paula Jones's attorneys in Dallas. He told me he had just received my fax. Cryptically he asked, "L. D. have you filed this yet?" I told him I had and faxed the motion to all the lawyers involved in the case. Quietly as if someone may have been listening, he asked, "L. D., are you all right, have they gotten to you?" I assumed that meant the Clinton lawyers or someone acting on Clinton's behalf. I wanted to answer I had been 'gotten to' by Bill and Hillary Clinton for the last fifteen years but I didn't think that it was the right venue to tell my life's story. I simply told him I prepared the motion on my own with no help from the Clinton lawyers. He still suspected I had been pressured but I insisted I hadn't and that ended the conversation.

I thought that the call was improper, coming after I had filed a motion with the court that was still pending and due to the fact that I was under a subpoena. I thought of a way to get the Jones lawyers off my back. I telephoned Bennett's law firm in Washington, DC and asked to speak to Katherine Sexton, the name on a letter sent to me along with a subpoena for all documents related to Bill Clinton that I may have in my possession. This included any 'contracts' I may have with the *American Spectator* magazine. They were apparently trying to prove I had received money from the magazine for telling my story on Bill's womanizing, an allegation that was patently false. I must say, however, that if they would like to pay me now, after all my family and I have been through, I sure wouldn't turn it down.

Ms. Sexton came on the line and I could tell she was a little apprehensive about talking to one of the 'evil doers' that had accused her client of misdeeds. I set her mind at ease by asking her exactly what it was that they wanted from me in the way of documents. I told her I had a lot of things like the signed photos and books that Bill had given me, did she want them too? She said those sort of things wouldn't be necessary, I should bring things such as contracts. I assured her I didn't have anything like that and the conversation was just about to come to a close when I brought up the other matter. "Is it appropriate, Ms. Sexton, for Mrs. Jones's lawyers to be calling me on the telephone asking me if I had been 'gotten to' by the President's people?" I inquired. She hesitated for what seemed an eternity before coming back on the line replying, "I don't believe we have any comment on that." I had gotten the message across. Or so I thought.

I had a hearing on the motion—it was over the telephone. Judge Susan Webber Wright's clerk had telephoned me to set it up and the logistics were quite complicated. The court had to get all of the parties on the telephone at once, make sure we could all hear each other and then direct who could speak and when. It all went quite smoothly, however, and we were all connected by the time Judge Wright came on the line. She introduced herself and made sure everyone could hear and then gave me the floor to explain my motion. I had a copy in front of me, so I naturally went through each issue I had raised as to the propriety of my testimony. The thought that was going through my head, still does, that the defining moment of Bill's potential downfall was linked to a sexual allegation that I didn't buy into. With all the things I knew about personally that were illegal or unethical, it all was going to come down to this?

Bob Bennett chimed in a few times. He agreed with a couple of my points, as I expected, but surprised me when he complemented me on the quality of the motion I had drafted. Bob Rader threw in his objections as Jones' lawyer. They were quite good and relevant. He pointed out that I did have knowledge of Bill's prior sexual peccadilloes and that I had spoken publicly about them before. Anyway, I lost the motion rather quickly as Judge Wright commanded I present myself for the deposition. It would be scheduled at a later date and I would definitely be there. I wasn't arguing, since I knew full well that one of the most powerful people beyond Saddam Hussein is a United States federal judge. If you don't believe that, just take one on. Susan McDougal is perfect proof of that.

The judge had issued a 'gag' order that commanded all 'parties' in the suit to remain silent about what was going on. I wasn't a 'party' to the suit as I was only a witness. Both sides in the lawsuit put their own 'spin' on what was really meant by the gag order. My friends who sided with Bill told me it meant I too could not say anything about what I had said in the deposition. Jones's lawyers told me I could walk outside and call a press conference and tell everything that had been said in the matter. I think they still did not grasp that I wanted to stay totally out of the fray.

The deposition was set for a most unusual place, I thought. It would be the first time I would give a deposition in a hotel. Then again, I had been interviewed by the Office of Independent Counsel once in a hotel, but more on that later. The site for this episode in the ongoing saga of my involvement with the Clintons was the Doubletree Hotel in downtown Little Rock. A recently renovated structure just across from the Pulaski County Court House, the Jones lawyers had rented a salon off the main ballroom on the second floor. It provided more than enough room for the lawyers, the court reporter and me since it was designed for use for private parties or diners.

Bob Rader and David Pyke, the Jones lawyers that I had previously met with to attempt to avoid the deposition, were already there. Bob Bennett and Ms. Sexton, whom I had already talked with, arrived and both shook my hand. Bennett seemed friendly and Sexton was a little uptight looking—like a 'woman on a mission.' The court reporter showed up and the machinations of setting up her equipment started, an extension cord here and there. Everything revolves around the court reporters since they are the ones that swear you in and take down every word that is spoken. If they can't hear you or don't understand something you say, they stop the whole line of questioning until they are sure they get it right. They also sit at the center of everyone in order to get a better pickup through their microphone of what the participants have to say. Invariably they are female. That made me a little nervous—especially in this case where we would be talking about all the sex and lies (no videotape).

Bill Bristow, Trooper Danny Ferguson's lawyer, arrived last. I had seen him on television before, when he ran for public office. In 1998, he was the Democratic Party's nominee for Governor of Arkansas, losing to Republican Mike Huckabee. He is an interesting man, Harvard educated, but comes across more like Mr. Haney on the Green Acres television show. The one that always had a product that Eddie Albert's character needed. I had been told the 'country lawyer' routine was a charade but in reality he was a top notch lawyer. I did, however, not see anything that day that would indicate he was a legal eagle.

We had arranged by mutual agreement that my lawyer, Justin Thornton of Washington, DC, would be allowed to participate in the deposition by long distance, using a speaker phone situated at the center of the table. Although we lost contact with him several times, the system seemed to work out okay. It was all I could do, I could not afford to fly Justin down for the deposition. Justin was aided by another lawyer in Washington, Bill Aramony, a man with a keen legal mind whom I had met through Justin. I was glad he would be helping Justin during the next few hours.

The Jones team had first go at me. We went through the entire list of women they knew about. They asked me details of a Boca Raton trip where Bill had an encounter with a girl in a car. All of it. I was a bit embarrassed at the presence of the court reporter, but I answered every question truthfully. Then came what the Jones lawyers apparently saw as their coup de grâce. I knew that one of the strategies that Paula Jones's lawyers were implementing was to try to establish that Bill was a 'sexual predator'. There was no doubt that he used women.

Did he stalk them and force himself on them like they were animals? I don't think so, but that's a matter of opinion.

Bob Bennett jumped in with an objection when Bob Rader asked me if I thought Bill was a sexual predator. Objections don't mean a whole lot in a deposition since there is no judge present to rule on the issue. The objection is noted so that the judge may determine later whether or not to allow the testimony or not. Justin started to chime in about the issue when I said I would answer that question. Did I think Bill Clinton was a sexual predator? "No, Mr. Rader, I don't. I think he just likes women," I replied rather matter of factly, much to Mr. Rader's chagrin. It was an obviously welcome relief to Bob Bennett, who had tensed up when I offered to answer the question. Too bad I didn't have the full benefit of knowing the details of the Lewinsky or the Juanita Broaddrick matters at the time of the deposition. I would certainly have answered differently if I had.

Bob Bennett had his turn now as the Jones lawyers were done for a while. We had already been there for hours due to the sheer volume of questions about women, some of whom I had never heard. Bennett introduced himself for the record, and pulled his chair right up to mine. His strategy became clear very soon. His line of questioning centered around the motion I had filed attempting to quash the subpoena.

Bennett produced a copy of the motion and began to question me on its content. He first pointed out it was clear the motion was made under oath and so clearly I was under oath to tell the truth. I agreed with him, stating I knew full well I was under oath now but the motion contained the truth as well. He seized on that statement and began to read directly from the motion.

"Were these statements true when you filed them?" he asked, to which I replied they were. "Are they true today?" He went on in a methodical fashion with every point I had made in the motion. I answered again they were true, as we continued this dialogue throughout the questioning. I had stated that the deposition was designed to harass and embarrass me. I thought it was, since I had cooperated with Jones' lawyers at my office answering every question they would ask of me.

But Bennett would have a surprising set of questions to ask of me before his portion of the deposition was over. "Did you have sex with Gennifer Flowers?" he asked. Justin and Bill, my attorneys on the speaker phone, objected. They stated that the question would not be answered and Bennett asked on what grounds they had based their objections. Justin cited the rule chapter and verse and Bennett, clearly trumped by Justin's research, didn't say another word about it. He went on to ask if I had ever had sex with every woman who had been mentioned during the deposition. I refused to answer every time a question was asked. It was obvious he was trying to demonstrate I felt the questions were designed to embarrass and harass. A claim he hopes he can substantiate for his client Bill Clinton. I felt like reminding him I wasn't the defendant in this case, Bill was.

Bill Bristow, Danny Ferguson's lawyer, had his chance at me. He took a cue from Bennett and pulled his chair right up to me. He had buffalo breath and I scooted back just a little so I could breathe. He pointed out I wasn't there the day the alleged confrontation between Jones and his client occurred. He also made the relevant point that Danny Ferguson worked at the Governor's Mansion after I did. That was about all he had to ask.

All sides have a chance to ask further questions of the witness and the Jones lawyers asked a few more. Katherine Sexton began whispering in Bob Bennett's ear and Bennett signaled he too had one more question. "Had I ever met with Jones's lawyers before today?" he asked, knowing the answer was yes. "Had Jones's lawyers ever contacted me after I filed my motion to dismiss?" he asked again, knowing from Sexton they had. He then went on to ask what Rader had told me about his concern that the Clinton lawyers "had gotten to me."

It embarrassed Rader that he had been caught in the act but I hoped it served another purpose, to leave me alone.

The deposition ended after about four and one-half hours. Much of that time was spent arguing about whether or not I would answer questions. After the deposition was over, I learned there were reporters downstairs waiting for me to come out. I took the stairs but they found me at the basement garage. I jumped into my car as they shined the television lights inside while I drove out, nearly causing me to hit a concrete pillar. I guess I evaded them well enough, since the evening news did not carry any footage of me. The newspapers apparently did not see who I was either.

✻    ✻    ✻

Paula Jones' lawyers still weren't done with me. Even though a reasonable person would have known to not antagonize me further, in February of 1998 I received an envelope from the Rader, Campbell, Fisher and Pyke law firm in Dallas, Texas. It was postmarked February 25, 1998 from Dallas. I opened it and found it to contain a photocopy of a column written by Joseph Sobran for the Universal Press Syndicate. In it, Sobran paints a picture of Bill Clinton as a psychopath, one who lies without a conscience. He indeed quotes Dr. Robert Hare's book *Without Conscience* which was not written about Clinton. He writes of Hare's indication of the psychopath who lies without remorse but is totally sane and rational at the same time. Egocentric, sexually promiscuous and power-hungry, Hare writes that the psychopath may strike others as being 'a little slick.'

This sure sounded like Bill to me, but I'm no psychiatrist. One thing I did agree with in the column was Sobran's thought in closing. "The psychopath may be sane," writes Sobran, "but his flunkies are nuts." Dead on correct. Thanks for the letter, Jones' lawyers.

✻    ✻    ✻

There is one incident involving Bill Clinton's behavior that may be relevant to both the Jones and Lewinsky cases. It happened to my dear wife Becky once after Bill had come home from a late night function in Little Rock.

Becky had been baby-sitting Chelsea and had already put her to bed. Bill, after getting a beer, found Becky watching television in the upstairs part of the Mansion. He slouched down next to Becky and offered her a beer. Incredibly, he began his 'I'm so bad' routine with Becky! I had seen him use it time and time again trying to get a woman to comfort him— comforting which he would then manipulate into eventual sex. Becky got out of there in a hurry. When she told me of the incident, I wanted to take Bill out and administer the punishment to him that he has escaped from so many of the 'significant others' of the women he has used over the years. I let it pass, but I never forgot the incident. It was just one of the many reasons I eventually left the Mansion.

The circumstances of Bill's occasional disciplining by Hillary would always be the same. Bill inevitably would have gone without a sexual fix for some time and the 'urge,' as he would call it, came forth at the most inopportune times—the times where Hillary was present. Bill invariably liked younger women (like Lewinsky), which he would meet at gatherings such as fund raisers for campaigns. Hillary would attend many of these functions and accompany Bill while shaking hands with the crowd. On one occasion, Bill was having an extensive handshaking episode with a young buxom blonde. This episode was very typical of such encounters. While firmly grasping the young woman's hand (and not letting go), Bill's eyes would be transfixed on the woman's bosom while he was talking to her. Hillary finally—and ever so gently—would place her hand on Bill's arm and lead him away. If we stayed around long enough, Bill would ask me to find out who the woman was and get her telephone number. It was when we got inside the Lincoln Town Car that all hell would break loose. Hillary, who always sat in the back, would begin with the line, "Hell Bill, why didn't you just go ahead and fuck her right there!" Bill would offer no apology as he sat there and took his medicine like a good boy. Sometimes I would deliver the antidote in the form of a telephone number I had gotten at his direction during the function when we arrived back at the Mansion. This always made him feel a little better since all was not lost in the ordeal.

Many such fund raisers were the source of controversy as Bill tried to expand his ever-increasing stable of sexual contacts. At one fund raiser he targeted a young woman who, as we would say, was 'a little on the young side,' maybe twenty-one years old. After being given my mission to get the all-important telephone number, I returned with bad news. The poor girl was the daughter of Clinton's county coordinator who was sponsoring the party. We didn't pursue her—if there was one thing Clinton had mastered, it was the art of fund raising. He wouldn't even let a potential sexual encounter get in the way of that.

These types of encounters were no fun. Being a part of the subterfuge directed at Hillary was. As we will see later, Hillary was no saint. In her private interactions with Bill, one may have observed she was cold toward him to the point of frigidity. Humiliating him in front of me seemed to be a sort of sport. My empathy with Bill stemmed from my miserable marriage and Bill knew it. But I never experienced the humiliation that Bill did once, as he ruminated over a lawsuit involving Arkansas and another state. With Hillary in her back seat command position in the Lincoln, Bill offhandedly asked Hillary, "In lawsuits against the states, who has original juris-diction, Hillary?" Hillary exploded and lashed out with, "Goddam it Bill, the Supreme Court, Bill!!!" Adding "L. D. you knew the answer to that didn't you?" After I confirmed her suspicions, she admonished Bill never to ask a question as stupid as that in front of me again.  Yes, Hillary—Ms. Personality.

Covert action plans were resorted to when Hillary was in town.  They often took place when Bill was feeling down after a row with Hillary.  One method we used was to drop Bill at a fire station on Shackleford Road in west Little Rock.  I would leave him there and wait for the trooper to call me on the radio to advise me to "pick up GS-1," meaning the governor, at 'the location.'  I knew what that meant, and picked him up straight away.  After suffering through the same line of questioning, "Has Hillary called?" we would then go on about our business as if nothing had happened.

A particularly interesting trip occurred when we made one of our many one-day excursions to Bill's hometown Hot Springs.  It was the occasion of his 20th high school reunion. We were accompanied on the trip by Bill's cousin, Liz Burks, and his childhood sweetheart, Carolyn Staley.  Now, Bill wasn't the most popular band boy at Hot Springs High, but I really didn't know just how unpopular until that night.

The party was held at the Hot Springs Country Club where Bill was to be the obvious special guest.  We arrived with little fanfare and without Hillary.  I expected the entire senior class to be in awe of their most successful alumnus, but instead found a lot of unbelievers in the group.  The guys kept taunting Bill about how he played the saxophone in the band and bringing up embarrassing anecdotes that he obviously would rather forget.  We didn't stay nearly as long as I had expected and the four of us headed back to Little Rock.

When we reached the city, instead of going to the Mansion we drove to Liz' home.  While Liz and I went inside for a nightcap, Bill and Carolyn stayed in the car for a little quiet time.  Carolyn was Bill's childhood sweetheart.  Liza Ashley, the old cook at the Mansion, always said that Bill should have married Carolyn instead of 'that woman, Ms. Hillary.'  They indeed would have made the perfect couple.  Carolyn was one of the nicest caring people you would ever want to meet.

*    *    *

Bill's relationships did not always fall as far away from the tree as this, however. When the Clintons came back into office, they brought with them their own staff which included a new Governor's Mansion administrator. Robin Dickey was a tall, blue-eyed brunette beauty queen who had been a friend of the Clintons for years. Robin was as cordial as she was capable in fulfilling her duties at the Mansion, which included managing the day to day affairs of the sprawling estate. She was particularly adept at preparing the Mansion for dinner parties, special events and making sure the Clintons' every need was taken care of.

Robin was married to former Arkansas Razorback football star, David Dickey, who shied away from the hustle and bustle of the Governor's Mansion. With three children, including the oldest, Helen, who later would work at the White House with her mother Robin, was a busy woman—very busy indeed. Robin and I became very good friends. Intuitive and understanding to the point of actually claiming a certain sixth sense like her sister, a professional psychic, Robin and I would spend social hours away from the Mansion whenever time permitted. She also enjoyed spending social time with Bill Clinton.

Robin eventually left the Mansion due to Hillary's apparent suspicions over an affair between her and Bill, an affair both Bill and Robin would share with me in our deepest conversations. The liaisons between the two were not as easily negotiated as the covert operations treated earlier. These meetings would occur only when Hillary would be out of town on business. The methodology would be simple. Bill would call down and say that Robin would be coming into the back gate and going in the back door. After she was inside, Bill would give me strict instructions to tell Hillary I could not find him if she were to telephone. The 'do not disturb' light was definitely lit. This continued even after Robin left the Mansion job. She eventually would follow Clinton to the White House but would leave to go on to the Pentagon only days after I told the truth about Robin and Bill's relationship in my Paula Jones deposition. Shades of Monica Lewinsky. Strange coincidence, you may ask? If there is anything a reader may learn from this book, it is that the Clintons' methods of subterfuge, intimidation and lying have not changed one iota from governor to president. The only difference between now and then is when you leave Bill's employ, you now get a top secret clearance.

Gennifer Flowers sparked the public controversy of Bill's paramours and deserves special treatment here. I, too, knew Gennifer very well. She was a well known night club singer at the Capital Club at the top of what is now the NationsBank building in downtown Little Rock. Gennifer was a seductress, plain and simple. With a voice like a nightingale and an alluring sex appeal that I have seen in few women, she lived at the Quapaw Towers, a trendy location with a popular private club on the first floor where all the power brokers would go after the legislative session. Gennifer maintained a condominium in the Quapaw as did many friends of Bill.

Gennifer was telling the truth when she said she had an affair with Bill. I was in her condominium once when Bill called. The answering machine kicked on and Bill left a message asking her to call him back. I thought that was pretty brazen and so did she. She told me how much of a risk-taker he was and of his, shall we say, shortcomings, long before she ever went public. Although she's been vilified by the press ever since, Bill has now admitted to the affair in his Paula Jones lawsuit. But Bill was not the only powerful person Gennifer was known to have taken a liking to. In fact, there was a mad rush to the local book store when her book came out. It was particularly painful to some, since the thing wasn't indexed— making it tedious work for the former paramours to see if their name was in there or not. A few people who had as much to lose as Bill drew a collective sigh of relief when they finished that book.

# CHAPTER FIVE
## Women of the World

Some of the best opportunities for Bill's extracurricular pursuits came while we were out of town with Hillary and Chelsea. Boca Raton, Florida was like no place I had been to in America at the time. Designer shopping, exquisite golfing and private beach front recreation were the highlights of this resort community. Situated on the Atlantic coast in south Florida near Fort Lauderdale, it was always these type of destinations that were selected for some of the conferences we attended, especially if the family was to go along as well. The Southern Regional Education Board based in Atlanta held their conference there one year and Bill, Hillary, Chelsea and Becky McCoy, Chelsea's nanny (and now my wife) would be making the trip. After the conference, the family, along with Becky, was to stay in Florida and drive up the peninsula to Disney World. On most of these trips, two security people would travel with the family and this was no exception. This would be a good one, Bill said, so we wanted someone 'cool' that liked to party to go with us. The perfect candidate was Ralph Parker.

Ralph was one of the troopers assigned to the Clintons during the last campaign because of the threats that had been made against them. Ralph, God bless his soul, died of cancer some years ago. Part of his full life was spent with Bill and me since he could be trusted explicitly. A Vietnam combat veteran, Ralph was one of two African-American troopers on the detail. He was well thought of by the family. Bill could trust him and Hillary knew he was a real man since he wouldn't put up with any of her attempts to humiliate the 'guards,' as Hillary called the troopers.

As we left the Governor's Mansion in Little Rock, Ralph and I looked at the hotel brochure where we would all stay. The five-star Boca Raton Hotel Resort and Yacht Club was right on the beach, close to the night life and to top it all off, we were on the state's tab. This was going to be a great trip indeed.

Traveling with little Chelsea Clinton during those years was a chore at best. Hillary, the former Arkansas 'Mother of the Year' whom I will treat later, left the hands-on machinations of corralling the child to Becky. Worst of all, the airport was the last place you wanted to be with this group. Bill was busy trying to scam first-class seats for the family and Ralph and I were just glad to get them all on the plane on time. Mister 'let's hit it!' Bill Clinton, with his constant tardiness and disregard for schedules, always thought we could call the airports and have planes delayed (can anybody say L.A. airport haircut?). As Ralph and I filled out forms to pass our pistols through security to get on the plane, Bill would invariably be schmoozing some babe. Chelsea would be looking for her 'Ba Boo,' a nasty little stuffed animal Becky couldn't find, and Chelsea couldn't live without. All the while Hillary sat on her fat—well, anyway the trip was going to be a good one since I could finally answer that question for Bill I recounted at the beginning of the book.

The Boca Raton Hotel Resort and Yacht Club lived up to its promotional billing. Pink stucco buildings situated next to a championship golf course and all within a ferry's ride to the pristine private beaches made this a setting for some prime time fun. Bill's schedule was loose. I already knew that, and so did he. It wasn't long until his commitments to the few meetings he had to attend were met and we were off to the races. The pool at the hotel was beautiful and Bill and I had to walk right by it to get to the meetings. Becky and Chelsea practically lived in the water and Bill would never miss a chance to spend time with Chelsea at the pool. Not knowing at the time he was speaking to my future wife, Bill would give the then-twenty-three-year-old Becky compliments on how she always had a 'nice tan.' This, of course, would be with a wink and a nod toward me and only after he had addressed the comments toward her bosom and not her face. This wouldn't be the last time he would step over the line with Becky or her family, but more about that later.

But we weren't in Florida to swim in the pool. As everyone knows, you have to get to the beach and we did. Unfortunately, Bill asked everyone if they wanted to go, thinking Hillary would back out. I didn't know the strategy behind that tactic, but I deferred to his judgment. Ralph and I knew full well that if Hillary went with us, the only thing that would happen would be that Bill would get chewed out by Hillary for gawking at other women. Ralph, knowing this as well as I did, joked he had his full tan and would skip the beach trip. Actually a short straw doomed me to the trip. One of us had to go due to the fact we were still officially on the job.

The ferry ride to the beach was a short one. I still could not figure out why Bill was so cheery. I mean, we had the whole family with us, which would certainly mean his roving eyesight would be myopic on this trip. As Hillary stripped down to her suit (I needed a drink) Bill whispered to me, "I sent Ralph out to find a club for us tonight. We'll go out and have some fun!" As I watched Hillary slather on what must have been 900 SPF sun block while Bill glared at Becky, I knew Ralph was working hard to find us a real rock and roll spot to take Bill. Bill always had a plan.

Bill, Hillary, Chelsea and Becky had a two-bedroom suite just two doors from our room in the old section of the hotel. Bill had told Hillary what I thought was a pretty good lie for

him. He had said we were going to meet with one of the other
governors downstairs at the bar. "Heck," he said, "We may
even take a drive and look around." He knew full well Ralph
and I had already tipped the valet and had the car warmed up
with Ralph at the wheel. Ralph had already driven the route
and knew exactly how to get us to the club in the shortest
amount of time possible. We all knew Hillary possessed the
cunning to investigate our whereabouts if she really wanted to,
and that our time out was at a premium. Ralph made a beeline
to a disco club he had advanced located near an undeveloped
area in Boca Raton. We turned the rental car over to the valet
and charged headlong into the mating games like one of Bill's
favorite horses at the Oaklawn horse racing track back in Hot
Springs.

Now, Bill Clinton may be a heart-throb to many women but
at least during this time frame he had a deep-seated insecurity
problem meeting women in bars. Ralph and I always thought it
was because he felt he stood out in a crowd so much since he
was so tall, something Bill told me he worried about growing
up. At any rate, I would always be the one to approach the
women at another table.

After ordering one round of drinks, the only one Bill would
have since he didn't want to get in trouble with Hillary, Bill
told me to go over to a table full of good-looking girls who
were obviously alone. "Ask that one if she wants to dance with
the Governor of Arkansas," a line I've heard over and over
again. Now, I've always hated that line since my take on that
was 'who gives a rat's behind who the governor of Arkansas
is?' And even if they do, who's going to believe this guy is
really that governor in a disco in south Florida, trying to pick
up women?

Ever the obedient servant, I nevertheless obliged Bill and
produced one of my state police cards as I asked the woman he
had selected the fateful question. "Yeah and I'm Queen
Elizabeth!" she responded with deserved incredulity. Just as I
was about to fall back and regroup, it happened, as it always

did. "No, that's Bill Clinton!" another of the girls at the table injected. I heard, "I've seen him on television!" as they stampeded over me like lambs to the slaughter to our table—including the chosen one.

On second thought, maybe Bill's insecurity with women is exhibited when he is in a position to dance with them. Bill Clinton, trying to be cool with these twenty-somethings, looked like he was doing the eighties' version of the monster mash. This didn't seem to bother the chosen one. She was mesmerized by the young governor from Arkansas.

The night wore on and Ralph and I were doing very well for ourselves. Drinks and dancing with the Governor's bodyguards wasn't actually dancing with the Governor, but with a whole table of women, no one wanted to sit and watch. Bill had retreated into his close conversation mood with the chosen one. She listened intently to whatever he was shouting into her ear, attempting to override the music. Just as the party was coming to its fruition, duty called. Bill had given us the 'high sign' which consisted of an index finger pointing upward making a circular motion. That meant 'Get the car, I'm ready to go, *I've scored!*'

The chosen girl was clearly eager to follow Bill anywhere. She, too, had the valet pull her car around and Bill told us to follow him in the rental car. Bill must have told her we couldn't go back to the hotel, because the girl drove to the undeveloped area near the club. Ralph and I pulled around and in front, stopping after about twenty feet. Bill and the chosen one leaned toward each other and began kissing, wasting no time as if she had been told by Bill that time was at a premium. Maybe the girl was sleepy—all these gubernatorial moments being too much for her—since she then laid her head in his lap. Ralph and I knew 'something was up' as Bill was enjoying this 'cat nap in his lap.' The gubernatorial goober lasted about five minutes as Bill made his exit (no kiss) and jumped into the back seat of the rental car.

"Let's hit it!" came the familiar command and Ralph made for the hotel like a horse for the hay barn. After a sophomoric "Damned that was great!" he asked, "Has Hillary called?" having not completely come down from his high. Since this was the age before cellular phones Hillary couldn't possibly have called. Although if she had screamed as loud as I knew she could, we would have definitely been interrupted on the dance floor. Bill settled down into his introspective mood as he always does after extramarital sex.

"You know guys, I really enjoy paling around with you." Then came the fateful line I would always hear during Bill's effort to reconcile his guilt. "L. D. you're a smart guy, do *you* consider oral sex adultery?" he asked almost boyishly.

Quickly trying to drown out Ralph's snicker, I answered, "No, not necessarily." Knowing what he wanted to hear I followed up with, "But don't try that with Hillary!"

"You know L. D., I'm with you on that!" Even after Monica Lewinsky, apparently so is Hillary.

Bill, Ralph and I flew back to the hotel at light speed. As the valet took the keys, Bill darted upstairs to check on Hillary. She was fast asleep. Not one to miss an opportunity, Bill realized he could stay out a little while longer with the boys. The Boca Raton Resort had several bars which were first class and full of patrons. With the conference being over, Bill felt a little more at ease in the hotel, not fearing being seen drunk or womanizing by any of the other governors. We met a couple of people in the bar and Bill stepped out for a few minutes, long enough for me to become concerned. As I went to look for him, I first checked the bathroom. I called his name but got no answer. Just as I was about to leave, I saw his number 13s protruding from under one of the stalls. "Bill, are you okay?" I asked, knowing there couldn't be another foot that big in Boca Raton. "Yeah, yeah L. D., these damned sinuses are killing me!" As I retreated to the bar, I realized what was going on. You see, Bill knew that with my prior experiences in drug enforcement I didn't tolerate illicit drug use—particularly 'nose candy.' I didn't care what he did in private regarding coke, but he knew not to try to use it while we were out making our way through bars in his quest for women. Cocaine would figure into our relationship later on and eventually contributed to the ruination of our friendship.

I think Bill became a little spooked after the bathroom incident, so we decided to take our drinks upstairs. We all three retired to my room where Ralph mixed a nightcap. We had a great night and I decided to take a few snapshots. Bill was zonked and that candy must have been flavorful. I sure hope this photo can be reproduced in color for this book (on the rear cover).

The rest of our trip was spent on the golf course. Ralph not being an avid golfer, I jumped at the chance to drive Bill the short distance to the Doral Country Club to play with Hillary's brothers Hugh and Tony who lived in nearby Miami. Bill thought the pudgy duo a little goofy and christened them Huey and Louie after the Disney duck characters. They were really nice guys, though, which increased my suspicions that Hillary must have been adopted. Bill is a dangerous golfer and you must play behind him in order to live. I had played with him before and opted to watch from the cart as he gave a new meaning to the word 'mulligan.' Rank does have its privileges—just ask Vernon Jordan.

The rest of the trip consisted of meetings that even I didn't much care for. Ralph and I headed back to Little Rock as Bill and Hillary along with Becky and Chelsea drove up to Disney World for a private vacation.

Becky told me after the group returned form Disney World that Bill had just barely missed getting a speeding ticket from one of Florida's finest. Bill, always the lead foot and vehicular maniac, had been speeding up the Interstate on the way to the resort when they were pulled over. Hillary was in full chastising mode as Bill explained he was the Governor of Arkansas, never one to miss an executive privilege. At any rate, he didn't get a ticket.

✻   ✻   ✻

Dallas, Texas is a fun town.  It's the closest really fun town to the burg of Little Rock, Arkansas.  Bill loved sports, but couldn't even dribble a basketball.  Being Governor, he had passes to all the Arkansas Razorback football games in Little Rock, Fayetteville and even on the road.  One of the best trips we ever took in the eternal quest for the ultimate good time found itself in the combination of booze, women, football and Dallas.  Even some of Bill's good friends and contributors knew a good trip when they saw it and signed on for this one. Bill Clark, a Clinton appointee to the powerful state Highway Commission, and Chris Burrows, a long time Clinton ally, were good guys and equally fanatical Razorback nutsy fans (I call them Razornecks).  So we tramped off to Dallas in hopes of seeing the Razorbacks trounce the Southern Methodist University Mustangs in Texas Stadium.  Everyone there had already been drinking, but since this was a NCAA-sanctioned game, no liquor or beer was allowed to be sold in the stadium. With the Governor going first class we were to be in a private sky box replete with cushioned seats and television monitors for those replays.  But there was still the problem of the booze. Bill and his cronies had the idea of me bringing it inside the stadium in a paper sack.  Now, as you'll see later, that's not all I carried illegally in a paper sack, but I thought this was a little too out in the open.  I was proven right when, as the last person in the entourage through the turnstile, I was asked by security what was in the bag.  As I showed the guard the Crown Royal, Jack Daniels and other assorted liquors, I told him I was with the Governor of Arkansas.  Not as easily impressed as a Boca Raton bimbo, he proceeded to share with me his disdain for politicians, Arkansas politicians and Arkansas politicians who tried to break the law.  I bet he didn't vote for Clinton in the presidential race!

Anyway, as I was trying to keep us in booze, Bill and his buddies left me high and dry walking off from me as if to say "L. D. who?"  I guess I should have known what would follow in the years to come by what happened that day. Regardless, I left the booze and caught up. Bill's buddies told me not to fear, they had a full night planned. Boy were they ever right.

That night proved to be so eventful that I don't even remember who won the game. The only thing that struck me was how Clinton wanted to go down to the locker room and talk with the Razorback football players, something we had never done before. By the time we made it down into the bowels of Texas Stadium, where otherwise the Dallas Cowboys dressed on game day, the Arkansas players had already undressed and had begun to shower. Thinking it was time to leave, I started out as soon as I saw we were too late to do any political glad-handing. To my shock, and apparently to the dismay of Clinton's cronies, he insisted on staying in the locker room shaking hands with naked jocks. He even ventured off into the showers causing him and his suit to get that 'sweaty, tropical' look. We finally left, ending what was certainly one of the weirdest episodes I have ever experienced with Bill Clinton. If it weren't for his alley cat libido with women I might have thought—no surely not.

Bill's tag-alongs were to be taken at their word. The night was well-planned. We had rooms booked at the Westin Galleria Hotel, a beautiful atrium style complex located at one end of the Galleria shopping mall with its indoor ice rink and dozens of upscale shops and restaurants. But the fun to be had was all near the Texas Stadium site where the game was held. Texas Stadium is not actually in Dallas, it's in Irving, Texas as any Cowboys fan knows. As any true hell-raising Cowboys fan who has actually attended a game at Texas Stadium knows, there is a proliferation of strip bars all along nearby Northwest Highway. With all that time in the stadium sky box away from good-looking women, Bill needed a fix. I knew it, Bill's cronies knew it, and Bill felt it. I was assured the strip joints we were to visit were to be the 'high-dollar' ones, no trashy strippers for our governor. As we entered, Bill's eyes lit up like a kid in a candy store. With the spotlights whirling and reflective balls turning, Bill dragged us to the table nearest to the stage where "Debbie" was doing her thing. We were right there with the guys in the raincoats that put five dollar bills in the G-strings. It was like Bill had never been to one of these before. Certainly not a veteran of a strip bar scene, I still knew the answers to such questions as "Do you really think these girls would do anything if you paid them lots of money?" Bill didn't have a clue and I sensed if we didn't get him out of there he would be up on the stage doing the monster mash a la Boca Raton within five minutes. Failing that, he would be asking me to ask them if they wanted to dance with the Governor of Arkansas. I knew that would only drive up the price if he just *had* to touch the goods. Given that scenario, I knew since he didn't have his billfold and he still owed me money (and still does) I would be paying for that non-refundable expense. Charging off booze to the state under the guise of legitimate expenses was one thing, but this was another. After lots of ca-joling and promises of 'maybe we'll come back,' Bill placed a borrowed five-dollar bill in 'Debbie's' G-string. On the way out Bill asked me, "L. D. do you think you can get her number?" Giving him some advice I'm sure he's recalled since during the Monica Lewinsky scandal, I advised, "No Bill, that kind of girl would get your number." Come to think of it, I don't think he had a clue as to what I meant.

✱    ✱    ✱

I had never been to Denver, Colorado. Bill invited me to go on a trip where he said he would be raising some money. He told me that he was to meet a Mr. Lyons, the individual who would later for the 1992 presidential campaign prepare a report showing that the Clintons lost money on Whitewater.

In Denver we stayed at the Brown Palace Hotel. A turn of the century opulent structure, the Brown Palace had a gilded atrium that was gorgeous. I can't remember who paid for that trip but it must have cost a pretty penny. The meeting with

James Lyons was to take place in a tall office building near the hotel and next to another skyscraper that was being built.  Lou Kilzer of the Rocky Mountain News once reconstructed the meeting place from the location of Lyons's office at the time and found that I was exact on my description of the location.

What a lot of people never realized was that Bill was always running for office, with the goal of the presidency always in his mind.  He raised money everywhere we went.  Many of the people who supported him for President had been cultivated over the years and this meeting was one of those instances.  I stayed long enough in the room with the group of about seven men to realize that this was one of those Kodak moments I didn't want to be around.  As the discussion turned to money, I left.

On the way back to the hotel, Bill and I were joined by a young woman who was the wife of one of the participants in the room.  He gave me the 'something's up' look as she wasn't looking and I saw them go into his room when we got back to the hotel.  I never knew exactly which one was her husband, but I bet he would be interested to know now that his contribution was more than just monetary.

# CHAPTER SIX

## The True Loves of Their Lives

To say Bill and Hillary had an 'open' marriage would be an unfair characterization. Bill and Hillary had an 'understanding.' It was this understanding that bound the two together in agreeing on the extramarital parameters within which their marriage would exist and indeed be sustained all these years. Bill had a recognized 'significant other,' as did Hillary, and it was only when anyone strayed from these bounds of the agreement that trouble erupted. It was only in Bill where keeping this agreement failed.

Hillary had open disdain when she learned of the affair with Robin Dickey and clearly was outraged at the girls whom Bill would undress with his eyes. But Hillary understood the "getting something from others that we can't get from our spouses" as she once told me. That 'significant other' for Bill Clinton was Beth Coulson.

Beth has been described as a 'Kewpie doll with brains,' being diminutive with sky-blue eyes while an intellectual lawyer as well. Beth was always there for Bill and was indeed his soul mate. Married with no children, Beth lived in Little Rock in the fashionable Heights section about fifteen minutes from the Governor's Mansion. Whenever Bill really needed to talk to someone, he would tell me, "Let's go to Beth's." Bill was assured I knew the way as we had been there many times before. Sometimes late at night after a function at the

Excelsior Hotel, I would drive up into the driveway of the small brick house and follow Bill inside, watching Beth and him retreat to the back room. Other times it would only be for fifteen minutes and I would wait outside in the car while he would go inside for a "mental or physical fix" as he termed it.

Beth was also a visitor to the Governor's Mansion. As with Robin, this would only occur while Hillary was out of town. Using the same methodology, Bill would ring, alerting me to Beth's approach, knowing I would allow her in the gate and to the back door for the visit. I always wondered what her husband thought or if he even knew what was going on. It took a visit to a friend of Bills' restaurant to find out.

Charlie Yah Lin Trie, currently under indictment for illegal campaign contributions in the campaign finance scandal, owned two Chinese restaurants in Little Rock. A tall, engaging gentleman, Charlie's place was a spot we would all go to frequently when the crowd consisted of only Bill, Hillary and personal friends. On this particular occasion it was Beth Coulson, her husband Mike, along with Hillary's law partner Vince Foster and his wife Lisa.

Bill, Hillary and I had met at a residence near the restaurant where everyone converged for the night out. It would be a night that would demonstrate just how the 'understanding' worked. It would also serve to confirm in no uncertain terms who Hillary's 'significant other' was.

The night started out different from most with Bill and Hillary drinking more than usual. We all, in fact, were drinking more than usual as we decided to walk to Charlie's restaurant. There was a private room downstairs and we were ushered in by Charlie himself. The drinks really began to flow as everyone laughed and talked. Beth and Bill sat together, Vince with Hillary and, as the night grew on, Mike Coulson and Lisa Foster. The most sober ones among us gravitated to each other, obviously, in order to have someone to talk to.

Hillary, in a rare moment of levity, pulled a joke on me—the likes of which I've only seen while she was drinking. About an hour after the dinner, while everyone was enjoying yet another after-dinner drink, the entire Chinese staff of the restaurant appeared at my table with a huge birthday cake. They all joined in a chorus of 'Happy Birthday to Roo,' which the rest of the group found hilariously funny because it wasn't my birthday. By this time Vince and Hillary were looking like they were in the back seat of a '57 Chevy at the drive-in. Hillary was kissing Vince like I've never seen her kiss Bill, and the same sort of thing was going on with Bill and Beth. Mike's and Lisa's oblivion to the escalation of the amorous activity left me bewildered. No one seemed to notice me, except for Vince who would give the occasional furtive glance, sometimes accentuated by a wink.

When we left the restaurant, the pairs remained locked together. Mike and Lisa led the entourage with Bill and Beth shortly behind. Vince and Hillary brought up the rear as Vince was really getting a handful of Hillary's. Bill and Beth kissing did not bother me as much as seeing Hillary attempting to reciprocate with Vince. Vince, good looking, tall and suave obviously knew what he was doing, but Hillary looked awkward and unbalanced.

After witnessing this, I fully expected some marijuana, group sex and a 'Big Chill' night. When we reached the car, however, everyone broke loose of their strangleholds, kissed and said good night. That night was strange and uncomfortable enough without the ride home. Bill and Hillary obviously had a hormonal high going that they weren't ready to quash. Bill, uncharacteristically, jumped in the back seat with Hillary and the wrestling began. This is the only time I have ever seen the two passionate with one another—and I know no one else that has. For fifteen minutes I struggled to keep the Lincoln Town Car on the road. You would have thought two elephants were doing their best to produce a new baby Dumbo for the zoo back there. Not a pretty picture.

When we arrived at the Mansion, it was as if someone had thrown cold water onto them. Hillary fixed her hair as only

Hillary can do, and Bill concealed his 'little governor' enough to make it in the back door. I didn't even go into the guard house that night to say goodbye to the trooper on duty. This was one weird night and I was ready to go home.

Hillary Rodham loved Vince Foster, let's put that issue to rest right here. It has amazed me that the subject has been taboo in the 'mainstream media.' Especially after he committed suicide, a serious discussion of motive could not be undertaken until that variable had been included in any hypothesis. Hillary and I would talk often about our problems in our marriage in general terms. She knew that I was in a miserable marriage and had an eye for an attractive woman. Her line was, "L. D. I know personally that we have to get some things from other people that we cannot get in our own marriage." She was always talking about him and would even give Becky advice on how to pack her bags based on what Vince had showed her. "Now Becky you should roll things up like this. It makes for more room. Vince showed me how."

More specifically, at the point I was to divorce my first wife, Hillary told me, "L. D., sometimes you have to make that leap of faith." She traveled with Vince often, once even to London. They were soul mates, and I actually felt sorry for Hillary as I saw her come down the steps of the church at Vince's funeral. He deserved better.

*    *    *

Many people have asked me whether or not Hillary is bisexual. I was always surprised to hear this question since I never had any indication that she liked women in a sexual manner. In that vein, I have struggled over whether or not to ever tell the following story since many consider Hillary to be, well, not pretty.

The occasion was a trip to Pine Bluff, Arkansas. I drove Hillary to a speaking engagement there. It was during this trip she gave me the speech about 'getting things' from other people besides your spouse. We were obviously having an intense conversation that day. As we neared the Mansion, Hillary asked me if I ever went anywhere just to think. I told her I did have one place which was up on top of a building overlooking the Arkansas River downtown, a roof you could drive your car onto. She asked me to show it to her. I thought it a little odd, but agreed.

As we pulled up on the roof, Hillary was clearly relaxed. The view overlooks the Interstate 30 bridge into North Little Rock, ironically where the future home of the Bill Clinton Presidential Library will be. Not much to look at until you get high above it all.

I don't know whether it was the conversation we had been having or just the moment, but Hillary—out of the blue—told me she wanted me to start traveling with her, not just on the one hour trips, but out of town on the overnight ones. This was a big step for her since she traveled alone on all of her business trips that were out of town. At that moment she slid to the middle of the front seat of the Lincoln and gave me a big kiss on the cheek. I didn't utter a word. I saw my entire career, or what was left of it, fly past—as in out the window. I restarted the car and we drove back to the Mansion. She didn't say another word.

I had forgotten the incident until the next time Bill, Hillary and Vince were together in the kitchen one night after I had driven them back to the Mansion. Hillary, Bill and Vince had been drinking wine and Hillary asked me to join them. I always felt a little uncomfortable when they all had been drinking because I never knew what I was about to be a witness to. Bill and Vince walked into the breakfast room. They were not even out of sight when Hillary walked over to me a planted a juicy one on my lips. I say juicy because Hillary never was a particularly affectionate person. I backed away quickly as I knew Vince and Bill could be back at any minute. At times, Hillary was as unpredictable as Bill and these two episodes, and others, are testaments to that fact. As Forrest Gump would say about these experiences, "that's all I'm going to say about that."

＊        ＊        ＊

Bill Clinton had a big problem with women—I guess he still does. I shared that problem with him, and although I don't like to think that was even a minor reason he and I became such good friends, I know it was a factor in gaining his trust, a sort of mutually assured destruction, or MAD in nuclear arms parlance. If I talked, I would be damaged, and he surely wasn't going to say anything.

Bill's craving for women was not the result of him being a 'sexual predator' as Paula Jones's lawyers tried to get me to say during my deposition in her case. Although women were obviously to be dominated, I rather saw Bill as needing to prove to himself that he could overcome the female dominance he had felt growing up. Marrying Hillary perpetuated that dominance (and a war between Bill's mom, his Chief of Staff Betsey Wright, and Hillary for their shares of that dominance). It wasn't so much a means of getting back at women as it was just a means of proving he had chosen the coalitions he built with Hillary and Betsey and he could overcome them by dominating other women sexually in an almost 'I'll show you who's boss' mentality.

We would often talk about how 'bad' we were. But at the time we thought we were just really good old southern boys out to have a good time. Bill thought you would be judged on *everything* you did in this life and in large part I believe that as well. I've heard psychologists say that the term for this is 'compartmentalization.' I think this may have some validity, since he had a tendency to put aside doing badly to get good things done. The end justifying any means? Consider that question after you've read the following chapters. You will see that the scandals of today are a mere continuation of the ones from the 1980s.

# CHAPTER SEVEN

## Politically Savage Animals

Bill Clinton liked Ronald Reagan. He also adored John Kennedy. Go figure. When we talked about Reagan, he saw in him a man who made it to the White House without having to go through the armed forces to get there. "L. D. why does a man have to serve in the military to be elected President of the United States?" he asked more than once. I waited till probably the second time he asked me to point out Reagan had not taken that route *per se*.

As the question about law suits between the states he asked in front of Hillary showed, he was not incapable of asking a stupid question. I remember once, walking up the Capitol steps, he was worried about the consequences of harvesting ivory. "Do they kill the elephant when they get the ivory L. D.?" he would ask in almost little brother tone. As I clued him in, I wanted to tell him the elephant was just put to sleep, but I realized I was, after all, talking to the Governor of the state and not my little girl. So it didn't surprise me that the Reagan mystique had engulfed him as well as the rest of the nation. Through our conversations it was clear that Reagan was everything he wanted to be politically—popular, well-loved and forgiven for all his mistakes. From the current polls and his evasion of an impeachment conviction, I would say that Bill has taken up where Reagan left off and has become the 'thermonuclear Teflon' President.

With George Bush the situation was curiously different. I never met Reagan, at least not with Bill, but he did introduce me to George Bush, whom he liked as well. It was the occasion of the National Governors Association meeting in Portland, Maine near Bush's Kennebunkport home. Robin Dickey was there along with her daughter Helen, Bill, Hillary and Chelsea. The family and I had taken a circuitous route by way of Wellesley, Massachusetts where Hillary was to give a speech at her alma mater.

I took in Fenway Park instead of being around some of Hillary's flower children friends, but more about them later. We drove from Boston to Portland in one of the most horrendous trips of my life. Chelsea and Hillary in the back was okay, but *Bill* driving! This would scare the ever-loving heck out of a grown-up! Bill Clinton drives like my old Aunt Jackie—accelerate and decelerate, swerve and weave. All the while Hillary would be ignoring Chelsea screaming at the top of her lungs about her 'Ba-Boo' toy I had retrieved from the bottom of the escalator after Chelsea had thrown the thing down two flights of stairs. While Hillary screamed, "Get the goddam thing L. D.!!" I apparently had allowed some escalator grease, if there is such a thing, to come into contact with the toy. We arrived alive.

✳   ✳   ✳

The first thing you notice about George Bush is his height. When Bill introduced me to him at the Portland, Maine Holiday Inn, Bill knew I was a big fan of his. He was a former Director of Central Intelligence, and little did I know I would later be more directly involved with the agency with Bill's help. I also would meet and talk with Bush many more times and fly Bush's children around Arkansas in the 1988 presidential campaign. To this day I cannot prove where the closeness of the relationship between Bill and George is derived from. Chapter seven will present information from which a reasonable person will be able to draw conclusions.

Hillary was not as impressed by Bush. Then-Vice President Bush hosted a clam bake and lobster boil at his home near Kennebunkport at Walker's Point. Hillary flatly refused to go and a major cat-fight ensued at their hotel room. "Fuck him, Bill," she admonished, "He's Reagan's goddam Vice-President!" she screeched for the whole world to hear. One time at the Mansion, when I had forgotten about Hillary's hate for Reagan, I showed her a photograph of Nancy Reagan and me at the Little Rock airport. "You ought to burn the goddamned thing L. D.," she told me.

I was really looking forward to this little side-trip and was just about to suggest to Bill we leave the antisocial, paranoid cadaver at the hotel when she stormed out of the room dragging Chelsea. Robin, her daughter Helen and I loaded into the rental car with Bill, Hillary and Chelsea for the short drive down to Walker's Point. All the way Hillary said not one word.

We arrived at the secret service checkpoint where we had to show identification. To my horror the agent said that only the Governor and his immediate family would be allowed down to the compound for the dinner. Right there on the middle of the road Hillary declared, "Okay, L. D., Robin and Helen—just get out!" I spoke up and told the agent I was the family's security, but Hillary starting screeching so much that in the end, I just got out, knowing my protests would get Bill into more trouble than he was already in with Hillary. I hope she had a good time.

* * *

When we arrived back in Little Rock after the Maine trip, I took a couple of days off, as we usually did after a trip out of state.  As I returned back to the Mansion there was a function going on inside.  One of the guys had told me that Chelsea's new baby-sitter had been hired.  I didn't think much about it until I went inside and started looking for Robin Dickey, the Mansion administrator, to ask her a question.  When I came into the stairwell area at the front of the Mansion, graced by a Tiffany chandelier, I saw Robin standing there with a young petite brunette.  Robin introduced me to Becky McCoy, Chelsea's new nanny.  "So you're L. D." she said.  "I've been hearing L. D. this and L. D. that, I've been wondering who L. D. was," she remarked.  She had never met anyone called by his initials.

Becky had baby-sitted for Vince and Lisa Foster for years and Vince had recommended Becky to Hillary.  Besides being a nice guy and letting me drive his Jaguar, Vince introduced me to my future wife.  I owe him for that.

Becky and I were to become good friends, and as my wife and I separated, even better friends.  We traveled with the Clintons on business and vacations and shared some great experiences working for them.  Becky's mother Ann and father Grady were like family to me and even though we have split since the Clinton debacle, I hope that one day we will be reconciled.

Becky and I were married after I left the Mansion and we would have three children.  As Bill would say, I know I've caused pain in my marriage, but this woman has stood by me through thick and thin and has been the best person I've ever known in my life.  She took in my daughter from my first marriage and raised her for her own.  She'll have a special place in heaven for her.

I don't believe Hillary hated Bush as much for whom he was as for what he was.  Being the Vice-President of Ronald Reagan, the leader of the evil Republicans, was his greatest crime.  Hillary actually *hated* Republicans.  When she would ask me about a person in a crowd, she would say, "L. D. who's that Republican-looking person over there?"

Becky remembers one time when Hillary, Chelsea and Becky were in a taxi in Washington, DC while Bill was at a meeting. The taxi drove by the south lawn of the White House en route to meet Bill, when Chelsea became excited at the sight of the executive Mansion. Bill and Hillary were to attend a dinner there that night with the Reagans. Having never seen the inside, Chelsea begged her mother to take her on a tour as they arrived back at the hotel. I've often wondered what this brilliant little girl thought when her mother admonished her with the retort, "Chelsea, we'll take a tour when someone *decent* lives there!" Becky, the most wonderful person you'll ever meet, was astonished at Hillary's comments. But as Becky will relate later, Hillary never really did deserve that Arkansas 'Mother of the Year' award.

Bill Clinton always had an idea of the conservative roots that were at the heart of the electorate in Arkansas. He knew how to champion causes close to the heart of his constituency —but only when they served his purposes. I always told Bill the 'law and order' theme was a winner. Champion law enforcement, pay them well, give them the tools to enforce the law, and the voters will follow. He was reluctant to follow my advice and with good reason. In a paper I wrote and delivered at the University of Manchester in England while studying for my Ph.D, I made a comparative analysis of the Waco Branch Davidian episode and a 'Cuban Crisis' Bill endured in Arkansas during his first term as Governor.

Jimmy Carter had relocated about 1,000 Cuban refugees, who had fled the Castro regime, in a federal complex in Fort Chaffee in northwest Arkansas. Clinton, in the midst of an election he would ultimately lose in part due to this incident, was furious with his friend Jimmy Carter. When the refugees rioted, Bill called in the Arkansas National Guard to quell the disturbances. When that proved woefully inadequate, he summoned riot gear-equipped Arkansas State Troopers (Waco anyone?). As a result, several Cubans were shot as they stormed the gates of the compound attempting to flee into the countryside. The Cubans probably would not have fared much better if they had succeeded and made it into nearby Barling, Arkansas since the locals were sitting on their doorsteps, shotguns at the ready, just waiting to get a shot at a stray 'Cuban Commie.'

The statewide *Arkansas Gazette*, the bastion of Arkansas journalistic liberalism and otherwise a Clinton supporter, slammed Clinton's hardball answer to the riots. After the smoke had cleared, Bill came out defending his Troopers, saying he was proud of them and if he had to do it all over again, he would do the same thing.

Many policy analysts saw it as a decisive move on Clinton's part, showing positive leadership qualities, still the event contributed to his demise. In the election that booted Bill and Hillary out of the Governor's Mansion, Republican Frank White, the first Governor I worked for, chastised Clinton for allowing his Democratic buddy Jimmy Carter to use the state to house Castro's refugees. Some of the boat people were clearly a mix of criminals and mental patients. Although White offered no alternatives to what should have been done, the damage that was inflicted by liberal policy analysts and by the media had been devastating. Combined with Hillary's refusal to change her name to Clinton along with the realization by conservative Arkansans that Bill and Hillary had brought in a bunch of liberal weirdos as gubernatorial staff (read first term White House), the election of Frank White was ensured.

Bill told me he had learned his lesson about championing the Arkansas State Police from that loss. He had gone to great lengths to effect the changes needed to make sure he would never be defeated again. Hillary Rodham was now Hillary Clinton ("call me Hillary, not Mrs. Clinton"), and Maurice Smith, his new chief of staff was an old political hack who had experience in dealing with the 'old guard' Southern Democrats in the Arkansas legislature. In fact, to demonstrate his neglect of the agency, the Arkansas State Police had fewer troopers working the highways of Arkansas when Bill left office as Governor than when he first attained the office fourteen years earlier. He believed he didn't need the state police—except in his speeches.

My good friend Ralph Parker was on duty at the Mansion when Becky and I received the news that his brother-in-law Louis Bryant, a trooper in rural De Queen, Arkansas, had been killed. I telephoned Ralph at the Mansion and told him I would come in and relieve him on his shift. Ralph refused my offer. Being the man he was, he said he would his finish out the night so as not to inconvenience anyone. This tragedy would be exploited by Bill as a means toward his political end.

Louis was killed by a man named Richard Wayne Snell, who had been dubbed a 'White Supremacist' by the media. Louis Bryant, who was black, had stopped Snell for a traffic violation near De Queen in southwest Arkansas (not far from Hope, Clinton's birthplace). Louis had tried to radio his position to the state police troop headquarters but due to an antiquated radio system could not make contact. As he approached Snell's vehicle, he was met with a hail of bullets. Louis never had a chance.

Bill made preparations to attend the funeral which would be held in Texarkana, Arkansas, near De Queen. Police officers from nearby Texas, Louisiana and Oklahoma, along with the expected contingent of Arkansas troopers and other law enforcement officers, jammed the Ramada Inn in Texarkana after the funeral for a reception. As I escorted Bill down a hallway of the hotel I asked, "Bill, do you want to go in the ballroom and shake hands with some of the troopers?" Bill incredulously shot back, "Fuck those ignorant sons-of-bitches, I don't want to go in there!" I was shocked and angered, but also embarrassed for Bill since he didn't see the other two people behind me. On seeing them he quickly changed his tune and meekly said, "I mean, let's get to a phone and make some telephone calls."

It was with this hypocritical attitude that Bill 'championed' the Arkansas State Police in the next legislative session — only to line his own pockets and those of his drug-dealing friends.

Dan Lasater should need no introduction to the followers of Bill Clinton's political career. He's the man who, when testifying before Senator Alfonse D'Amato's Whitewater Committee, stated that he thought giving away cocaine was not as bad as selling it, a crime for which he was eventually sentenced to federal prison. Dan was a frequent visitor to the Governor's Mansion, but only while Hillary was away. She hated him. She knew he represented opportunities for Bill to have sex with women Dan had at the ready, and for cocaine use. Dan would arrive in his limousine with the ex-felon chauffeur who loved to show me his pearl-handled pistol. We would also go to Dan's house when the conditions were right (a party was going on and Hillary was out of town) where the women were loose and, unfortunately, so was the cocaine. Once, as Bill and I walked in the door to Dan's house, I saw a sterling silver candy dish full of nose candy. I didn't see Bill partake. He had his mind on the girls, and I didn't waste any time getting him out of there.

Lasater's name would reappear some time later as Bill's justification for getting me into the worst mess of my life, a mess I'll describe later.

Dan Lasater had his own brokerage firm. When combined with the fact that he provided Bill with campaign contributions and parties laden with coke and girls, you can see that Dan was one of those 'special friends.' After Louis Bryant's death, Bill saw a way to take care of Lasater and himself.

The Arkansas legislature was to meet just a few months after the death of Louis Bryant. Dan had ingratiated himself with Bill and the state police by providing us with use of his private box at the Oaklawn thoroughbred horse track at Hot Springs. Free trips to Angel Fire, a ski resort in New Mexico, sweetened the pot. The trips to the Mansion by Lasater increased and I knew by overhearing conversations between Dan and Bill that something was up.

That something was a bill introduced in the Arkansas legislature to authorize a multimillion dollar bond structure to build a new radio system for the Arkansas State Police. The legislation would allow certain bonding houses to market the bonds, which purportedly would pay to correct the problems such as Louis Bryant's inability to contact troop headquarters. Bill poured everything he had into the legislation, pushing for passage by pressuring legislators that it was the right thing to do. Knowing the real impetus behind the bill, I still was not in a position to oppose it openly since I was already active in the newly founded state police labor group. Because of our obvious mutually assured destruction, I couldn't oppose Bill openly anyway.

The bill sailed through the House and Senate and Clinton signed the finalized version which authorized the bond structure. Needless to say, Dan Lasater made a lot of money, more than $750,000, selling the bonds. Bill received more campaign contributions and we enjoyed the perks of soon-to-be felon Dan. Bill told me that that was the way it worked. I knew by then I was learning from a master of political corruption. And in the middle of it all, Bill and Hillary continued to ask me why in the world I wanted to be a part of the state police which was full of nothing but idiots. And about that new state police radio system—it still doesn't work right.

Bill would occasionally have me drive down to Lasater's office in downtown Little Rock. He would admonish me to 'be careful,' which I knew to mean 'don't screw this up'. I knew then that it was important. I would walk up to the receptionist's desk at Lasater and Company and pick up a plain manila envelope. Immediately when I picked it up I knew there was money inside. Nothing else is shaped like banded money that keeps it form inside an envelope—try it sometime. I would take the money directly back to Bill. I never saw it again unless it was some of the 'black money' we would spread around periodically.

I was later questioned by the Office of Independent Counsel about other pickups I would make as Bill's trusted 'bag man.' Several times I would drive to the Little Rock Air Center or Central Flying Service to pick up a 'package' for Bill. The same manila packet was used to conceal what I knew to be money. The same look, the same feel. I never opened it, as it was sealed just like the Lasater packet. The one the OIC questioned me about was reportedly from Don Tyson. I didn't ask.

*       *       *

Bill showed his disregard for the Arkansas State Police, the only police agency over which he had any direct control, in another significant event. The Arkansas State Police Commission is one of the more than 300 state boards and commissions to which the Governor may appoint members. Some of the boards are insignificant but the State Police Commission is a prestigious one especially for someone who wants the position for power. Gene Raff of Helena, Arkansas was one of those people. I knew Gene from my days as a narcotics investigator in Eastern Arkansas. Gene was the elected prosecuting attorney for a twelve-county area I worked. He had a keen dislike of the Arkansas State Police since he had no direct authority over the officers. That flew in the face of his need for power. While I worked as a narcotics investigator in his district, Gene would routinely decline prosecution of drug dealers and once even stated that seizing vehicles from drug dealers was against the law.

Once, after I had amassed a volume of evidence against a local sheriff (who eventually died in the federal penitentiary no thanks to Raff), Gene refused to follow up with prosecutorial action against the sheriff or his cronies. I had worked this twelve county area along with one other investigator who had suffered the same results. At an impasse with Raff, the state police transferred both of us out of his district to Little Rock, thus severing the state police's presence in that area. This was ultimately how I came to serve at the Governor's Mansion. But I would not be rid of Raff that easily.

Gene Raff was a power broker in Eastern Arkansas. He helped deliver the vote for Clinton for several years. When a vacancy arose on the Arkansas State Police Commission, Raff jumped at the chance. I learned at the state capitol one day that Bill had been approached by Raff for the spot. With this feather in his cap, Raff would be able to exert influence on the state police in his prosecuting attorney's district at will. After returning to the Governor's Mansion that day, I had decided to confront Bill. He knew of my narcotics work in the area controlled by Raff, having discussed the problems in the district some time before. As he came out the back door with the familiar, "Let's hit it, L. D.," I knew this may be a tough sell since Raff still had a firm grip on the political situation in that area of the state. This was a predominately rural and poor black electorate where half-pints of whiskey were still handed out at the polling booths to get out the vote. "Bill, I hear Raff wants on the State Police Commission," I said, trying to get a feel for his level of commitment. Knowing the answer to his own question, he asked, "You knew Raff when you worked over there didn't you?" I jumped at the chance to remind him that although I had made hundreds of cases in his district, I never was able to send anyone to the penitentiary while he was the prosecutor. I also stated my opinion that if Raff were appointed to the commission, Bill would lose any hope of garnering further state police support in the Eastern Arkansas area.

Bill never made a decision quickly. It was when he grew completely silent I knew he was in deep thought about the issue. I had hopes he would consult with someone who knew the situation over there better than he, someone who, if telling the truth, would confirm my take on the potential appointment. Just before leaving our 'zone of privacy' that was the Lincoln Town Car he dashed my hopes with, "You know L. D., I've just got to give him that job. Now, I know you're right, but $5,000

is a lot of money!" Continuing with his familiar theme of compartmentalization he added, "We've got to look at the bigger
picture of running these campaigns for the greater good." A
political payoff? You bet, and I knew not to force the issue.
The common good? Read instead "my political success and ultimate presidential bid." This wouldn't be the only political
appointment sold or the worst—and the future Office of
Independent Counsel may as well have been in the car with us.

✸    ✸    ✸

Bill and I would let our hair down a little one night as we
got away from Hillary for a while.   Bill's fascination for
celebrities was evident already in his Arkansas days.   There
was a Lionel Ritchie concert in town at Barton Coliseum and
Bill really wanted to go. Trooper Mark Allen and I told Bill we
would go and 'advance' it in the security parlance, meaning we
would check it out and see if it would be plausible for Bill to
get in and out okay. The show was a sellout. Ritchie was at
the height of his career and we wanted to make sure we could
get back stage as Bill wanted. Another caveat to the concert
was that the Pointer Sisters group was to perform with Ritchie.
They were from Arkansas and Bill wanted to say hello.

Mark and I arrived at the concert before the crowds and
went to the back stage area flashing our badges to get in. We
were taken to an area where the dressing rooms were and told
to wait. I told Mark that Bill really wanted to get out that night
and that we needed to do everything we could to get him in
back stage. We waited for about fifteen minutes and began to
think we had been forgotten when we saw a black guy with a
flop hat come our way. He had his head down and we couldn't
see his face until he came up to us. "Lionel Ritchie," he said
softly and we shook hands. He said he would love to meet the
governor so we made plans to bring Bill in the back door that
night.

Robin Dickey wanted to join Bill and who were we to stop her. Robert Felcher also mashed in, so we all loaded up and went out to the back stage area. Bill was gawking at the performers, particularly one named Sheila Esposito, a percussionist who later would perform on her own successfully as Sheila E. Bill shook everyone's hands and he stayed much longer than he should have. It was one of those instances when working for Bill was a good time. He clearly admired the celebrity status of these people and mingled easily with them. It didn't surprise me at all when as President of the United States he filled the White House with his Hollywood friends.

Becky and I did get to meet a few more celebrities while we worked for the Clintons. Bill has always felt comfortable around these people but he considered them a ready source of cash more than anything else. He proved that all the way to the White House as he has milked the celebrity money for all its worth.

One day Mary Steenburgen showed up at the Mansion with her child to play with Chelsea. I had seen her there many times and she even tried to get Becky to go to work for her once. But this time she had that weird husband of hers, Malcolm McDowell, with her. He looked as if he had just stepped off the set of his movie *A Clockwork Orange*. McDowell's eyes were as wide as saucers and looked like he was freaked out on something. He didn't speak, even when spoken to, and looked to be in a daze. I don't know if Bill had ever met the man but he was clearly as uncomfortable with the guy as I was.

After McDowell walked into the kitchen Bill leaned over to me and said, "Don't let that son-of-a-bitch near Chelsea." Now that Steenburgen and McDowell are divorced I see that Mary has had a few visits to the White House since.

Another odd bird celebrity was Norman Mailer. He married a woman from Helena, Arkansas, Norris Church Mailer, who was a friend of Bill's. They came to the Mansion a few times and I tried to talk with Mailer but he just stared at me. I was beginning to wonder if he was in a trance but in the end I realized he just didn't talk to the help.

Elizabeth Ward, the former Miss Arkansas who went on to win the Miss America pageant, has been in the news as someone Bill allegedly forced himself upon. I never knew Bill to have a relationship with her but since then Ward has admitted that they had an affair. One extraordinary coincidence did happen to Becky when she was with the Clintons in New York. Elizabeth had gone to New York to study acting and Bill, Hillary, Chelsea and Becky were there on a trip. Becky went with the family to a taping of Sesame Street and took some nice photos as Chelsea got to meet all the characters.

One day as they all were walking down the street, the whole family bumps into Elizabeth. Becky said it was very uncomfortable and could tell Bill was a little embarrassed. Funny who you run into in the middle of Manhattan.

Webster 'Webb' Hubbell was a nice enough guy. He would accompany Vince Foster to the Mansion frequently when Hillary and her law partner Vince would drive to Heber Springs to a cabin they kept there. I always turned down the invitation since I thought I might witness another Chinese Restaurant episode I might not be able to get out of. Worse yet, I was afraid there may be one I might be asked to participate actively in. There actually were some things I wouldn't do, especially with Hillary.

Webb also had Hillary's liberal streak and on one occasion shared those views with the world by composing a guest editorial for the *Arkansas Gazette*. The thrust of the article was anti-capital punishment, a real hot topic with Hillary. I've heard her tell Bill more than once that if ever a death warrant came to him for his signature, she would leave him if he signed it.

Hillary was excited that Webb had been so prolific in the editorial. It was almost as if she had written it herself. She may well have. Webb was a nice guy but no legal eagle. Soon after the column ran, the position of Chief Justice of the Arkansas State Supreme Court became vacant. According to the Arkansas constitution, the Governor was allowed to fill the position for the unexpired term. The nominee would not be able to succeed himself. Therefore, the position was an honorary one more than a political commitment to serve as an elected official.

Hillary's eyes sparkled as she said to me, "L. D. don't you think Webb would be great for that job?" I immediately thanked God that I did not have a case pending before the state Supreme Court. I don't even remember being able to come up with a reply. Just as soon as Bill and I were alone I reminded him about the guest editorial in the *Gazette*. He agreed that since the conservative electorate in Arkansas overwhelmingly supported the death penalty, given Webb's recent journalistic project it might not be politically advisable to make the appointment. Of equal concern to him was that Webb was one of Hillary's law partners. This one would not be easily decided.

The next day there was speculation in the newspapers as to whom Clinton would appoint to the prestigious position. There was open jockeying among the trial lawyers who knew the appointment would be a major career-enhancing coup.

The decision was made as Bill and Hillary got into the Lincoln. We were to drop Hillary at the Rose Law firm before making the run to the Governor's office. There was a distinct chill in the air. The normally talkative Bill was silent. As we reached the Rose firm and Hillary reached for the door handle, she finally blurted out, "Well goddam it Bill he's my friend, you can appoint him by law, so do it!" It was at times like these I witnessed in his public life, which continue to this day, that I have had the most compassion for the man. I really felt sorry for him but knew someone was about to pay. Hillary had humiliated him again and he knew he had to make a politically and policy-wise flawed appointment again. He had compromised himself again but I knew he could see the lack of political sense this would make. He appointed him anyway.

Webb was a true athlete. I think Bill was always jealous of that. Even though Bill was tall and husky, Webb was even bigger and had played football for the University of Arkansas Razorback football team. The three of us used to take in ball games whenever the schedule allowed. One in particular sticks in my mind.

The date was February 12, 1984 and the top ranked University of North Carolina was playing the very much underdog Arkansas Razorback basketball team. The game was to be played at the Pine Bluff, Arkansas Convention Center where Frank White had introduced Sam Walton as the head of K-Mart instead of Wal-Mart.

We would all agree later this would be the best basketball game we had ever seen in our lives. We had seats on the floor right behind the Razorback team and Bill yelled himself hoarse. It was so funny to see him take an active part in the game, first pretending to coach and then chastising the referees. It stood in stark contrast to his inability to get off two consecutive dribbles on the asphalt court in the driveway of the Mansion.

The Razorbacks won the game with a last-second-shot 65-64, I noted in my (subpoenaed) day book. Bill wanted to go back stage and see the team that night, like he did in Dallas at the Razorback football game, but we didn't have time. It would have been nice since the star of the North Carolina team was a young man by the name of Michael Jordan who had a little basketball left to play.

✳    ✳    ✳

It is at this propitious point that I introduce the political woman in Bill's life, Ms. Onie Elizabeth 'Betsey' Wright. If Bill Clinton would have listened to this woman he would not be in the trouble he is in right now. That's how politically savvy she was. It's not that Betsey just knew that a politician shouldn't have extramarital affairs, eat like a hog or make crooked deals to win elections. More important than that, she knew that Bill Clinton had the propensity to do all the above—with a vengeance.

Betsey was always mothering Bill about what not to do, what to do and how to do it. Bill had an unnerving habit of crunching ice with his teeth. He took care not to do it around Hillary as she would call him down immediately. Betsey would tell him flat out to stop and that he was ruining his teeth.

Since Betsey ran the Governor's office and pretty much stayed at the Capitol, she couldn't travel with Bill to make sure he didn't screw up on the road. After every trip, when we would return to the office, Betsey would corner me for a debriefing about Bill's activities. "Who did he flirt with?" she would ask. "Did you take him by Beth's last night?" She knew Hillary was out of town.

Knowing how we dealt with cash and campaign checks, she would demand, "Did you all pick up any cash?" She was a mother hen who couldn't be all places at all times and she knew that meant trouble.

Bill took the same grilling from her as she dished out to me—to a point. The day Hillary forced him to commit to the Webb Hubbell Supreme Court appointment fiasco was one of the days that Bill was not to be bullied. I said someone would pay dearly for Hillary's tongue lashing that day and it was Betsey's turn in the barrel.

Bill and I had been to some function the night before but did not go out and play afterward. I think the Hubbell appointment was really playing games with his mind and he was worn out. As we arrived at the office and I briefed Betsey on our good-boy behavior from the night before, she charged off into Bill's office to grill him and compare our stories. I considered warning her but I didn't much like her, so she received both barrels of Bill's pent-up anxiety.

"What did you and L. D. do last night?" she asked. She was going to add a caveat to the interrogatory when Bill shot back, "Get out of my goddam office, it's none of your goddam business—Get out!!" The normally nerves-of-steel backbone of Bill Clinton's political career burst into tears and fled like a wounded animal. In a way, I was proud Bill finally put one of his keepers in their place. Unfortunately, it would never happen to the one who needed it the most, Hillary Rodham Clinton.

\*    \*    \*

Hillary's parents, especially her mother Dorothy, were nice people. Her father Hugh died some years ago and Dorothy now lives in Little Rock, a long way from the Chicago suburbs where Hillary grew up. Given their pleasant demeanor, it's a given that Hillary didn't get her acerbic tongue from her parents. Hillary could cuss like a sailor and the levels of her attacks knew no bounds. Characteristic of the way she would run roughshod over people was the abuse she meted out to the troopers at the Mansion—that is if you let her.

Hillary respected people who stood their ground and who would not take her verbal barbs lying down. I am convinced our first encounter on moving in day laid the groundwork for our cordial relationship. She justified including me in their most memorable moments by concluding I wasn't like the other troopers. To her I was far more intelligent than 'those idiot guards,' as she would call my buddies. She would often tell me she didn't want that 'fucking idiot' or such to ever drive her again after a trooper had driven her somewhere by a route not at all to her approval.

She would tell troopers this to their face as well. Typical of the Clintonites who would take a slap in the face and then ask for another, Trooper Mark Allen was prone to crying spells after incurring Hillary's wrath over the most minuscule miscue. Many troopers would stay only one day on their new assignment at the Governor's Mansion after a run-in with Hillary. They preferred to return to highway patrol rather than to suffer the humiliation at the hands of Hillary.

Hillary possessed a deep-seated insecurity unlike any other I have ever seen. She felt awkward and inadequate around the more poised and beautiful people she was forced to interact with as 'First Lady.' She was especially jealous of attractive women . Anne Jansen, a local television anchor with the CBS affiliate in Little Rock, was her target one day. Anne is a beautiful statuesque blond with a perennial short haircut. Hillary, in all seriousness, once asked me about Jansen, "Who's that Quaker looking woman over there?" I always thought of Anne as an attractive journalist and not someone on an oat box, but I did tell Hillary who she was.

Hillary never missed a chance to strike back at those she considered to be inferior. A perfect example came when she was on a compulsory campaign outing with Bill and me in north Arkansas. It was the county fair and all the common folk were in town to have their jams and jellies judged and their hands pumped by all the politicians running for public office.

Hillary had just shaken the hands of one of the obviously poor families dressed in bib overalls and cotton dresses. It was time to go, and we retreated to the travel car none too soon as Hillary broke into her familiar spiel. "Goddam L. D., did you see that family right out of *Deliverance*?" alluding to the hillbilly representations of the Burt Reynolds classic movie. "Get me the hell out of here!" she commanded. It sickened me to see her perpetrate the fraud of asking for votes from people she obviously detested and to whom she felt superior.

I told Ralph back at the Mansion about the episode. He had seen it all before and like me he just felt sorry for the woman.

✸  ✸  ✸

Bill had a real connection with the black voter in Arkansas. The only way to describe it is in terms of a political machine. By the time Bill Clinton left Arkansas he had appointed every member to the some 300 state boards and commissions. He had made political deals with legislators to enact every sort of piece of legislation one can imagine.  He had thus built coalitions with Republicans and Democrats alike at all levels of government.  Almost everyone was riding on his coattails, even in federal races.

The black vote, however, needed special attention and a separate framework had to be devised to ensure the most re-liable and active voting block in the state would go his way.  At the heart of that machine beat the 'black money.'

Bill had a capable staff of African-Americans on which he relied extensively.  They were so reliable he took them all to Washington, DC with him and placed them in his cabinet or in the White House.  Bob Nash headed up that team as the Governor's staff member for economic development.  Bob traveled to Washington, DC and currently serves in the White House as director of personnel.

Rodney Slater and Carol Willis were Clinton liaisons to the black community and knew their job well.  Rodney has moved on to greener pastures far from those in rural eastern Arkansas and currently is Clinton's Secretary of Transportation.  Carol earned a top job with the Democratic Party in Washington for his loyal efforts.  Each of them were products of hardscrabble Arkansas and worked hard to maintain ties to the black elec-torate that were phenomenally Democratic in their voting preferences.

But the key to getting blacks out to vote in Arkansas was the black preachers.  The black community largely saw Bill as the new savior.  I've heard many black preachers tell their congre-gations just that.

Once we attended a fundamentalist black church in Little Rock that was packed with worshipers who were swaying to and fro in a frenzy as the preacher worked up the crowd.  The theme was the need for the poor depressed black communities in Arkansas to rise from the ashes like the mythical Phoenix.  Since Bill was the guest of honor, we sat at the front of the church.  The entire sermon was about Bill and his attributes as the finest leader and friend to the black race the preacher had ever known. The minister prophesied, "And like Jesus, Bill Clinton will lead us into the Promised Land!!" (I think he meant Moses.) "And very soon we will be calling him *President Clinton*," he intoned as the crowd went wild. With everyone in a fever pitch, one guy in the back stood up and screamed as if the devil himself had taken a bite out of him. He ran to the side aisle and at full speed, eyes closed tight, ran 50 feet to the end of the aisle toward where we were sitting. Hand firmly on my gun, I watched as this guy ran straight into the closed door at the end of the aisle knocking him unconscious. *That's* a Clinton endorsement if I ever saw one. And believe it or not I saw that replayed all over the state. Quite frankly, it scared the heck out of me.

The 'black money' campaign financing scheme was taken all the way to the White House—and in Arkansas I was the bag man.

Robert Fiske and Kenneth Starr's people have grilled me about this patently illegal technique of 'getting out the vote,' as the Clintonites so antiseptically term it. I, among others, have been the source of the reporting of it in many books, newspaper and magazine articles. It remains to be seen if the independent counsel will do anything about it.

It was all really very simple. Cash money was placed in the hands of black ministers charged with making sure black voters reached the polling booth knowing how to vote and who to vote for. The preachers would even pass out what I called 'crib sheets' with 'Bill Clinton' on them for the illiterate voter to use in finding the correct lever to pull, a sort of voting 'match game.'

I never carried more than $5,000 at a time. Betsey would bring the money out to the Mansion for some trips to the counties where Bill would be traveling. At times, Bob Nash, Rodney or Carol would already have the money on them. When we arrived once in Lee County, traditionally the poorest county in Arkansas with unemployment near 20%, Bill met with a group of black ministers who had one hand out to shake

Bill's hand while the other was being fed cash from the bag I had passed to Bob. That's how open and frankly how well known and accepted the practice was.

When I say a bag, I mean paper bags like you get at the grocery store. As incredible as it may seem a paper bag was the safest way to carry the cash and the least likely to attract attention.

As the Whitewater affair heated up, I worried the word had gotten out I was Bill's 'bag man' while working at the Mansion. This was confirmed when Bill Simmons, then the Associated Press bureau chief in Little Rock, telephoned me one day after Robert Fiske's agents had interviewed me. "L. D. I hear you were 'caught' carrying a bag of cash on an airplane for Clinton once." I had no comment and sensed I would be receiving a subpoena any day. About that I was right. As I reveal later there would be no stone left unturned by special counsel Robert Fiske and independent counsel Kenneth Star in their questioning of me.

As Bill and I traveled the state we were always campaigning. At that time in Arkansas, gubernatorial elections were held every two years. Only states like New Hampshire still had two-year terms. Ours was a holdover from the antiquated 1874 state constitution that was designed more to prevent another Reconstruction era than for the effective operation of state government. This meant we were always in campaign mode—soliciting and accepting campaign contributions, not all of which made it to the campaign kitty.

Betsey was continuously worried about where the money Bill and I or anyone else collected would go. She devised a system using two boxes placed near the back door inside the Mansion. When we arrived at home from our trip, Bill and I would empty our pockets of the cash and checks onto the table. Some of the proceeds from our excursion would go into the boxes, some of it would be passed from Bill to me as "L. D., here's the twenty bucks I owe you." I took the money, but theft never being one of my vices, I put it back or gave it to Betsey.

Bill would pocket some of the checks and leave others for the campaign. He also stuck cash in his pocket. And all of this would be of interest to Kenneth Star.

Bill never had a sense of money, how it was needed, made or spent except, as a means toward a political end. He knew he needed it in order to be reelected and he worked hard to raise every penny he could. Most of it was spent fighting imaginary demons in nightmares of another loss such as the one delivered to him in the person of Frank White.

A political unknown, Woody Freeman came forward in 1984 to challenge Bill for the Governor's office. Bill had amassed a sizeable campaign fund but did not want to take any chances. He turned to his old buddy and husband of one of his paramours, Jim McDougal, to secure a loan to buy a last minute flurry of television commercials.

Bill would often say of Jim, "L. D., He's one goofy son-of-a-bitch, but he's sure good for a lot of money." After stomping Freeman in the overkill election, Bill had to pay off the loan and it surely wasn't coming out of his pocket. Bill pulled what we called a 'made-up fund raiser.' This involved calling upon a major supporter to send out invitations to a fund raiser for Bill, in this case to retire his campaign debt. The *made-up* aspect of the fund raiser lay in the fact that no one was really to be out any money. Bill told me Jim would cover it all. I don't know how the final investigation will shake out, but when I was deposed under oath by the independent counsel investigator, I could tell they knew the fund raiser was not on the level. I even gave Bill a small donation for that campaign and was assured by him it would be turned into *much more*. The fact that my name was on file, he told me, would allow more money to be given in my name. What the independent counsel did not know, until I told them, was that all the campaign funds were itemized in computer files.

*       *       *

Bill already had a nationwide network of political friends. He was frequently in Washington, D.C. testifying before congressional committees or for other business. One of the politicians and statesmen we both admired was Averell Harriman. Once during a trip to D.C., when Bill was to make an appearance before a committee of Congress the former ambassador to the Soviet Union was in ill-health. Bill had an idea of dropping by Mr. Harriman's brownstone in the fashionable Georgetown area where he had completed his undergraduate work to see another friend, Harriman's wife the late Pamela Harriman.

The former wife of Winston Churchill's son, Pamela was a first-class fund-raiser and socialite for the Democratic Party. A native Brit, Pamela was to be a key supporter of Bill's in his upcoming presidential bid.

Bill always had his eye on the women but little did I know that included aged women as well. "You'll like her, L. D," he said with the sex-based wink and nod as we were driven to the walk-up in an old convertible. "She's a little old, but she's a looker," he added as we arrived. As Pamela greeted us, it was obvious that Bill adored her. A gracious host in her mid 60s, Mrs. Harriman was mesmerizing with aristocratic style. I later would review a book for the *American Spectator* magazine on Harriman. In *Life of the Party*, the author Christopher Ogden points out that in her political fund-raising career, Pamela rarely became involved in presidential campaigns until Bill's came around some years later (p. 8). From the chemistry I observed between the two it did not surprise me she embraced Bill's presidential run and that she would end her life as his United States Ambassador to France.

Jesse Jackson was seen recently at the White House to comfort the President during l'affair Lewinsky. They have come a long way since the cool relationship I witnessed.

One weekend at the Governor's Mansion, Bill telephoned me and said Jesse Jackson was on his way to see him. "Jesse Jackson?" I asked, knowing nothing was scheduled all day. In fact, Bill and I were alone that day with no staff at the Mansion. Bill asked me to open the front gate, an entrance usually locked except for use on special occasions. A couple of minutes passed and Bill rang me again with another humble and apologetic request, "Listen, L. D., I know this guy's an ass, but would you mind making some coffee for him and meeting him at the front door since there's no one else here?" I assured him it would be no problem and I would enjoy the opportunity to meet Reverend Jackson.

I was busy making a pot of coffee while watching for a car to enter the front gate. Bill called down to the kitchen and asked me to tell Jackson to have a seat in the living room when he arrived, since he was not yet ready. This obviously was not a scheduled meeting. Just as I finished, I saw a black Cadillac pull through the gate. As I opened the front door, I saw two men jump from the car and open the back door of the Cadillac. Jackson emerged and flashed a look around, apparently expecting a welcoming party. He strode in the front door where I stood. I was casually dressed as always on weekends when there was no official schedule. Jackson sneered at me as I announced, "Hello Reverend Jackson, I'm L. D. Brown, good to meet you." Sensing my outstretched hand was for some other reason, Jackson turned on his heel and dropped his topcoat over his shoulders for me to take. Playing the hey-boy, I politely took his coat. He had yet to say a word.

As if to add insult to injury I asked the gentlemen to wait in the living room for the Governor who would be downstairs in a few minutes. The men stood and looked at each other as if they had been slapped in the face. They hadn't seen anything yet. Bill suddenly burst into view at the top of the stairs clad only in his jogging shorts and a t-shirt. Hand outstretched and about halfway down the stairs he yelled, "Hey Jesse, how ya' doin?" Equally indignant at Clinton's appearance and demeanor Jackson and his entourage stepped into the living room, insulted that we had not rolled out the red carpet. As Bill followed them in for their meeting, he looked over his shoulder at me and rolled his eyes. He was right. Jackson was an ass.

\*     \*     \*

Gary Hart, on the other hand, was a really nice guy. Then-Senator Hart was in town for a talk on the Ides of March, 1984, and had invited Bill to breakfast at, you guessed it, the Excelsior Hotel. A pleasant man, Hart and Bill talked about presidential politics and the race in 1984. I could see they had more in common than just presidential aspirations. Hart and Bill both noticed how cute our waitress was. It did not go unnoticed by Hart that the Excelsior Hotel seemed to be a hot spot for good-looking women. That is a fact that has been painfully obvious to Bill. Bill was smarter than Hart as he would prove later. Bill had the sense not to dare the media to catch him fooling around during his presidential campaign. But as evidenced by Flowers, Lewinsky, Willey *et al.*, Bill should have heeded the advice given to Caesar on the timing of his meeting with Hart. We were there on March 15.

This was the era in Bill Clinton's life when he was really building the coalitions that would take him to the presidency. Even during these earlier days, however, Bill was entertaining ideas of offering himself on a national ticket. Once Senator John Glenn was in town and had invited Bill over to Jack Stephens' home. Jack is a billionaire political power broker who owns the largest brokerage house off Wall Street. Glenn had declared his candidacy for president and Bill and he were talking about the possibility of Bill joining as his running mate. I left the room to give them some privacy but not before talking with the Senator at length. His mild manner belied the fact that the man took part (and is taking part) in making history. I felt history indeed was being made that night. Bill dashed all my hopes that he and Glenn had forged an alliance when it became clear that if Bill was to be on a ticket, he would be the top name. As we left the Stephens home he asked yet again, "L. D., why is it a man has to have a military record to run for President?"

We would go to Jack Stephens' home several times while I was with Bill. On one occasion we met with Hamilton Jordan, a confidant of President Jimmy Carter. On that occasion, as I drove Jordan back to his room at the Coachmen's Inn in Little Rock, Bill and he talked of the possibility of Bill running as Senator Glenn's running mate in 1984. It was no surprise to me that ten years later Glenn would be an insufferable apologist for Bill in the Senate Committee investigation of campaign finance illegalities that would take place on Capitol Hill.

✻   ✻   ✻

With all the turmoil in his political and personal life, Bill has loved his family—his blood family, Chelsea, his mother Virginia and brother Roger. He has stood by them and coveted his relationships with his family though at times, they were politically dangerous.

Virginia Cassidy Clinton Kelly was a wonderful and colorful individual, full of life. Virginia loved her sons equally and suffered through the problems of her youngest, Roger, as intensely as she was proud of Bill's accomplishments. Virginia adored her only grandchild Chelsea as well. Preferring to visit when Hillary was not at the Mansion, Virginia was in a war of personalities with the first lady. In that battle, Hillary was unarmed.

Virginia often would invite us to her lake house on the shores of Lake Hamilton in Hot Springs for a visit. At every chance, while in the area, Bill and I would stop in—announced or not. Virginia would tell us how she was doing at the Oaklawn horse track where she spent an inordinate amount of time. She did the best she could in bringing up the boys in what she related were 'difficult circumstances.' With a streak of white through her hair and her love of more than just a dash of makeup, Virginia cut a striking figure. She lived life to its fullest.

Her youngest boy, Roger, would be a source of heartbreak for Bill and Virginia. I befriended Roger. He would come to the Mansion often. To the consternation of Hillary, Roger would stay at the guest house where special guests such as Harry Truman had stayed. Roger was a screw-up, plain and simple. Where Bill's weakness was women, Roger treated his deep-seated problems with cocaine. Bill didn't help matters when he got his good friend the cocaine dealer Dan Lasater to give Roger a job working with Dan's thoroughbred horses. It was obvious Roger had a severe problem. Although I knew Bill had dabbled in the drug that was running rampant through the excess-of-the-eighties culture of bond daddies in Little Rock, Roger was something else. The state police was working a case on him that eventually involved the Drug Enforcement Administration as well. Bill confided in me he knew there was a case being worked on Roger but he had been admonished by Hillary to, "leave him to his own devices." It killed Bill's soul he could not intervene in the case on Roger's behalf. The real story of why he didn't lies not in the fact it would have been the wrong thing to do, but in the realization it would be political suicide if he did. I knew it, Betsey Wright knew it, and eventually with a little help so did Hillary. That's when I knew for sure Bill would stay out of it.

Hillary, who realizes her place in history lies in the public perception of Bill's position in public office, demanded Bill keep his hands off Roger's troubles. Bill complied, although reluctantly, but amazingly Roger still had the run of the Mansion while Hillary was not there. Even after Roger was indicted by a federal grand jury he still brought his girls out to the Mansion, and he obviously had not given up the coke either. At times, Hillary would find out and there would be hell to pay. Bill was not doing the boy any favors and I told him so. Bill depended on me to talk to Roger. I counseled Roger by telling him how much he had hurt his brother and his mother while not forgetting to mention the political fallout that was occurring over his drug use. I could get nowhere and told Bill so. Bill did not become involved to the point of saving Roger. He would have to do some time.

The Fort Worth Federal Correctional Facility is not exactly Alcatraz. Bill and I were met at the airport in Dallas by a Texas Ranger who would drive us to the function we were attending that day. But that was not the real reason for the trip. Bill had come to see his brother. On the way, Bill told me he was worried that Roger was at a facility where organized crime family members were being housed, a concern of which I could not make much sense at the time.

The facility looks more like a high school than anything else with its sports fields and lack of security around the perimeter. Roger knew we were coming and was hustled out to meet us without much delay. There were no security cameras watching us as the unusually cheery Roger talked with Bill about how things were going in Arkansas. We didn't stay that long and after a long brotherly hug we watched Roger disappear out of the open courtyard.

As Bill and I sat in the rear seat of the Ranger's car, I witnessed a rare moment from a man whose emotions were prone to wild swings. Bill began to cry incessantly as we cleared the grounds of the complex. As a good friend would naturally do, I put my arm around him but was violently rebuffed as he threw my arm away from him while covering his face. I sensed then a well-deserved deep-seated feeling of guilt in the man. I knew his own brother, in large measure, had become another victim of the excesses of the Clintons.

✳    ✳    ✳

Bill would exhibit this compassionate side every so often, especially with people who appeared to be downtrodden. Once we were at a function where I noticed a little boy about eight years old standing patiently near the governor, waiting to shake his hand.  He seemed very shy and reluctant to call Bill's attention to himself,  but finally Bill saw him and bent down to shake his hand.  The frail looking boy shook Bill's hand and started to cry incessantly.  I walked over and tried to find someone who may be with the boy.  No one knew him. He must have come there just to see Bill on his own.  Bill was clearly concerned the boy may be in some type of trouble.  He stayed down on one knee and talked to the boy who would wipe the tears from his eyes and nod his head to Bill's questions.  Bill had me take down the boy's name and follow up on where he lived and to make sure he was okay.  I don't remember what the circumstances turned out to be with the boy, but I remember that Bill wouldn't rest until he knew he was all right.

I would always have a pocketful of notes after a trip like that.  Bill had me take down information about people we had met, and they weren't always pretty girls.  While traveling the state we would meet people who would obviously be down and out, jobless and in need of some help.  Bill would have me take down their names and pass on the information to a staffer back at the Capitol when we returned to Little Rock.  I spent an inordinate amount of time putting these people in touch with staffers.  And it would never fail that Bill would follow up and ask me if I had taken care of the man we had met who needed a job.  He never actually said it in so many words, but I knew he cared for people like that.

❋     ❋     ❋

Bill could tell Chelsea the best stories.  Whenever we were in Little Rock, we would take Chelsea to her preschool.  She would sit on Bill's lap as he strapped them both in their seat belt.  Chelsea would have a book at the ready.  The twenty-minute ride would be too long for the selected story and Bill would pick up where the book left off with a newly fabricated story of his own. Laced with animals, heroes and heroines, Bill would weave a story that would mesmerize the little girl. The timing would be just such that the hero would be about to ride into the sunset as we arrived at the preschool. He never did anticipate the myriad of questions Chelsea would have about where the hero went and whether he had any children. Chelsea, a bright child with a vivid imagination of her own, would long for another story. It was deeply disturbing to Bill that he had to spend so much time away from the little girl. We often talked of how he had been away from his mother so much while he was growing up. He was determined to spend as much time with Chelsea as he could. As a result we were late for many office appointments.

As many parents whose time with their children is limited, Bill tended to spoil Chelsea while they were together. When the limit had been reached, Bill would attempt to put his foot down on 'time to go' or 'no, you may not have that' but was not very successful in his efforts. Becky would always be around to tend to Chelsea as Bill invariably had to leave for an appointment.

# CHAPTER EIGHT

## Bill Clinton, the C. I. A.
## Recruitment Officer

I had seen enough of the Clintons and the Governor's Mansion. I had gone through a divorce, met the woman who would become my wife and grown weary of the scandalous behavior that shrouded my life with Bill Clinton. It was time to move on. My first effort to get another job would strangely turn out to be the beginning of the end for our relationship.

Hillary always received the New York Times Sunday edition at the Mansion by courier. I would take the paper to her and carefully monitor when she would be done so I too would be able to read it. On April 1, 1984 I retrieved the paper and began to look in the employment section as I had begun to do since I had decided to leave the Mansion. I was startled to see a large advertisement for positions with the Central Intelligence Agency right there with the corporate announcements for available employment opportunities. As I finished the advertisement, Bill came out the back door of the Mansion and out to the guard house. I immediately showed him the announcement with my first question being if it was real. "L. D., I've always said you would make a great spy." He went on to encourage me to apply with, "Answer the ad. I'll help you with it."

Bill was always reading spy novels from authors such as John Le Carré when not devouring more serious fare. Bill had a connection to the Agency. A contact which he never revealed to me but which he was about to call into action.

The Central Intelligence Agency is a different sort of people to deal with. My initial contact with them involved receiving volumes of paperwork to complete concerning everything about me and my family. When I showed Bill the first stack that had arrived, he seemed not at all surprised. He encouraged me to complete it as fast as I could so he could "start making some calls for me."

With the preliminaries out of the way, I was contacted by the 'personnel representative' in Dallas, Texas, Kent Cargile. Mr. Cargile explained that I would be contacted by letter and given a number to call collect at a specific date and time. He would rarely call me outside of this special arrangement. Ultimately I was sent an entrance ticket to an examination that was to be administered at the University of Arkansas at Little Rock on May 5, 1984. I was advised the test would last approximately eight hours with a one hour lunch break. Once you were allowed in, you could not leave. These people always had a flair for the dramatic.

I arrived at the test to find myself in the company of about ten others. No one seemed to dare speak to one another—I don't know why—and the test began. The test was not easy. It had strict time limitations and included foreign language abilities. I knew I would do well on that part, having studied Spanish for many years. Bill had also encouraged me to study Russian at the University some time before, which I had found curious. Although it has been useful in a novel sense, I knew the primary advantage I reaped from having studied it lay in my potential employment with the Agency.

I couldn't wait to get back to the Mansion to tell Bill about the test. He had strangely warned me I would have to write an essay during the testing procedure, and I did. I chose the Beirut bombing as my topic. I told Bill that I thought I'd done well, which seemed to excite him as much as it did me. Throughout this entire process, and the activities which would follow, Bill always would exhibit almost as much excitement and knowledge about what was going on as I did—curious still.

I apparently did well on the test. The next letter I received from the C. I. A., in Dallas, told me to report to there on August 30, 1984. I was to meet with an operations officer who would interview me for possible employment. When I told Bill, he acted as if he already knew it. I never knew whom he had called about me and who was keeping him informed on the process, but someone obviously was. That is one of the unanswered questions that dogs me to this day.

In the correspondence from the C. I. A., was a request to prepare a 500-word essay on a current event. When I showed this to Bill, he had a quick suggestion. "L. D., write it on the 'conflict' in Central America. Make it an anti-Marxism paper. That's what they want to hear and I'll help you with it," was his advice. I was of course familiar with the Sandinistas and the Contras and it didn't really matter to me what the topic was. I accepted his idea as my own and went to work.

A couple of days later I picked him up at the back door with a draft in hand. As he got into the car I handed it to him. After a brief glance, the former 'law professor' went to work with, "Can I write on this?" I realized I had not made a copy of the essay. Embarrassed, I timidly answered, "Sure, go ahead." He pulled the felt tip pen he always kept, the one that would write on photographs, and started to make corrections, suggestions and deletions. As we arrived at the office, he handed me back the paper. Fortunately I have kept it until this day (see appendix).

I was told by the personnel representative to ask for Mr. Dan Magruder's room at the Hilton on Commerce Street downtown. He would either come down to see me or I would be invited up to his room. I was a little apprehensive about the meeting, but Bill had admonished me to just cooperate with the

Agency and do what I was told. I felt I needed to keep my mouth shut and answer, not ask, questions. Still, it was curious to me the meeting was being held in a hotel and not in the 'personnel office' with which I had been corresponding. Mr. Cargile had told me on the telephone that the operations officer would reimburse me for my expenses at the hotel. I was to keep my taxi receipts, anything that would be connected to the trip.

Magruder answered my house phone call and told me to come up to the room. Dan Magruder was an Ivy-league looking guy, buttoned-down, polite and articulate. He displayed his C. I. A. credentials, which I examined carefully with a sense of admiration. He already knew everything about me and said he liked my essay on 'Marxism in Central America.' We talked almost as much about him as we did about me. Magruder told me he was an 'Asia expert' and had last returned from Korea. He made sure I knew this job would not be a law enforcement position as I was used to. He knew Bill and referred to him casually as 'the Guv.' Magruder was most interested in my Drug Enforcement Administration schooling and law enforcement experience in the narcotics field. He asked me if I was up to a little work, and I said I was. Magruder assured me I had a very good chance at employment with the Agency. Having done my research, I knew the operations officer's position was a plum. The C.I.A.'s Directorate of Operations carries out covert operations and intelligence gathering abroad. I was a little let down when he asked me if I might consider working in a section that involved security and paramilitary operations. He said working in those areas often led to an operations job. I quickly agreed since Bill had told me to cooperate in every way and show I was a team player. The last words Magruder would ever say to me were that I would be called by someone later on what to do and when to do it. Magruder paid me in cash and as I left he assured me, "I think you'll do fine."

Magruder must have known from Bill or someone else I was team player and took orders without fail. I always felt Magruder knew Clinton from some past association. I wanted to ask Bill about it when I returned to the Mansion, but I was still committed to not asking any questions and just doing what I was told—I wanted that operations officer job. As Bill came out the back door he knew I was excited about the Dallas trip. As he was fond of using the 'old boy' expression he asked, "Are you having fun yet?" I told him everything while trying to contain the question of how  Magruder knew him. It's a question I have always wished I had asked.

Bill was loving every minute of living this association with the C. I. A. through me. Just as he enjoyed the womanizing, going to bars and doing his best to dribble a basketball like one of the guys, he was getting his vicarious jollies through yet another source. But by using the C. I. A. and me, he would push my ability to follow orders to the breaking point - and destroy our friendship.

I had only received one telephone call from the agency after I had met with  Magruder in Dallas. It was from someone named Compton at headquarters in Langley asking me a couple of questions about whether or not I was willing to serve overseas, a contingency I had already planned for. Bill told me when I was hired I would have to move to another country since the Agency (supposedly) did not have any authority to operate within the United States. He kept reminding me I was to cooperate and not rock the boat. They were testing me, he said, and I would have to prove myself.

As I began to be concerned whether they would call back, Bill said not to worry, I would be getting a telephone call. What I didn't know, was the next call I received was the one to change my life forever.

✱    ✱    ✱

Barry Seal was a crazy man. He was also everything Dan Magruder was not. Happy-go-lucky, irreverent and loud,

Seal telephoned me and told me he was the man I was told would call me.  It was time to meet and he chose a hangout with which I was readily familiar.  It was the mid-1980s and with the decadence of that time and the free-flowing cocaine, Cajun's Wharf was a hangout for the bond daddies such as Lasater and company.  With a live band and lots of good-looking women, Bill and I would go there whenever he had a total disregard for the consequences of messing around in public while in the state.

I asked Seal over the telephone how I would know him. "I'll know you," he said with a matter-of-fact tone that made me wish I hadn't asked.  It was another reminder that these people made the rules and that Bill's advice was all I could depend on—just don't ask questions and do what you're told.

The first words out of Seal's mouth, "How's the Guv?" re-minded me of Magruder's apparent familiarity with Bill.  An overweight, jovial, almost slap-happy man as my next contact with C. I. A. was not exactly what I expected.  Seal, too, knew everything about me.  He focused on my D. E. A. training as Magruder had done in Dallas.  He knew of my meeting with Magruder and declared, "I'm the man they told you would call."  He had an extensive knowledge of airplanes and having been trained on Beech Barons, a twin-engine pas-senger plane on which we ferried Bill, I knew he was an experienced pilot.  He was planning a trip.  The 'operation,' as he called it, would be an airplane flight and I assumed, since all he talked about were jets, that we would be traveling first-class.  He said we would only be gone one day and he would call me later with the details.  I again had a million questions I wanted to ask this guy and following Bill's advice was hard.  I would later wish many times, I had demanded some answers from both of them.

✳   ✳   ✳

Mena, Arkansas is a tiny town near the Oklahoma border in far western Arkansas.  I didn't know why Seal wanted to meet me in such a far away place for an out-of-the-country trip. I had expected to leave from Little Rock as Seal had led me to believe he had flown an airplane into the Little Rock airport for our meeting. He told me to be at Mena before dawn which meant I had to leave my house in Little Rock around three-o'clock in the morning. I had only told Bill I was being tried out on an assignment. "Don't worry about it," was his advice I will never forget. "You can handle it," were his parting words. That was easy for him to say. I was about to go through a real test of my commitment to getting this job.

As I drove through the open gates of the Mena Intermountain Regional Airport, I recognized the buildings that made up the flight center from a previous trip to the town by air with Bill. What shocked the heck out of me was the huge dark airplane with engines already running waiting on the tarmac. I had driven my white unmarked police car on this trip and as Seal had said he would, I saw him waddling over to meet me. I was dressed casually as he had told me to. As I started to ask about the plane, he grabbed my arm and yelled for me to leave my billfold, watches and rings, anything I had on me, in the trunk of my car. He then said to leave the car keys over the front tire. I didn't realize why at the time, but I complied, re-membering Bill's advice of doing what I was told and not asking questions.

What I came to know as a C-123 cargo airplane reminded me of its big brother the C-130s assigned to the Little Rock Air Force Base. This plane was warmed up and ready to go and I had a sense I might have been late. Seal led me into a side door of the low-slung idling airplane, obviously just waiting on me. I stepped into a hollow cavernous shell of a plane as Seal struggled to speak over the noise. "Sit here and don't get up," he said as he directed me to a bench seat on the copilot side of the plane. Seal climbed up a small set of stairs and into what I supposed was the cockpit area. As I buckled up, I looked to the rear of the plane and saw two Hispanic men already sitting down and strapped in. The men were sitting near a huge pallet covered by a dark tarpaulin. Over the tarpaulin was a netting of sorts attached to some straps. They just looked at me and I at them. It was obvious from their relative calm, however, they had been there before.

One cannot imagine the noise this airplane made as it lumbered down the Mena airport runway. I had been there before on the trip with Clinton and knew the treacherous terrain a pilot had to negotiate just to get in and out in a small plane I was used to flying in. As I struggled to look out what I knew to be windows, I quickly found out they were all covered—no one could see in and I couldn't see out. I assumed Seal was flying the plane and I hoped at least half of the skills as a pilot he had boasted about were true. As I was to learn, I hadn't seen anything yet.

We made it off the ground somehow as I drew strength from the two Hispanic guys at the end of the plane. I wasn't sure if they were really as confident as they acted or if they just put a different valuation on human life than me. We flew for about an hour, it seemed. I couldn't be sure since Seal had commanded I leave my watch in the trunk of the car with everything else. Seal would not appear from the cockpit area and I finally was relieved to feel the plane start to make what I realized was an approach to land. We touched down in what Seal later told me was New Orleans for fuel. Declassified intelligence reports indicate we were actually at an air base in Mississippi.

No one got off the plane and we again were rumbling down the runway but without as much obvious strain on the plane. All the while, these guys in the back seemed as calm as ever. I began to wonder what their function on this trip really was. I knew I hadn't a clue as to why I was there.

This airplane must have had one big gas tank. We flew for what seemed like hours . The airplane at first took off in what seemed to me to be a normal manner but then dropped down to what I could tell by the plane's attitude was a lower altitude. We stayed at that level for the majority of the time we were in the air. The drone of the engines was my only company until the boredom was broken by a sudden flurry of activity with the Hispanics in the back of the ship. They began to pay particular attention to what I would eventually call the 'pallet,' which was lying in the center of the plane's belly. I couldn't tell exactly what they were doing but it was obvious they had done it before. As they worked on the web and tarpaulin-covered pallet I sensed the airplane was gaining altitude again.

This would be the first time I was to see Seal since we had taken off at Mena. As he squeezed his way through the door that led to what must have been the cockpit, he yelled to me, "Hang on L. D., we're gonna rock-and-roll!" I had absolutely no idea what he meant, but I was soon to find out what this whole 'mission' was about and what the role of the quiet Hispanics was. About five minutes after Seal retreated back into the cockpit and as the Hispanics, or 'Beaners' as Seal would later call them, increased their activity, a new sound pierced the constant droning of the engines. The whine of what was obviously an electric motor of some kind filled the shell of the interior of the cavernous airplane. To my horror the entire rear section of the blunt-ended aircraft began to open up. A sort of tail gate as one might see on a pickup truck was lowering and I could for the first time see daylight—and a rush of warm, humid air. The Hispanics were on each side of the pallet and with the newly available light I could see they had some sort of headphones on. I supposed they were talking with someone up front. I was sweating bullets at this stage of the game. I don't believe Mike Tyson could have pulled me out of that bench seat as the pucker factor was at plus ten.

But I wasn't prepared for what would happen next. My appreciation for the Hispanics and their level of skill was to be sealed forever as I watched wide-eyed while they actually pushed this huge pallet from the middle of the airplane—*and out the back door while we were flying*! Now, I was no stranger to being in tight situations, but I must say, since I still didn't know what I was doing there in the first place, I began to wonder if I may be the next thing out the door. Moreover, I was seriously reconsidering my level of commitment to and desire for this association with the C. I. A. "Just do what you're told and don't ask questions," was Bill's admonition. That was easy for him to say since he was back in Arkansas on terra firma. In reflection, it was probably about then I started to really question his motives for furthering my involvement with this group of people.

As slowly as the back door had opened, it began to close. While the motor sounds accompanied the Hispanics' return to their seats, Seal (or whomever was flying the plane) sharply turned the airplane to the left as if evading something or someone. This was accompanied by a discernible rise in altitude. In an unpressurized airplane these maneuvers are easy to perceive, and Seal was leaving no room for doubt. I remember thinking during the flight about how Seal had bragged about his flying abilities when I first met him at Cajun's Wharf. I again hoped some of the claims were true.

It was not long before we would be landing and none too soon for me. I was dying to confront Seal with questions as to what had happened and why, but knew I wouldn't then or ever. I still wanted that job that badly. Seal would later tell me we had touched down in Tegucigalpa, Honduras. It was obvious that after the uneventful landing we had stopped to refuel. I remained in my seat as the Hispanics left the airplane through the same door I had used at Mena. They seemed to not even notice me as Seal himself came down the short set of stairs that led to the cockpit. After making sure I was alive, Seal went out the same door.

The two Hispanics would return just behind him. Each of the two had what looked to be an army duffel bag, the kind you may see in a military surplus store, over each shoulder. As they took the bags back to their position at the rear of the airplane, I remember thinking this was their laundry or personal belongings in the bags—boy was I wrong.

Seal landed the huge plane at Mena after we had seemingly retraced our route back, including the refueling stop. As the plane parked at the same spot from where we had left in what seemed an eternity ago, Seal came down the stairs and opened the door. He motioned for me to follow as I realized we were back in Arkansas. He followed me to my car as I retrieved my keys from the front tire. I told Seal that I was expecting something like I flew Clinton in, a twin-engine small Beech Baron or even a jet like he talked about at Cajun's Wharf. Seal, seeing I was obviously still shaken up, told me to just sit back for the ride. He then handed me a manila envelope which I found to contain $2,500 in used American bills, my payment for sitting back for the ride.

All during the long drive back to Little Rock, I was filled with anticipation about telling Bill. I was hesitant on the one hand to even mention any details since I knew I was being tested as to my suitability for the job. I especially didn't want Bill to convey any ideas of my being over-inquisitive back to whomever he was talking to at the C. I. A. When I returned to the Mansion on my next shift, I never had the chance to break the news. As we met each other on the walkway between the guard shack and the back door of the Mansion he yelled, "You having fun yet?" I took the opportunity to speak freely and told him the airplane I had been on was quite big and not exactly what I had expected. His only answer was, "You're a big boy, you can handle it." The admonishment he had given me earlier to 'do what I was told and not to ask questions' was what I read from that. On my next trip I was to find out why.

Seal kept his word and telephoned me for a meeting. We actually had at least two more. One occurred at the Cajun's Wharf bar with another curiously at Charlie Trie's restaurant near the state capitol. On one of the occasions, the Secretary of State in Arkansas at the time, Bill McCuen, remembered I had introduced Seal to him at Cajun's Wharf.

Seal was more forthcoming with information now and for whatever reason, increased trust or confidence in me, proceeded to share with me why we had made the flight, and we would make another.  Guns, more specifically U. S. made M-16s were in the crate covered by the pallet, according to Seal.  He even asked me if I wanted one, which at the time I thought was crazy.  They were going to the Contras, the rebels fighting the Sandinista government in Nicaragua[3].  All of a sudden the essay on 'Marxism in Central America' Bill had suggested for my C. I. A. application made sense.

The next trip I was to take came in December.  My initiation to Seal having occurred in October, I was anxious to move this thing along since my contact with the agency consisted mostly of telephone calls and of receiving a letter of nomination for employment.  I was going by what Magruder in Dallas had promised.  I would first have to work at a 'lower level' before being considered for the operations officer spot.  I didn't mind.  Contract work, as I then saw it, paid well and 'sitting back for the ride' was not very hard work if you could keep your eyes shut and your ears plugged—and of course your mouth closed.

I was going through a very traumatic time in my personal life.  Becky, who would marry me within the year, had a younger brother Read who was severely ill with cancer.  Read and I were very close and I knew the prognosis was not good.  'Duty' called, however, as at the end of December Seal told me we would need to make another trip.

I drove my personal car to the Mena airport that day, a Datsun 310 hatchback, and hoped we would be taking a different airplane this time.  As I drove through the now-familiar gate in the still-dark morning, I saw what looked to be the same dark airplane sitting in the near-identical spot, engines running.  I knew the routine and in fact had already cleared my pockets of what I now knew would be damning evidence of my identity.  I stashed my keys over the front tire and joined Seal as he led me to the airplane.  Although I don't know if the exact route was the same, the attitude of the airplane resembled that of the first trip.  The interior of the airplane, its cargo and contents were identical as well, as were the Hispanics who were now somehow comforting to me since I now knew their purpose and skill. I wasn't nearly as surprised as the back door opened and, perhaps sensing my level of comfort, Seal this time didn't warn me of it either.

The major differences in this trip lay in the appearance of whom I thought to be the copilot of the airplane. A white male about thirty-five years old sporting a baseball cap, he casually asked how I was doing. I assumed he knew I was along for the ride and he asked me nothing else. I never saw that man again; but later, others thought he had to die for some reason. I've always wondered if he is alive today.

The other difference was that Seal himself would carry on two of his own duffel bags and place them near the door. We seemingly retraced our steps back to Mena when another change of plan unfolded. This one would cause me to confront Bill Clinton with evidence of a crime he knew was being committed.

# CHAPTER NINE
## Bill Clinton and the Crimes of Mena

From the start I thought it curious that Seal had brought on two duffel bags. This brought to my mind images of Seal staying, in what he said was Honduras, long enough to carry such a large load of clothes. All sorts of things ran through my mind as to the reason for these trips. Was I to be trained to be qualified as a 'kicker,' as Seal called the jobs of the Hispanics in the back of the airplane? Perhaps I was to be trained to fly the C-123. The final difference in the second trip was that Seal grabbed one of the duffel bags as we exited the airplane and headed toward my car.

Seal swung the bag over his shoulder like a toy and followed me to the Datsun hatchback as I popped the door open. Seal threw the bag top first into the back of the car. I thought he was going to ride with me to Little Rock. I had to lay down the collapsible back seat for the bag to fit. I knew I was going to have to make the front seat fit for the big guy as well. I opened the passenger door first, more to make adjustments for his girth than to be polite, and quickly adjusted the seat. Seal walked to the front of the Datsun and got only partially in the door. It was already dark and the inside light stayed on even after I had closed my door. Seal reached back to open the duffel bag in the back. He removed a manila envelope identical to the one he had given me after the first trip. I knew what was in the envelope but there was something else. He reached deeper into the bag and gave me the shock of my life.

Seal's face had a sly, smirky, almost proud look as he removed a waxed paper-wrapped taped brick-shaped package from the bag. I immediately recognized it as identical to bricks of cocaine from my days in narcotics. I didn't know what to think and began demanding to know what was going on. I cursed, ranted and raved and I believe I actually caused Seal to wonder if I might pull a gun and arrest him. Seal threw up his hands and tried to calm me down saying everything was all right and quickly exited my car. He removed the bag from the back and hustled back toward the plane.

I at once felt a sense of panic and relief that Seal was gone. Had he left something in the car? Was I about to be surrounded by the police? Wait a minute I *was* the police and furthermore this was an operation sanctioned by the C. I. A. and I was recruited by them—and by Bill Clinton. It was a long drive back and I had lots of time to try to rationalize what had happened. I would become furious with Bill for shepherding me through this mess, indeed for getting me involved. I would then as quickly think of explaining it all away as a 'sting' operation designed to trap the people on the other end of our flight who maybe had sold the drugs to Seal. Through my narcotics enforcement experience this seemed to be the most logical explanation. But surely as much as Bill had known about this whole operation, he would have told me, warned me. He was having a good time living this thing through me while not facing the dangers inherent in the work. There had to be an explanation, but I would not hear it until another tragedy would unfold.

Becky's brother Read was terminally ill with cancer when I made the flight and Becky did not want me to go. She knew I was traveling out of the country for the C. I. A. but she did not know where I was going. She also knew it would not be for long, but as feared by her, it was too long. The day after my return, still shaken from the incident at Mena, I called Becky to tell her I was back, hoping to confide in her my concerns about what had happened. It would not be possible since her brother had died during my absence. I immediately went to her side at her family's home in Little Rock. While I wanted to share with her my fears of being involved in an illegal operation and of how Bill had initiated this chain of events, I knew this was not the place or time to do so. I realized I had to wait until after the funeral to approach Bill since he was to preach the service at the church for the family.

I had to restrain myself as Bill conducted the funeral ceremony for Read at the Second Presbyterian Church in Little Rock. I had so many questions that needed to be resolved before that telephone rang again. I needed to know what to say to Seal, Magruder, the Agency headquarters or perhaps the Drug Enforcement Administration if they knocked on my door. At the cemetery, Mark Allen, at that time my close friend, accompanied me as we watched Bill and Hillary pay their respects. Mark knew I was doing something covert for a new job but knew no details. He also knew how close Becky and I were and how distraught I seemed to be about something beyond Read's death. As Mark looked at me with a puzzled expression, I could hold back no longer. I began to cry under the pressure and asked Mark, "What am I going to do now?"

I confided in my brother who knew I had been making trips out of the country for the C. I. A. He didn't know exactly what I was doing, but when I returned from the second flight with Seal, he knew something was severely wrong. I told Dwayne I had become involved in what I thought was a drug operation. We were at the Mansion, sitting in my car. When he asked who was behind the deal, I simply nodded toward the Mansion. He knew whom I meant.

I did what I thought was right and decided to confront Bill directly. He had known about the first trip and had facilitated my involvement with the C. I. A. I did not have a telephone number or any way through which to contact Magruder. The personnel office in Dallas would be of no help and I couldn't tell anyone in law enforcement. What if it was a legitimate sting operation? I had to talk to Bill personally. If he didn't know, I knew he would be able to ask the people that did know.

When I arrived at the Mansion I had already determined Bill was going to be there alone. The justifications I had made in my mind, for what I had seen and experienced, faded as I pulled in the back gate of the Mansion. The tension was building up inside me as I saw Bill coming out the back door. I was getting mad all over again as I got out of my car and he strode over to me. It was the first time we talked since the trip, the trip he knew I was going to take. His mouth opened and the words, "You having fun yet?" were already forming on his lips when I burst out, "Do you know what they're bringing back on those airplanes?" He immediately threw up his hands in a halting fashion and took a couple of steps back. I know he thought he was in danger of receiving a class A state police ass-whipping. My hopes of an innocent explanation to the whole sordid affair were dashed with the now-famous line, "That's Lasater's deal! That's Lasater's deal!" he whined as if he had just taken a tongue lashing by Hillary. "And your buddy Bush knows about it!"

Bill had done to me what I had seen him to do to so many other people. I, too, had now been used and severely betrayed. I immediately ran to Becky, who lived in a small house on the Mansion grounds. I told her of the incident and cried with the pain it had caused me. She was still grieving from the loss of her brother and I knew it was unfair to pile all of this on top of her, but it was as if someone had just stuck a knife in my back. I had never before felt so used and lied to.

I have wished I had stayed on and continued that conversation with Bill many times over the years. It's not clear if I had it to do all over again exactly what I would have done differently, but I could have done one of two things. I could have either given him the class A treatment which would have probably been the worst thing I had ever done in my life, or I could have demanded further explanation for what 'Lasater's deal' meant. Although I didn't give him a chance to explain the comment, I felt that I didn't have to. It had all fallen into place. The only place I had ever seen Bill in a room where cocaine was available was at Lasater's. Was the cocaine on the airplane really 'Lasater's deal'? I can't say for sure, but Dan was involved and convicted of distribution of cocaine— Colombian cocaine. It would not be the last time I would hear of Colombian influence in this miserable sequence of events.

And what of the 'my buddy Bush' comment? What was I to make of that? Did the cozy and pleasant relationship Bill had with Bush have a connection to all this? Is that why, years later, I was allowed to fly the Bush kids around Arkansas and openly campaign for him in the 1988 presidential election? I wish I had the answers. The country deserves to know the truth.

I received one more call from Barry Seal after the trip. I had already called the C. I. A. personnel office in Dallas and told them to withdraw my name for consideration. As I explained this to Seal, he countered, not with an explanation that would legitimize his actions at Mena airport, but with the line, "there's lots of money to be made." It was not until then that I started worrying about the two $2,500 payments I had received from him for the trips. While worrying about the consequences of my actions, I, at the same time, wished I had gotten a lot more because of the trouble I had been through. Losing my friendship with Bill, being away from home when Read died, and discontinuing my relationship with the C. I. A., thus losing the prospect for a job. By then I wished I had never applied with the agency. I simply told Seal never to call me again. He never did.

Bill and the C I. A. were obviously worried about what I knew and what, if anything, I would do with the information. Bill and I never spoke again about that plane trip or his claim of Lasater's involvement.

But I was not done with the C. I. A.. In early 1985, I received a telephone call from a man at the Mansion who identified himself as Felix Rodriguez. A man who claimed he was Barry Seal's boss. He asked if he could come to Arkansas and meet with me and I agreed. Could it have been that Seal was doing the drug transports on his own? I was more curious than anything else and had to find out. Rodriguez was the man to tell me.

Felix Rodriguez is a Cuban-American with a long history of intelligence work. He had telephoned me at the Mansion and wanted to meet me there in the parking lot. When he arrived, he drove in the back gate as if he had been there before. We sat in his rental car and shook hands. Felix was a polished, articulate man and it was obvious he did not like Seal. He had already been told by someone about my experiences with Seal and was obviously upset with what Seal had done. I am still puzzled over how Rodriguez found out about the incident. When I telephoned C. I. A. personnel in Dallas, I never mentioned what had happened with Seal. It must have come from Bill through whomever his contact at the Agency was. Rodriguez made me feel comfortable. He had C. I. A. credentials which he showed me. "Don't worry about him. We'll take care of him," is how he assured me of the 'problem' with Seal. Indeed Seal would die a violent death a year later-at the hands of whom is still a point of controversy in some circles. This lifted a great burden from me as I now felt Seal was a renegade contract employee who was making money on the side while dropping guns for the Agency. It still did not explain why Bill had offered the 'Lasater's deal' defense or indeed why he even was involved in getting me into the situation in the first place. I would have been content with the explanation Rodriguez had given me but there was more. Rodriguez was apparently trying to smooth things over by offering me another chance to continue my involvement with the Agency. Whether or not Bill had influenced this decision, I have never known. Rodriguez did talk as if he knew Bill and it always puzzled me that he knew how to get in the back gate to the Mansion. He never asked directions on the telephone and only people familiar with the Mansion knew the back gate to be the easiest point of entry.

Felix and I had some mutual friends. From my days in attending Drug Enforcement Administration schools in south Florida, I had come to know a couple of his Cuban associates. Nick Navarro, who was an instructor at one of my schools in Miami was a friend of Felix's. Raul Diaz, a narcotics officer in Miami, was also an associate of Felix and Felix wrote of them in the autobiography *Shadow Warrior* he published three years later. Rodriguez indeed wrote of meeting with Diaz around the time he met with me in early 1985. In that same book, Felix also discloses he was in the United States to meet with Donald Gregg (Dan Magruder) as well. Felix had asked me if I wanted to meet again with Magruder, a meeting that never occurred.

The next assignment for me would be much different from the last—and thank God it wouldn't involve a C-123 airplane.

# CHAPTER TEN

## Leaving the Mansion, Bill, Hillary and the Agency

Grand Bahama Island is a wonderful place. I would come to see all of it over the next ten months as Rodriguez placed me in an apparently ongoing operation that involved guns as well. I would enjoy the place so much that, like Campobello Island, I would later take my friends and family down to enjoy the gin-clear waters and friendly people. This time I would have a real job to do. The island was apparently an important cog in the wheel of supplying guns to Central America as was Mena airport. Rodriguez would pay me $1,000 per trip. I would make three of them in the spring, summer and fall of 1985.

All during that year I was distancing myself from Bill personally. He had promised me a good job in state government away from the Mansion. I always assumed that Bill was behind my getting the Bahamian job, but never asked, for fear he might come up with some other new revelation like the 'Lasater's deal' comment.

In this, my last association with the Agency, Rodriguez would telephone me when I was needed. I would then fly commercially to Miami where a pilot would meet me and take me down a flight of stairs at the Miami International Airport to the awaiting plane, a puddle-jumping Cessna. He took my bag, said hello and never said another word to me until we got to the island. I remember being surprised that the flight was so short, not realizing Grand Bahama was so close to the Florida coast. When we landed the pilot taxied to an area beside the main terminal to an awaiting jeep.

'Bull,' as he was called, was waiting for me. A man of few words, Bull took me to a hotel located in the interior of the island and handed me a room key. He said he would be back to pick me up that night and told me to charge anything I needed to the room. I explored the hotel and casino across the street and found the food to be great—all in all a nice place to visit. I wondered what I would be doing this time. I was still a little worried this may be a setup to get me out of the country and out of their hair permanently after what had happened with Seal.

That night Bull rang my room and I came out to find him in the same jeep he had been driving earlier in the day. After we had driven out of the Freeport town center, Bull reached into the back of the jeep and gave me another shocker. Bull produced what I now know to have been a Soviet-built AK-47 assault rifle with a collapsible stock. The thought did occur to me that I might have been right about my fears of being put out of this business for good. To my relief, Bull handed the rifle to me and asked me if I knew how to use it. He knew I was a policeman, but I had never fired an AK before. I lied and said I did and placed the weapon on the floor between my legs.

This assignment would be much easier than the last, but it wouldn't pay as much. Bull dropped me off on a paved road at the end of which was a boat dock with one fluorescent light illuminating several boat slips. He didn't clearly tell me what to do as he said, "Don't let anyone come down this road." He had driven to the end of the road by the time I wondered what he meant by that. Fortunately I never had to find out since all three times I was in the Bahamas that was all I had to do, just stand there and watch.

About fifteen minutes later I could hear a boat coming closer to where Bull was sitting in the jeep. A sleek tapered 'cigarette' boat pulled up to one of the boat slips and I could see movement inside. Bull met two men at the boat slip and they proceeded to unload several metal containers onto the dock. Bull would later tell me these contained guns like the one he had given me. The boat left as quickly as it came. A few minutes later another boat similar to the first, but definitely not the same one, entered the slip. Bull, still standing on the dock, helped the men in the second boat load the same canisters back onto their craft. As the boat left the dock, Bull jumped into his jeep and drove back to me. As I jumped in, Bull took the AK and put it in the back of the jeep.

The same process would be repeated on my second trip. Again Bull gave me $1,000 in U.S. currency and identical boats took part in the transfer of whatever was really in those canisters. For my last trip, Bull told me there was a change in plans. Instead of driving to the remote area with the boat slips, this time we would drive directly to the ocean front. We arrived at dark near what looked to be some sort of oil transfer station with a huge pier. Bull dropped me off at the entrance to the platform where he waited for another boat like the one I had seen on previous trips. It wasn't long before the switches between boats had been made and we were out of there. When I returned to Arkansas after my last trip to the Bahamas, I realized something about those operations. I had never asked Bull what I should do if someone did come down that road. And, perhaps most important, I never even checked to see if that gun was loaded.

Becky and I were ready to leave the Mansion. Bill was still running hard trying to recruit any woman he could bed and I was tired of being the chief procurement officer. He and I were drifting apart over the way he raised money and all the rest of the dirty politics. For example the way he betrayed his so-called friends in deference to the 'high bidder' in making political appointments. Robin Dickey was leaving as the Mansion administrator, a move sparked by Hillary's finding out about Robin and Bill's relationship being more than just a professional acquaintance. Robin was sick of Hillary but needed the job. She would later be recruited back into the fold during the 1992 presidential election as Bill tried to keep everyone silent about his 'affairs of state' in Arkansas. Robin would ultimately follow Bill to the White House in a paid position. After my Paula Jones deposition in which I testified under oath to my knowledge of the affair between Bill and Robin, she was transferred to the Pentagon a la Monica Lewinsky. One has to wonder about the efficacy of the practice of dumping Bill's ex-paramours into top-secret clearance positions.

Bill and Hillary had met with Ann McCoy, Becky's mother, about taking Robin's job. I was there the day Bill met Ann and saw him admiring her redheaded good looks that belied her age. Ann's husband was there as well, and Bill came up with one more insult after he had met the two. He asked me, "She's a looker L. D., but what's she doing with that goofy son-of-a-bitch?" I looked at Bill with what must have been a look that could kill. He backed up on the statement by saying they just didn't go together and that was all he meant. Here this guy was talking about my future in-laws and grading my mother-in-law. That's how sick everything was getting at the Mansion.

Desperate to get out, I found a position at the Arkansas State Crime Laboratory. A former trooper named Jim Clark, who had worked at the Governor's Mansion with me, was moving up to the director's position and we had talked about me coming over to fill his old post as assistant director at the lab. Jim had signed off on it and Hillary had as well. Bill promised me the job saying that with my narcotics experience, it would be a good position for me to take.

The time came in June for Jim to take over the director's position. After the ceremonies had been completed and Jim had assumed his new duties, I asked Bill when we could make the move. He told me I needed to talk it over with Jim. Bill seemed nervous as I headed for the guard shack and the telephone. What Jim had to tell me would floor me. He said he had decided he didn't need an assistant and that the deal was off. I hung up the phone and went immediately to Bill. I demanded to know what had happened. Bill said in his ever-so-meek voice, that he acquires when he has been caught red-handed, that he had to defer to Jim's wishes. "Defer hell!" I shouted at the top of my voice. I felt like round two had begun and I should make up for not giving him the class A butt-kicking I should have done back in the 'Lasater's deal' debacle. Instead, needing my job and not wanting to get Becky into trouble, I turned and left—I had quit to his face. After calling him a few assorted (and appropriate to this day) names that apply to his heritage and lack of veracity in just about anything he says or does, I drove out of the Mansion—I had worked my last day for Bill Clinton.

The director of the Arkansas State Police, Tommy Goodwin, had been a friend to me. I drove directly to his home, as this was on a weekend, and pleaded with him to transfer me out of the Mansion detail. He knew I had planned to go to the Crime Laboratory job and asked me what had happened. When I told him of Bill's lie, he wasn't surprised. He too knew Bill Clinton. Tommy told me he had only a position in the auto theft unit and I jumped on it. It was dirty work, inspecting stolen vehicles for the confidential serial numbers located on the engine and transmission, but I took it. The job was Monday through Friday and I could spend more time with my daughter. But I was still in the Arkansas State Police.

Becky soon quit the Mansion but stayed on long enough to find her own replacement as Chelsea's baby sitter. She cared deeply for the little girl and wanted there to be as little disruption in Chelsea's life as possible. Bill, always thinking everything is about him, became irate that Becky was leaving the Mansion as well. He couldn't understand that his betrayal of me was equally offending to Becky. One night after Becky came home to the house we were refurbishing, Bill telephoned to 'have it out' as he would put it. He started off with his calm flourishing tone by making small talk. Then he got to the point.

"Goddam it I told you I'd get you another job!" he shouted at me in his attempt to portray me as the one who was being irrational. "You're taking Becky away and Chelsea's the one who's suffering!"

I knew how to calm Bill. I simply handed the telephone to Becky. If Bill thought he (or I) could run over Becky, he was sadly mistaken.

"I helped get L. D. on at C.I.A. and Chelsea needs you!" I could clearly hear him yelling as Becky held the receiver.

"You just don't understand that what you did to L. D. you did to me," Becky retorted. "I'll find a replacement for Chelsea, don't worry."

Bill was satisfied and hung up the phone. Becky found an old sorority sister of hers who was perfect for the job. She introduced her to Bill and Hillary and they hired her. As soon as the girl was settled in, Becky left. She has never heard from the Clintons again. Just another person they used up, disregarded and discarded. It was their loss.

The fallout from the split hit immediately and from an unexpected source. Ann McCoy, Becky's mother, who was now serving as the Governor's Mansion administrator, a job Becky and I had gotten her, remained loyal to the Clintons. After Becky quit the Mansion, a deep divide was formed between Ann, her 'goofy' husband, and Becky. We had planned to be married at Becky's church and have a reception at the Mansion. Ann eventually 'demanded' we return to Bill on bended knee and we both refused. Ann, to this day, is by Bill's side as the deputy social secretary at the White House. Ann has never seen or held two of her grandchildren and Becky hasn't seen her father in twelve years. Sound bizarre? It should come as no surprise because ever since Bill and Hillary have been in public life, their die-hard followers have lied, cheated and stolen to keep them in office. The 'deer-in-the-headlights,' almost cultist loyalty, in the face of jail or even family break up is what has held these people together. The tragedy of my wife's family is a perfect example of what the Clinton's can do to otherwise wonderful people like Becky's parents.

Tommy Goodwin, who had given me the job away from the Mansion, would be pressured as well. Betsey Wright, Bill's fixer for 'bimbo eruptions' in his entire public life, didn't start her career of intimidating people in the 1992 presidential election. Shortly after I left the Mansion, Tommy called me and asked if I would meet with Betsey at her home in Little Rock. He said that Betsey had called him saying Bill was worried I would 'talk,' since I was mad at Bill when I left. I didn't want to be in the same room with the woman, but in deference to Tommy's job I agreed.

I drove to Betsey's home on Hill Road to find Jim Clark, my former friend and now Crime Laboratory director, there with Betsey. Betsey got right to the point by saying that Bill would give me another job and she was worried I would tell what I knew about Bill. So there would be no confusion, I told Betsey I wanted nothing other than to be left alone. That was it. I left and would not experience this sort of intimidation until the 1992 presidential campaign when Betsey would send one of her workers to see me.

By this time I was finished with the C. I. A. for good, or so I thought. Becky and I had made the decision to stay in Arkansas and raise a family. I couldn't keep wandering all over with characters like Seal and Bull, protecting gun running operations. Rodriguez and I had parted company on good terms and I thought I would have good memories of my brief, but eventful association with the Agency. I was always to worry about that cocaine I had seen on the airplane and I wondered who else had known about it. Would it come back to haunt me?

I didn't find out until about two weeks after Barry Seal had been killed in February of 1986 that they knew for sure who had done the job. A Colombian hit squad had nailed him in Baton Rouge while he was living in a halfway house. It didn't surprise me to see him come to that end the way he played things fast and loose, especially with airplanes and cocaine. I remembered what Rodriguez had told me about taking care of Barry and I assumed the Colombians had just beaten the Agency to it until I received a telephone call from Felix in May of 1986.

Rodriguez had a sense of urgency in his voice. He told me they had found the guy flying the second seat of the C-123 I had flown on, the plane Seal used to fly the coke into Mena. The man was to be in Puerto Vallarta, Mexico on June 21 and I was to be there to take care of him. I could even take my wife with me if I wanted, they would pick up the tab. He told me it would look better to do it that way anyway.

My maternal grandmother was very ill with cancer at the time. My uncle Jon Phelps, who was like a brother to me, begged me not to go. My brother Dwayne understood, since I confided in him the urgency of the trip and that it was 'business.' He knew what that meant since he was privy to the operations I had been on before. I had to go. I was told to find the target at the Hotel Playa Conchas Chinas near the edge of town in Puerto Vallarta. After giving the person at the desk one of my old undercover name of Michael Johnson he would tell me where to find him.

Rodriguez had it all figured out. He sent me a manual for a 7.62 rifle, a Fabrique Nacional or FN that I was told to pick up at noon on the 20th of June from a soldier at a pier just across from the Dos Pajaros Restaurant in the middle of Puerto Vallarta. I wouldn't be seeing Rodriguez before the trip and therefore would have to be reimbursed for any expenses when I returned.

I was to see Bill one more time before I left for Mexico. I was at the state capitol one day after the trip was set and ran into Bill. I told him I was going to Mexico to 'take care' of the problem there. I wanted to see if he knew about the problem and what his reaction would be. He told me, "That's good L. D."

Becky and I booked flight 537 and connecting flight 535 to Puerto Vallarta leaving on June 18. I booked the return for the afternoon of June 21 to make a quick exit after doing the job. I didn't know if I was up to it, but I knew as long as there was anyone around to implicate me (or Bill) in the cocaine running out of Mena, I would never be safe.

Puerto Vallarta is not a pretty place. Smog laden air and the roar of old buses belies the fact that just a few minutes down the sea coast at Mismaloya, the village where Elizabeth Taylor and Richard Burton filmed *Night of the Iguana*, the beaches are pristine and the water clear. Becky and I had booked lodging at the Holiday Inn directly across the bay from the Hotel Playa Conchas Chinas. We had a couple of days to enjoy ourselves but I obviously had other things on my mind. My grandmother's health and the job at hand kept my mind off trying to have fun under the unpleasant circumstances. I telephoned my grandmother's home on the second night only to find out that she had died. I was in Mexico to kill someone while the woman who had become my surrogate mother was calling my name as she died. I told my uncle Jon Phelps I couldn't come home. It would be years before I could explain to him why I wouldn't be a pallbearer at her funeral.

On the day of the 20th, Becky and I ate lunch at Dos Pajaros restaurant as I looked across the street to the pier where I was to pick up the 7.62 rifle. I saw a soldier pacing the boardwalk around a building that looked like some sort of military installation. As we left the restaurant, I told Becky to go on to the nearby straw market without me. I would meet her back at the restaurant in thirty minutes. I walked across the street and up to the soldier who looked as if he was about to raise the rifle he had on his shoulders to protest my advance. I introduced myself as Michael Johnson, I even had an Arkansas driver's license in that name. The soldier never uttered a word and instead walked around to the seaward side of the building and came back with a large straw bag and handed it to me. I was expecting something else. I didn't know what kind of container I had expected, but definitely something else. I didn't even look into the bag but found when I got back to the room why Rodriguez had sent me a manual on the FN before I left for Mexico. The gun had been disassembled. I quickly assembled it and was counting down the hours until the next day.

The 21st was our last day in Mexico. I told Becky I was going for a walk as I grabbed the straw bag and caught a cab for the southern edge of town where I knew the Hotel Playa Conchas Chinas was located. I stood outside the hotel, still not sure what I would do when I saw the copilot of that airplane. I wondered if he would recognize me, if he might try to kill me. Had he been forewarned? I knew I couldn't back out now and walked inside and straight to the desk. I handed the clerk $50 American and told him I was Michael Johnson. He motioned for me to sit down. It was just a few minutes before the desk clerk motioned and nodded toward a dark-haired man headed out the door which led to the back of the hotel. Horror ran down my spine. I had never seen the man before in my life.

I left the hotel with the straw bag in tow. I didn't keep it long. I dumped the bag and gun in a ditch by the road back into town. It was a while before I could get a cab. I eventually flagged one down and made it back to the Holiday Inn. We left Puerto Vallarta that afternoon as I thought I would never see that man again. I was wrong. Ten years later I would be giving a deposition in a civil case he would bring in Little Rock, Arkansas. His name was Terry Reed.

When Rodriguez called me after my trip to Mexico, I immediately told him the man I saw was definitely not the copilot of the plane I was on with Seal. He seemed as surprised as I was. He was understanding of my wishes not to pursue any more employment with C. I. A. and let me out, no questions asked. From my dealings with Rodriguez, I believe he was as opposed to drug dealing as he was to Communism. He often talked about both. I still do not think he knew in advance of the drugs being flown into the United States by Seal or anyone else who had connections to the Agency.

Years later, Terry Reed  wrote a book titled *Compromised: Clinton, Bush and the C. I. A.* in which he details his alleged involvement with the Agency. Reed writes of training flights he participated in at Mena where he served as an instructor pilot. In that book, which someone sent me in the mail unsolicited, I saw to my chagrin Reed was the man I had been sent to see in Puerto Vallarta almost ten years earlier. Reed, who apparently keeps records like I do, had even kept and printed his hotel receipts from the Playa Conchas Chinas Hotel in Puerto Vallarta in June of 1986. If anyone ever found out about my trip on the very same days, it would be hard for me to deny I had a hand in some aspect of the same operation in which he was involved.

The book followed a 1991 lawsuit[4] Reed filed against Buddy Young, the chief of security at the Governor's Mansion for Bill Clinton, and Tommy Baker, a former State Police Sergeant, at the time a private investigator in Little Rock. Reed claimed the two had fabricated a criminal case against Reed and his wife because of damaging information Reed knew about Bill Clinton. Essentially, he alleged that Clinton knew of and actively participated in the Mena operation. On at least one occasion, Reed claimed to have met Clinton with Young present.

I first read of the Reed allegations in the Little Rock newspapers. His cause was being championed by David Henderson of the American Spectator Board of Directors. I eventually would get the story out about what had happened in Puerto Vallarta after the statute of limitations had run and only after it was apparent the story would come out anyway. I had been subpoenaed by Reed in his lawsuit.

I gave a five-hour deposition to Reed's lawyers and the lawyer for the state of Arkansas who was representing Buddy Young. I didn't know if Reed knew anything about my presence in Mexico while he was there. He apparently had been sent by Rodriguez as well on another matter he writes about in his book. The deposition ended without any mention of the Mexico trip but I knew sooner or later I would be found out. As soon as the statute of limitations had run, I would cooperate with the investigation and grant an interview to Bob Tyrrell of the *American Spectator* who would later incorporate the accounts into his book *Boy Clinton*.

Reed's lawsuit would never make it to court. Federal Judge George Howard, a Carter appointee in Little Rock, disallowed any mention of C. I. A., Mena or any other activities that Reed or I had testified to in the depositions[5]. The suit was effectively gutted. If Reed couldn't get the evidence about C. I. A. entered, the suit had no chance.

Congressman Jim Leach of Iowa in 1995 became concerned about what he had been hearing and reading. As Chairman of the United States House of Representatives Banking Committee, he had oversight authority in the matter of Mena if indeed money had been transported into the United States. Also, if any financial institutions were used to launder the money, he had a legitimate interest in seeing the matter investigated. Mr. Leach would eventually force the C. I. A. to make acknowledgments of the activity but it would take a lot pressure to do it.

I first met with Congressman Leach's investigators at Little Rock. Greg Wierzynski, Steve Ganis and Jim Clinger met me at a hotel to ask me questions about what had happened at Mena. I recounted the activities and the flights I had taken and of how Bill Clinton had gotten me involved in the process. They listened intently and it was obvious they were serious about getting to the bottom of what had happened and finding out who was behind it all.

In the many months to come, I would deal principally with Greg Wierzynski. That cooperation extends to this day as the C. I. A. is still making admissions of their involvement in the activities of which I was a part (more on that later). Wierzynski, a former journalist, telephoned me one day and said Chairman Leach wanted to meet me personally. My wife and I were invited to meet with the Congressman at his office in Washington, D. C.. It would be the first of two meetings I was to have with Mr. Leach at his office.

Jim Leach is a breath of fresh air in a city where there is a distinctly politically polluted atmosphere. As you read the remainder of this book, I think you'll see just a microcosm of the double-dealing and treachery that pervades the everyday machinations of the town. Mr. Leach is a calm, quiet and deliberate man who listens carefully. He had obviously studied the issue of C. I. A. at Mena well before Becky and I met with him. It helped that he had the benefit of a competent and hard working staff headed by the intelligent Wierzynski.

Becky and I arrived to a cordial greeting from the Congressman. Free from the sometimes pretentious manner that some members of Congress exude, Mr. Leach made us feel at home, especially Becky. She was not used to dealing with politicians in Washington and avoided telling her story on most occasions. She realized, however, we had to make the truth known. It was the reason we cooperated with Mr. Leach and it is the reason for the publication of this book.

With Greg Wierzynski and Jim Clinger sitting in, Becky and I told what we knew. Becky shared what she knew about the C. I. A. and that I was gone from the Governor's Mansion on the trips. She also confirmed the trip to Puerto Vallarta. I filled in with details of the trips I had made and we both committed to cooperating with any hearings his committee may hold in the future.

Over the next few months I would stay in contact with Greg Wierzynski, a contact which continues as this book is released. One reason for continuing cooperation is that Mr. Leach requested reams of information from the C. I. A. and called for an internal investigation to determine what had happened. Wierzynski told me several times the C I. A. was stalling on releasing any information to the committee and progress was slow. It could be a long time before the whole story of what happened at Mena was known, if ever, he said.

In the interim, the C. I. A. was preparing its own internal investigation, if you could call it that. On November 8, 1996 Inspector General Frederick P. Hitz of the C. I. A. issued a seven page tome, admitting in part that the C. I. A. had contact with me in the mid-1980s. The report erroneously states, however, that *they* decided not to employ me. The report went on to admit that in 1984 the C. I. A. did engage in a 'two-week training operation' at Mena. It denied the C. I. A. engaged in or was 'associated with money laundering, narcotics trafficking, arms smuggling, or other illegal activities at or around Mena, Arkansas at any time.' The report was signed by A. R. Cinquegrana, the Deputy Inspector General for C. I. A.

One interesting aspect of the C. I. A. report is its admission that the agency did interact with state officials (read state police) through another agency. My boss, Tommy Goodwin, who was director of the state police during the time period in question, has admitted to me he had been told there was a C. I. A. operation going on during the mid-1980s. I also had admitted to Goodwin I had been involved. The occasion was a trooper association meeting in Jonesboro, Arkansas as Goodwin and I talked of the revelations being made in the media about the operation. I remember Goodwin telling me at the time, "I'm surprised Seal let you on that plane."

Congressman Leach wasn't satisfied, and neither was I, with what the C. I. A. was admitting publicly. First of all, anyone with any degree of intelligence could reason that the only way Seal knew to contact me was through someone at the C. I. A., or Bill Clinton. The C. I. A. and Clinton were the only people who knew of the details of my application and status with the Agency. Other people in the intelligence community had come forward to confirm the name Gregg had used was in fact Magruder. Seal's wife had heard Barry talk of a state trooper he had worked with and there was absolutely no denying I was in Puerto Vallarta, Mexico with Reed. The C. I. A.'s report did not make any sense.

Wierzynski told me they were continuing to ask for more material from the Agency. On March 16, 1998 the C. I. A. issued yet another report to the United State House of Representatives Select Committee on Intelligence matters. In the unclassified summary of the report, C. I. A. now admitted the agency had a *signed agreement* with then-Attorney General William French Smith. The agreement stated that C. I. A. did not have to disclose any drug trafficking they might have un-covered or known about during the Contra supply operation of which the Seal flights I was on were a part. That was a sub-stantial admission and a departure from the report of November, 1996. I called Wierzynski the next day about the report. He was unaware of the finding but did know the current director of C. I. A. was on Capitol Hill that day to testify before Congress. The issue still remains shrouded in the bowels of the *classified* report which someday the American people who care will demand to be revealed.

It doesn't bother me that the C. I. A. stonewalls on the issue of Mena airport. I understand there is a need to keep the secrets of intelligence gathering, its methodology and findings. What does bother me is Bill Clinton, Governor of Arkansas, was involved, a man who would be President of the United States. What the heck was he doing and why did he get me in-volved?

In this space I will put forth my informed theory once and for all. I believe Bill had a close friend from his days in England, a friend who serves in his administration now and was his contact in the agency then. Bill essentially knew of the operation at Mena since it is inconceivable that if Tommy Goodwin, director of the Arkansas State Police, had been apprised of the operation, he would not have told Bill. It may have been just happenstance that Bill came out of the Mansion that day as I was reading the employment ads for the C. I. A. in the *New York Times*. It was not a casual interest he displayed in getting me in touch with the Agency and by shepherding me through the application process. It certainly was not a casual or distanced interest he showed in helping me with the essay I wrote for the Agency and in briefing me on the interview process and testing procedures. The key evidence lies in Bill being informed of my activities at Mena.

In the midst of all this activity, Bill was making telephone calls to someone on my behalf. It's obvious the C. I. A. investigated none of this. The telephone records at the Governor's Mansion would prove this. Two troopers have come forward to admit they heard Bill talking about Mena airport as well. Trooper Bobby Walker told me that one day, as Bill and he were landing at the Mena airport, Bobby saw the C-123 parked on the tarmac. He asked Bill if the Air National Guard was there and Bill told him no, the plane was used for 'something else.'

Trooper Larry Patterson also said he overheard a conversation concerning Mena between Colonel Goodwin of the state police and Clinton. Goodwin was telling Clinton that Senators Pryor and Bumpers had told him to 'back off' Mena[6].

So what happened? It is obvious to me Bill got me involved in that operation for security purposes. The security of denial would be Bill's, if and when it would ever be found out drugs were coming into Arkansas on his watch, if he had a more or less personal representative on the plane—me. A representative he and everyone else knew would never be involved in drug trafficking. What Bill or the C. I. A. had not counted on was the recklessness and greed of Barry Seal. As the C. I. A. is now admitting, the Agency had a written agreement with the Attorney General of the United States not to have to disclose such shenanigans as they found out about them, *in the name of national security*! When Barry did queer the deal, instead of playing along, I confronted Bill who offered the 'that's Lasater's deal' excuse. Whatever happened between Bill and Lasater is unknown to me. I leave that to the reader to piece together using the facts I have provided considering their relationship as it was known to me.

There was one more curious aspect of the Mena case that involves George Bush. Bill and I always agreed about Bush. He made it a point to introduce me to him at the occasion in Portland, Maine and never berated him like Hillary did. There was some sort of common bond they shared all the way to Bush's White House. Incredibly to me, Bush appointed Bill to a national education panel to study education in America and had Bill and Hillary over to the White House. Becky and I laughed as we saw George and Barbara take them in with open arms.

But even more strange was that the state police in Arkansas, with full knowledge of then-Governor Bill Clinton, allowed me to escort the Bush clan all over the state during the 1988 presidential campaign. Bush was seeking to continue the Reagan legacy and Bill was the national co-chairman of Democrat nominee Mike Dukakis.

I flew around Arkansas with Bush sons Marvin, Neil and George. George Junior, as we called him, is the current governor of Texas. Special guests who came into the state, such as Senator Strom Thurmond, were my charges as well. Bush's brother Bucky Bush came in from St. Louis and we all partied at the Capitol Bar to Bucky's rendition of 'George Bush for President' sung to the music of God Bless America. I have great photos of the events and when I look at them I still wonder how I was allowed to do all that on state police time.

Why did Bill allow this? Something was there but I never knew what. Was it Mena and some sort of partnership that existed a few years earlier? If Terry Reed's book is to be believed, one did exist.

Soon after the 1988 presidential election, when Clinton allowed me to work in the Bush campaign, I traveled to Washington, DC to meet with the future governor of Texas, George Walker Bush. The eldest son of George and Barbara Bush, I had accompanied George Junior, as he was called, around Little Rock.

George, Jr. was working in the transition office for his father. When the presidency passes from one administration to another, every incoming presidential team sets up an office to handle the myriad problems of assuming power. Much of the work concerns placing campaign workers and contributors, categories into which I fit well, into jobs in the new administration. Becky and I still didn't really want to leave Arkansas but I made the trip with a couple of other friends who had worked in the campaign. George, Jr. remembered me from his Arkansas trip and signed a photograph of his dad with his own signature, "the other Bush." My two friends had looked through what is called the 'Plum Book,' a paper bound compendium of all the jobs in government that are political appointments. I didn't have much in mind but did broach the subject of Central Intelligence Operations Officer with George, Jr. "I wouldn't touch that with a ten foot pole," he declared quite firmly. "We don't get involved in that," he assured me. I've often wondered whether his father had followed that procedure while he was vice president at the time Bill Clinton introduced me to him in Maine.

Regardless of what the complete story was, bottom line, I was used. I'm not surprised and neither is anyone else who has known Bill and Hillary for more than two seconds. Whether it is the woman who may be a potential mark, the unsuspecting poor guy at the county fair Hillary would glad hand, or their supposed friends like Vince Foster or Webb Hubbell who have been left in their ruinous wake, they all should know by now that anyone is expendable in the eyes of the Clintons. In Mena, that someone was me.

I was a little surprised at the lack of media attention concerning the story about the C. I. A. I did get a few calls from radio stations and newspapers around the country, but I didn't talk to most of them since I didn't know if they were out to do a hatchet job on me or not. I knew who I could trust and I preferred to just let them write their stories without me. I still get calls from Hard Copy, American Journal and the other tabloid news shows but one call did somewhat surprise me.

One day my wife told me that Mike Wallace from the television news program *60 Minutes* had telephoned. He wanted me to call him back and I talked with Becky about doing it. I grew up watching Wallace and *60 Minutes* and was curious as to what he had to say. We had decided we wouldn't do an interview with them since we somehow didn't trust a news program whose producer has bragged about 'making' Bill Clinton's presidency happen due to the producer's decision to spin the interview *60 Minutes* had conducted with Bill and Hillary in 1992. That was the one where they softballed the Gennifer Flowers issue and allowed Bill to get off with the 'causing pain' statement. The same interview in which he was obviously, and now by his own admission, lying through his teeth.

When I returned Wallace's call he wasn't in. His secretary said he would call back straight away. He did. "Please hold for Mr. Wallace," as I told Becky that he was on the line. "L. D. this is Mike Wallace," he said flatly as we made trivial conversation for about thirty seconds. He got straight to the point with, "We're thinking of doing a story about the C. I. A. and Bill Clinton. The allegations you have made are at the center of it and we can't do the story without you." He then went on to tell me of his friendship with Donald Gregg, also known to me in 1984 in the Dallas Holiday Inn as C. I. A. operations officer Dan Magruder. "I just find it hard to believe a man like Donald Gregg would be talking with an Arkansas State Trooper," he said with a sort of prissy tone. Well I know some Arkansas state troopers may seem to be a lower life form, but still the remark did upset me a little. He sensed this and decided to go for broke. "L. D., I hear you like to take a drink," he offered, obviously buying into a Clinton lie that I was Little Rock's answer to Mayberry's Otis Campbell, the town drunk. "Mr. Wallace believe what you will, I'm not doing your story anyway, " I told him flatly. Just before hanging up he told me to make sure I call him when I wanted to talk. Don't hold your breath Mike.

# CHAPTER ELEVEN

## The Clinton Intimidation Machine

Quite a few of the people Becky and I saw after we left the Clintons were still friendly to us. Becky and I would constantly run into people in Little Rock who had followed Bill and Hillary to Washington. We would know them from the Governor's office where we worked at the same time. Bob Nash, now Bill's director of White House personnel, was one of them. One Christmas back in Little Rock we saw him and his wife at a department store and said hello. Bob is a really affable person who, I've always thought, stuck with Bill for the political experience and to try to do some good through him. He knew how Bill fooled around and what Hillary was like but saw Bill as the agent for change.

The similarities between Bob and Henry, the lead character in the movie Primary Colors, are striking. Besides the fact that both are African-American, they both stayed on with the Governor in their respective lives even though they knew he was a seriously flawed individual. I thought of Bob when the Kathy Bates character (Betsey Wright) gives the first couple a dressing down toward the end of the film. The Henry character leaves with her but in the end comes back to stay by his

Governor's side. I was hoping the final scene would be of Henry with his feet propped up in his living room watching the Inaugural Ball of the former Governor, then President. Instead Henry had capitulated and made a Mephistophelian pact. He was in the crowd at the ball by his new President's side.

One of the last times I saw Bob was at the Capital Bar in the old Capital Hotel in Little Rock. He was in town for a function at the Excelsior Hotel in 1997 when he walked into the bar. He pulled up a bar stool and we reminisced about the old days when things were a lot simpler. But he had turned into Henry of Primary Colors by then and the strain of the Clinton White House was showing. He asked me how things were going and I said not well. "I know what you mean," he said with empathy. "I know what you mean."

During the presidential campaign of 1992, I found it amusing that Bill and Hillary would be running for the White House. I knew that somehow Bill's baggage, the women, Mena, the McDougals and all the rest of their scandal-ridden rise to power in Arkansas that I witnessed and was a part of would preclude them from ever reaching their goal. I had miscalculated, in I assumed the national press would examine his record in Arkansas and all this would bring him down. I was dead wrong but I felt that way when Cathy Ford, a woman whom I had known while she worked for Betsey at the Governor's office during my tenure there, came into Diego's bar and grill one day during the campaign. Cathy sat at the end of the bar and just looked at me. I was sitting with my good friend Mike McCormack drinking a beer and told Mike I would be right back since I wanted to say hello to Cathy.

I had left on good terms with many of the Clinton staffers, terms on which I still stand with many of them to this day. I asked Cathy how she had been. I knew she had left Little Rock to return to San Diego some time ago. Cathy was acting strangely, almost in a covert fashion. Cryptically she asked how I had been doing. We conversed as she ordered a beer, stayed only two minutes and then left. I didn't think much about her visit the first time, but in a couple of days she was back. My friend Mike was with me again and I went down to the end of the bar where Cathy said hello again. I asked her if she was in town for a while. "Sure, I'm working in the campaign for Betsey," she said as the alarm bells finally went off. That's when she popped the question, one I'd heard last from Betsey at the meeting just after I left the Mansion. "You're not going to say anything about Bill, are you?" she asked, half-heartedly. It was then I realized this was no social visit. It was damage control time and Cathy was acting on Betsey's behalf. I quickly reiterated what I had told Betsey years before, "I just want to be left alone." Cathy didn't even finish her beer. She left the bar.

The third visit Cathy would make was overkill. I had already said I wanted to be left alone but she obviously had something else on her mind—or Betsey's. I told my friend Mike I was going to follow her when she left the bar to confirm my suspicions. I walked to the end of the bar to Cathy's now familiar stool. She went straight to the point with, "L. D., is it a job you want?" I told her one more time I didn't want a thing from Bill Clinton and walked back over to Mike. She left quickly and I told Mike I would be back after my surveillance. Cathy got into her car and I followed her. Exemplary of the Clinton 'keystone cops' operation, Cathy drove into a convenience store parking lot where she got out of her car in a rush. She walked to a telephone on the wall and straight to a waiting Betsey Wright in all her glory. I laughed at their crude attempts at espionage and decided to blow my cover as I simply pulled in behind her, got out of my car and went in the convenience store. Just for good measure, as I went in, I yelled, "Hi Betsey!" Realizing she had been busted, she threw her hands on her hips and said, in an obviously frustrated tone, "Hi L.D.!"

✳     ✳     ✳

I am glad I kept a lot of the letters and day books of that era, especially the essay draft for the C. I. A. that Bill wrote on. I knew there would come a day I would have to give testimony on what happened at Mena airport. I cringed in the late eighties as I watched the Iran-Contra hearings and recognized 'Dan Magruder' as being in reality Donald Gregg, who worked for Vice-President George Bush as his national security adviser from 1982 to 1989. It also didn't surprise me to learn later Gregg was in fact Felix's boss in Vietnam when they both worked for the C. I. A. Remembering what Magruder had told me about being an 'Asia expert' and of his service in South Korea, it also didn't surprise me to learn he had been station chief in Seoul in the 1970s. He later even served as ambassador to Korea under his good friend Bush. These ties to Bill and Bush have always amazed me and I don't know if we will ever know the truth of their relationship. Even after I left the Governor's Mansion I would still have close ties to Bill for a while and eventually to Bush as well. It was a most interesting time in my life.

A few years later, Mr. Mike Chertoff, senior counsel to the Senate Whitewater Committee, investigating some of the wrongdoing I had witnessed as Bill's friend at the Mansion, would have Betsey Wright at the witness table and grill her about me. In particular, Chertoff would ask her if she had seen or talked to me. "I've seen him in passing and asked how Becky and the kids were," she would respond with a straight face, knowing she didn't care if my family lived or died. As Chertoff closed in for the kill to catch her in the attempt to silence me, Senator Alfonse D'Amato broke in and took over the line of questioning. He left the successful line of questioning Chertoff had been pursuing and began an inane inquiry that might as well have been a discussion of the weather. Later, I will reveal information about Al D'Amato that would have knocked him out of the Senate if it had been revealed before the people removed him in the November 1998 election.

✳   ✳   ✳

Becky and I were married in August of 1985 in Baltimore, Maryland. I had become more active in the state police Fraternal Order of Police lodge that we had formed while I was still at the Governor's Mansion. We were in Baltimore for the national FOP convention, having given up all our plans for a big wedding at Becky's church followed by a Mansion reception. I was to become more and more active in the FOP and ran for president of the lodge a few months later. This would eventually put me on a collision course with Bill politically. Knowing Bill's true feelings about policemen, particularly state troopers, from my witnessing episodes such as the one at Trooper Louis Bryant's funeral, I had my work cut out for me. It was in my position as president of what was by then the Arkansas State Police Association that I met Bill at the state capitol the day he talked with David Hale. But it was not until I had developed a legislative agenda that called for enhanced trooper retirement benefits that Bill and I would clash.

The 1987 state legislative session was one in which Arkansas struggled to cope with serious financial shortfalls. I realized it would be hopeless to ask for pay raises even though Bill had let our state police rot and decay to the point that our troopers were driving unsafe vehicles with more than 100,000 miles on them. The troopers were at the bottom of pay and benefits in the nation and the department wasn't hiring any new employees. I started a magazine for the association, which I edited and wrote, that raised enough money to pay for a dental plan for all our employees. That pushed our membership to almost 100% of the state police employees and established the association as a viable lobbying entity. It also gave me the resources to fund an actuarial study to see if our state police retirement system could afford to lower the retirement age from 55 to 52 while increasing the annuities the current and future retirees would receive.

I drafted two bills, one for the retirement system changes and one for the current retirees. People who had retired with 30 years service would get up to 22% increases on what was already a pitiful retirement annuity. I worked on getting sponsors from the 135 legislators with the help of a network of troopers around the state. We went into the legislative session with a mandate and actuarial findings that showed the retirement system could pay for the changes without any further contributions from the state. It seemed too good to be true. I even had a meeting with Bill in his office at the State Capitol. The vice-president of the association, Bobby Walker, and our attorney Darrell Stayton, attended as Bill and I looked over the legislation. We posed for photographs, made small talk and I spoke of the support, justification and need for the legislation. He promised his support. But I didn't know at the time that Bill Clinton would be out to undermine the entire process.

Passing the legislation was not an easy task. Retirement bills come under intense scrutiny and by law must be the subject of further financial study to determine their long-term impact on the retirement system. After spending thousands of dollars on lobbying and forging alliances with many influential legislators, both bills passed both houses of the Arkansas legislature. All we needed was the governor's signature and the benchmark legislation would be law. Bill had a few slaps in the face and intimidation attempts for me before that, however.

Tommy Goodwin, the state police director, told me at the office shortly after we passed the bills that the governor told him he was going to veto one of them. I expressed my disgust and disbelief at the mere suggestion, since we had worked so hard for their passage. Bill's statements flew in the face of the legislative mandate we had received in the legislature. I summarily told Tommy to tell Clinton to pick one out and veto it if he must, but I was not about to pull down two pieces of legislation that had received well earned support. I wasn't going to do that to the troopers and the retirees I was elected to serve.

Weeks passed and the legislative session was coming to a close. In Arkansas, if a governor does not sign a piece of legislation, it becomes law without his signature 30 days after the legislature adjourns. I had hopes that Bill would take this route and let the bills become law with a silent protest. My anticipation ended when my friend Trooper Bobby Walker, who still worked at the Governor's Mansion, paged me out of a movie Becky and I were attending. I immediately called Bobby at the Mansion and was not surprised at what he had to tell me. "L. D., the governor just came outside and told me to call you and tell you that he "signed the goddamned bills." Bobby, who was vice president in the police association, said Bill's face was beet red, the way it gets when he's either mad at me, is lying, or is doing coke in the bathroom of the Boca Raton Resort.

Bill had thrown away our opportunity to have a bill signing ceremony. I had planned to have all of our bill sponsors to attend along with my executive board. Bill knew he had missed a photo opportunity which would portray him as a police supporter even though he had done everything he could to see the bills die in the legislature. Bobby Walker passed on a message to Bill at the Mansion for me. I told him to tell Bill that since he had signed the bills, I would still agree to a signing ceremony even though he had snubbed me the way he did. Bill jumped at the chance and we agreed to meet at the governor's conference room at the state capitol for the staged ceremony. As you look at the photograph of the event in this book, just remember there is not one iota of sincerity in that smile on Bill Clinton's face - and that piece of paper in front of him isn't even the bill in question.

Bill was determined to get me out of the state police association and out of the state police. As Bobby Walker left Little Rock for another job assignment in Fort Smith, Arkansas, I took on Larry Patterson as the new vice president of the association. Larry also worked at the Governor's Mansion where he too would witness many of the liaisons between Bill and women, instances he would later report to the world along with his co-worker Roger Perry in the original 'Troopergate' stories. Larry would act as my conduit to Bill in my remaining years as association president and through the next legislative session. In that session we would ask for significant pay raises for the troopers and had secured 75 of 100 House of Representative members as sponsors. Bill would have a hard time with this piece of legislation. The Arkansas economy the national media never examined during Bill's 1992 presidential campaign, was still bad.

Bill was trying to raise taxes to pay for the shortfall in state government. We needed the bill to pass and I came to a compromise with Bill. He met me in the hallway of the state capitol and asked for my help in converting some of our legislative sponsors' votes to voting for his tax bill. He said he would make our pay raise bill an administration bill with his full backing if I succeeded in getting the three votes he needed to pass his own bill. A special legislative session would be called later in the year and he would personally see to it that our bill was on the agenda. Like a fool, I agreed.

State Representative Tommy Mitchum was our lead cosponsor of the state police pay bill. A Democrat from rural Arkansas, he was a typical 'Southern Democrat' who voted conservatively on taxes. Tommy agreed to change his 'no' vote to a 'yes' on the tax hike. Representatives Ron Fuller and Jerry King did the same. I reported to Bill we had the three votes needed to pass his bill. He was elated and the bill actually passed the House. It ultimately failed in the Senate but we had kept our part of the bargain.

The regular legislative session came and went with the promise of the special session to be held in October. As the month approached, the troopers' hopes rose incrementally. Bill had promised that our Bill would be made an administration bill and I was on top of the situation. When the list of bills that had been placed on the agenda for the session came out, our bill was not there. I called the Mansion and demanded to talk to the governor. It would, however, not be until I cornered him at the Capitol that the weasel had to answer to his inaction. "L. D. I don't know what's going on. I'll check on it," was all he could come up with. I knew he was lying. I had seen him do it hundreds of times. I would work the halls of the Capitol the entire session and each time Bill would give a lame excuse as to why he had not filed the bill. The last time I talked with him I made it clear that it was the last day a bill could be filed under the rules of the session. He didn't have an answer.

Having had enough of his broken promises and realizing the responsibility I had to my association members, I walked to a reporter for the *Arkansas Democrat* whom I had previously informed of the situation. I told her to go with the story that the governor had broken his promise to the troopers. It would be the beginning of the end of my career.

Bill's reaction to the news story the next day was explosive and typical. Lie and make counter-accusations, admit nothing. Privately, Patterson told me Bill was livid and that he was going 'to get me.' That's Bill rationale. Attack the messenger regardless of whether he is delivering the truth. It's how he deals with me and anyone else who tells the truth to this day.

From that day on, I made it my mission to spread the word about how Bill Clinton did not care for the police and would lie to your face when telling the truth would help him. And I had a new platform from which to do it. Our state police association had joined the National Troopers Coalition, a nationwide group of some 45 state police associations representing thousands of troopers. Bill knew this and was aware I had been elected vice chairman of the group. The coalition held three meetings each year and during the successful legislative session on retirement I had him commit to supporting our bill on retirement reform as the keynote speaker.

The next meeting after Bill's betrayal in the legislature was in Atlanta, Georgia. I was prepared with a speech and handout to all the state presidents from around the country. As I spoke to the state presidents, I made three points: that our governor hated police officers, that he lied pathologically, and that, most importantly, he was running for president.  I pointed out that this man would be asking for their support in the near future. Many of these presidents were from sure-enough unionized state police associations, the kinds that endorse candidates and make contributions.

When word got back to Bill, he was incensed.  He demanded a meeting at the Governor's Mansion.  I certainly had no qualms about meeting him and agreed to attend along with Larry Patterson and Bobby Walker. I took the opportunity to schedule a meeting of the 24 board of directors of my association for later that same day.  At that meeting, I planned to tell them what Bill had said.

As we arrived at my old stomping grounds of the Governor's Mansion, we were led in the front door, a route I was not used to taking.  To my surprise we were to have company.  Bill had his senior adviser Jim Pledger and his chief of state police governor's security Buddy Young there in the living room. Why Buddy would be there was a mystery to me since he took no part in the business of the association. This is the same Buddy Young who followed Bill to the White House and was placed in a senior management position as regional director of the Federal Emergency Management Administration even though he has never graduated from college—and it shows. The same Buddy Young who allowed White House aide Bruce Lindsey to talk to him about 'Troopergate' damage control on a speaker phone while ABC News rolled tape of the embarrassing conversation. If Bill thought he could use this as intimidation, he might as well have used his current lapdog named Buddy, for Young had no impact on me whatsoever.

Bill started things off by turning his natural shade of  beet red and cursing violently.  "I am tired of being called a goddamned liar!" he howled as he tried to appear as a man who had been wronged.  To the apparent shock of the others, Bill went on to imitate a 'real' man yelling at the floor. "Now goddam it I've tried to do everything I can for the troopers and all I get is being called a liar!"  I let him pause and regroup and finally asked him, "Are you quite finished?" I wanted to tell him to look at me when I talked to him as I had told so many other crooks I had interviewed over the years. Instead, I proceeded to lay out in chronological fashion the sequence of events that had led up to this meeting. Of key significance in the chronology was the point where he screwed the living heck out of the state police.

Confronted with the facts, Bill draws up into the insecure little shell he occupies as a boy-man. You've seen it many times in press conferences and in his grand jury deposition. It's the mode he goes into when he is caught in a lie. "Well, all I know is we've got to get this straightened out," he offered calmly and almost effeminately. I agreed, and offered him an opportunity to address my board who were waiting at the Hilton Hotel in North Little Rock. I told him he had to address that group and tell them he was committed to a pay raise for the troopers. I made it clear to him these troopers were from all over the state; what he told them would be taken back and passed on to the troopers. He knew the networking I had devised and that any commitment would be irreversible. He agreed to the opportunity.

As Bobby, Larry and I got into the car at the Mansion, I could tell they were still unsure whether they had just witnessed what they thought they had. Bobby said, "L. D., you sure put him in his place like no one else ever has." I told Bobby the way to deal with Bill is to catch him in the lie and stick it in his face, something the national media has recently done in the Lewinsky affair.

We arrived at the Hilton and went straight to the meeting room where the troopers were waiting. I announced that the governor would be arriving soon and that we had come to an agreement. Bill walked in and announced there had been a 'misunderstanding' in the last legislative session but that from now on he would fight for a trooper pay raise. Even as he spoke, I could sense he was plotting to take me out once and for all. But the troopers got the raise in the next session.

In an ironic twist, after that particular meeting, Bill called me over to the side and wanted to talk privately. He asked me, since we were now again on friendly terms, if I would be interested in letting him know what was going on inside the camp of one of his potential opponents in the upcoming general election. Congressman Tommy Robinson had announced his candidacy for the Republican nomination for governor. Tommy, an ex-state trooper and county sheriff in Little Rock, had openly solicited my support in the election against Bill. He assumed he could beat Sheffield Nelson in the Republican primary, an assumption that would in the end prove to be false. I listened as Bill made his pitch. He honestly thought I would go along with him as he promised to *really* help us out with a trooper pay bill. I took that to mean that what he had just told us in the meeting room wasn't really the truth at all. As he spoke, I thought of the old adage, 'fool me once, shame on you; fool me twice, shame on me.' I wasn't about to buy into any more lies from the guy but still didn't openly want to antagonize him any further. I just let him think I would get back to him. I never did.

In the interim I tried my best to get the best deal for the troopers I could get. Bill was coming up for reelection and two formidable opponents emerged, one of which would eventually occupy the Governor' Mansion. Jim Guy Tucker was Bill's opponent in the primary and was an outspoken enemy of Bill's. Jim Guy's office was just across the street from the association offices, and Larry Patterson and I had requested a meeting. As we did all gubernatorial candidates, we interviewed him to determine how he would treat the state police if elected. We didn't need to interview Bill, we already knew what he would do.

Larry and I met with Tucker at his office and Jim Guy would be cooperative. A vicious, vile man, Tucker was more interested in what Larry and I knew about Bill's love life than anything else. He craved every little tidbit that Larry and I knew from our years at the Mansion. We told him much of what we knew about the women, most of which was told by Patterson later when he and Roger Perry came out in the Troopergate matter.

Later, Larry shocked me one night, as he called me from the Mansion to tell me that Jim Guy was withdrawing from the race. He said Tucker was on the phone at that very minute with Bill. Before Larry put him through, Tucker told him to tell me the news. Tucker went on to say that Bill was going to run for president and Jim Guy would instead run for Lieutenant Governor now and walk into the governor's office after Bill was elected. I thought it ludicrous at the time. Little did I know it would prove prophetic.

We also met with Sheffield Nelson, the Republican nominee to face Bill in the general election. Sheffield solicited the philandering information as well. Neither of them used the information in their respective campaigns although I imagine they now wish they had.

I was tiring of the pressure of the constant fighting with a liar who held the power of the governor's office in his hands. He also could fire the state police director Tommy Goodwin any day, replacing him with a new director who would surely get rid of me. Clinton's minions were after me every day— even from inside the association. Mark Allen, the pitiful trooper Hillary had made cry, attended his first association meeting and accused me of misspending association money. The boy who was once my friend had turned into just another Clinton worshiper like Becky's parents. He was joined by other troopers loyal to the Clintons. Tommy Goodwin met with me and told me Bill and Hillary were pressuring him to fire me. When I asked Tommy if I needed to start looking for another job he replied, "I would, and preferably out of state." It had dawned on me that my career with the state police was at an end if I ran again for the presidency of the association. I was assigned to the special investigation section working white collar crime cases and had a good job. I decided not to run and keep my job instead. I was now convinced that Bill Clinton's corruption of Arkansas was complete. But I was not prepared for what would come next. Clinton started pushing for a criminal investigation of my past management of the Association[7]. Enter State Prosecutor Mark Stodola, a Democrat who had worked in Bill's first congressional campaign. Mark is an intelligent lawyer who weighs issues carefully. When presented with a case that was obviously politically motivated, Mark declined to look any further. He later told me that the Arkansas State Police investigator who was ordered to look at the case had submitted a handwritten note to the effect that there was 'nothing there.'

Even in the criminal division of the Arkansas State Police I couldn't escape the Mansion, Bill and the troubles that had been visited upon me. As a criminal investigator I investigated major crimes that occurred on state property. I also took on cases by special assignment as directed. Bryant, Arkansas is a small bedroom community ten minutes from Little Rock. With their own school district, police force and the accompanying drug problems and youthful indiscretions, the community was slowly looking more like the Little Rock so many of the people had tried to escape. Bryant also had its share of crime but usually the small stuff. The town certainly wasn't ready for the disaster that would befall it in 1987. A tragic debacle in which I would feel the tentacles of Mena again.

&ast;    &ast;    &ast;

Don Henry and Kevin Ives were two teenagers who attended Bryant High School, spotlighted the occasional deer and reportedly like to smoke pot. They lived near a  railroad track which provided a road map to their adventures after dark. One night in August of that year the boys got into much more than childish pranks or game and fish violations. A railroad engineer was the last to see them alive (or perhaps dead) that night as his train tore the seemingly lifeless bodies of the boys apart as they lay on the tracks. With the engine's horn blaring, the engineer would later testify that the boys did not move an inch. They lay on their backs with their rifle positioned beside them in an almost 'laid out' fashion. Indeed the scene made no sense. Enter the Arkansas State Police.

Homicides, even questioned deaths, were not my forte but drugs were. I was one of the first investigators assigned to the case, which had caused a public clamoring for an in-depth investigation. The boys' parents were indignant with the preliminary findings that showed the boys were in a drug induced deep sleep rendering them unable to hear the blaring horn of the railroad engine as it tried in vain to stop before literally tearing the boys limb from limb.

After interviewing several people at the boys' high school, I proceeded to examine the autopsy file. I had seen gory mutilated bodies before, but even the most experienced investigator feels pain when they are children. The state medical examiner Fahmy Malak had completed the reports, two of the hundreds of autopsies he had overseen during his tenure. Fahmy was no stranger to controversy. A Bill Clinton appointee, Malak had made a controversial ruling in a case that involved Bill's mother Virginia Kelly. Virginia was the nurse anesthetist in a case in which a man had died on the operating table. Malak cleared Virginia of any wrongdoing and Bill owed him.

I made an appointment with Dr. Malak but not before reading his findings in the case. Malak had determined that the boys were in a deep drug induced sleep due to the marijuana they had been smoking the night of their deaths. This was to prove to be the most controversial finding in the entire case. I found upon my examination of the file that Malak could not say to any degree of certainty the amount of THC, or tetrahydrocannabinol (the active ingredient in marijuana) that was in the boys' blood stream at the time of their death. The proper tests had not been conducted at the critical juncture of the autopsy. Without that determination, Malak would have a hard time sustaining his argument that the boys were so out of it as to not to be able to hear a deafening train horn bearing down on them.

After making small talk I pointedly asked Dr. Malak why the appropriate tests had not been conducted to make the determination he had made. Malak immediately hung his head and shrugged his shoulders. Soon tears came to his eyes as he admitted he had made a grievous mistake in the case. He talked of the embarrassment to his family the mistake would cause. He was clearly shaken.

Immediately recognizing the significance of the admission, I went to the commander of the criminal division to brief him on the developments. I knew Doug Stephens from my days at the Governor's Mansion where he was the first lieutenant I served under. Doug was clearly shocked at what I had found. After shuffling some papers on his desk he looked squarely at me and gave me a shocker of his own.

"L. D., I'm taking you off this case," he said, getting no sign of disappointment from me. It was the follow-up that floored me.

"This has something to do with Mena," he finished.

At that time I didn't want any information coming out about Mena, so I quickly obeyed his order to bow out.

The families of the two boys have since carried on a campaign for justice concerning the deaths of their sons. I have spoken only briefly on the subject with my remarks appearing on the editorial page of the *Wall Street Journal*[8]. I have always felt sorry for the families since the case has never been 'solved.' Other medical examiners have been called in and have stated categorically that the boys died of blows received before they were struck by the train. The boys are listed prominently on the list of people who have died under mysterious circumstances in Arkansas during Bill Clinton's tenure as governor.

✳    ✳    ✳

On one other occasion I would go along with the administration of the Arkansas State Police to look the other way concerning Mena. Former Congressman Bill Alexander became concerned with what had gone on at the Mena Airport. He called for a federal and then a state investigation into the activities several years after I was involved. Bill Clinton finally okayed a sizable sum of money to an investigation, money that was supposed to be funneled through the Arkansas State Police and a deputy prosecutor named Charles Black.

The appropriation of money made the newspapers and I was concerned about what may be uncovered. I was working directly for Colonel Goodwin in the white-collar crime unit at the time. One day, as I walked into Colonel Goodwin's office, he asked me a question out of the blue. After telling me he had received the okay to spend the money from Clinton on the Mena Airport investigation he asked, "L. D. I don't know of anything to investigate. Do you?" Although I had told Goodwin at a State Police Association meeting a little of my involvement at Mena, the statement and follow up question threw me off guard. It took me a moment to gather enough composure to agree that indeed nothing should be done. It was another case of the truth being put off at the sacrifice of justice. All in the pursuit of self-preservation, Bill Clinton's and mine.

✳    ✳    ✳

I was happy in my job at the state police investigating elected officials and public officials. There certainly was plenty of corruption to investigate. After all, we gave America Bill Clinton. When Bill decided to run for president, I felt a strange sense of relief. Although I shuddered for the fate of the nation, I had a sense that I might be relieved of some of the pressure that had been on me while Bill had been governor. However, signs that I was not to be left alone were confirmed with the visit from Cathy Ford at Diego's tavern. But there would be pressure from the Republican side as well.

Sheffield Nelson, the Republican opponent of Bill in his last gubernatorial election and whom I had met to discuss Bill's peccadilloes, contacted me through Tommy Mitchum, the state legislator who had changed his vote in that pivotal deal Bill made with me. Tommy asked me if I would talk to Sheffield about Bill. This was the week before the 1992 presidential election and George Bush was down in the polls. As Tommy and I entered Sheffield's office in the upscale TCBY Tower in downtown Little Rock, Sheffield was his usual intense self. He had a proposition for me. Somehow he knew I had information regarding Bill and drugs. I had told Tommy of some of the C. I. A. escapades years before and I guessed he had told Sheffield. The proposal was enticing. Sheffield was best friends with Jerry Jones, the native Arkansan and owner of the Dallas Cowboys football team. Sheffield told me if I came forward and told all I knew concerning Bill, his dealings with drugs and knowledge of philandering, I would be named the chief of security for the Dallas Cowboys. I should have taken it. Sheffield, a multimillionaire who usually gets what he wants, except in politics, did not get his way with me. I didn't like the idea of being paid off and, besides, I didn't want to live in Dallas. It was just like I told Cathy Ford at Diego's, I just wanted to be left alone.

On election night I stopped by the Holiday Inn West where the Bush people were holding their watch party. As I moved through the crowd, I couldn't help but notice how there was a somber mood even though the night was young. Bill was ahead and it looked bad. Sheffield motioned me over to him and declared, "L. D., you did the right thing. It wouldn't have made any difference."

Little Rock was going crazy. As Becky and I watched the returns on the election that night it was apparent that Bill and Hillary were on their way to the White House. Bill's dream had come true, and his nightmare and that of the nation had begun. My hopes that I would now be left alone were short-lived. Bill and Hillary left the Mansion in Little Rock taking my mother-in-law and Robin Dickey with them. They also brought the assortment of weirdos and policy wonks which were strikingly similar to the ones they had taken to the governor's Mansion in their first term in 1978. I wondered how long it would take for the American people and the press to find out what these people were really all about. I also wondered when they would ask about Vince Foster and Hillary.

I have read much about Bill's promise of having the most ethical administration in history. History has shown how ludicrous that vow was. I have also written quite a bit about how he mucked up his attempts to have his cabinet be 'representative' of all America. What he ended up with resembled more of the bar scene in the Star Wars movie. It was 1978 all over again indeed.

Becky and I were amazed that Vince Foster had decided to follow the Clintons to Washington. Vince had never been a political animal. He never entered into the fray during the campaigns. His wife Lisa was even more apolitical and it surprised us that she eventually moved to D. C. as well. I knew that he, in reality, could not stand to be away from Hillary, and vice versa. Given that, it was a shock to me when Becky told me that Vince had been found dead at Fort Marcy Park. My immediate thought was the conspiratorial 'they' had gotten him. I wondered when Vince and Hillary's secret would get out. Vince was a cool, level-headed fellow, the type you never figure for a suicide. But after thinking about it a long time I came to the conclusion that Vince could have killed himself if the right scenario had been played out.

First, Hillary would have told him the romance was off. Here he was being cut off by the woman he moved to Washington for when he had already left the lucrative law part-

nership at the Rose firm. He had moved his wife who was reluctant to do so anyway. To add insult to injury, Vince perhaps
was being sacrificed in the Travelgate scandal. Since I have
never seen the file on the suicide, it would be impossible for
me to give an opinion as an investigator. But considering that
the evidence was so mishandled, the statements as contra-
dictory as they are, one may never know the truth. The police
and prosecutors certainly laid the groundwork for many conspiracy theories to build upon, some of which may be true.
Knowing Vince as we did, and having the knowledge of how
the case has been mishandled, I think there may be some truth
in the theories that the official report is not altogether the whole
story. The alternative version I would accept would involve the
movement of Vince's body. The suicide may have occurred at
a place (and time) that was far more embarrassing to the
Clintons. I believe this to be so, since it is absolutely inconceivable to me that Vince would have killed himself without
first having said goodbye to Hillary. Of that, I will always
have no doubt. Unless Hillary starts telling the truth, we will
never know.

✻     ✻     ✻

Rumors were rampant at state police headquarters that Larry
Patterson was writing a book at the end of 1993. Larry had
transferred to the headquarters building where I worked, and I
saw him occasionally. The rumors proved true when he and
Roger Perry told their story to the *American Spectator* and the
*Los Angeles Times*. I was on the slippery slope to falling into
the entire mess all over again.

Enter my brother, Dwayne, who worked at Arkansas
Louisiana Gas Company (ARKLA) in Little Rock. He asked
me whether or not I would speak to Skip Rutherford about
what the troopers were saying. This story can now be told since
Dwayne has retired from ARKLA and no retribution can be
taken against him. The President of ARKLA before he went to

the White House as Bill's chief of staff was Thomas 'Mac' McLarty, an old friend of Bill's from Hope, Arkansas. I never asked Dwayne, and won't, who told him to ask me whether or not I would talk to Ship Rutherford, but the reader can make his or her own conclusions. Skip was a Clinton friend and confidant who currently is heading up the Clinton Presidential Library committee in Arkansas. He also was Mac McLarty's right-hand man at ARKLA before leaving to work on Bill's campaign in 1992. Dwayne knew I was getting intense pressure from the *Spectator* and the *L. A. Times* to tell my story and was trying to help me out of this mess. I didn't want to incur the wrath of Clinton and I was anxious to explore all my options. More importantly, I was interested in letting Clinton know I had not instigated this contact with the media and that they indeed had the story with or without me.

I initially refused the offer to meet with Rutherford since I didn't particularly care for the man and certainly didn't trust him. I became exasperated and after a few days finally agreed to meet with Skip at his office on Capitol Avenue in downtown Little Rock. Skip was glad-handing me as I entered the office as if we were old friends. "Want some coffee L. D.?" he asked. "What do they know L.D.?" he asked as he flipped his yellow pad into position. I had told him that the media had the story with or without me. Wattenberg from the *Spectator* had done the research necessary to make it impossible for me to refute the stories of Bill and me cavorting around America. Rutherford wanted a detailed list of the women the media knew about. He wrote them all down—Susan McDougal, Gennifer Flowers, Beth Coulson, just about all of them. I also told them there were questions about Madison as well. Rutherford put down his pen and asked an ominous question. "L. D., you know you're going to get subpoenaed over this don't you?" I leaned closer to him so I wouldn't miss a word. He continued, obviously on a roll with, "Now L. D., you have to lay your head down on the pillow at night. You have to live with yourself." I had finally had enough when he said, "And L. D., you wouldn't want all your credit card receipts splashed all over the front page of the newspapers now would you?"

Intimidation and threat? You bet and that's exactly what he was trying to get across. I left and was determined then and there I would tell my story.

# CHAPTER TWELVE

## The Office of Independent
## Counsel Comes Calling

When I received that telephone call from Warner Calhoun of the F. B. I., I was scared. As I dropped the phone onto the desk, my partner Danny Harkins could see I was shocked. Harkins, a decorated Vietnam War veteran, had been a friend who had stood by my side all through this debacle. "What's wrong L. D., you look like you've seen a ghost?" Danny asked. I told him who the call was from and he asked me what I was going to do. I was still reeling financially from having to defend myself against the Clinton attack machine several years before and did not have the resources to hire an attorney. I talked over with Danny what I should do. We both came to the conclusion I should just go over and tell the truth and demand the utmost in confidentiality and, above all, protection. I knew the Clintons would come back after me with a vengeance if they knew I was giving information to the newly appointed special prosecutor Robert Fiske.

I had met Steve Irons of the F. B. I. several times prior to this Valentine's Day, 1994. Steve is a cop's cop. Tall, red-haired and in top shape, he was and still is the independent counsel's biggest asset. Steve asked if I wanted a subpoena. Knowing that if I had one issued to me then whatever I turned over would be protected, I said yes. We chatted for about thirty minutes while they scrambled to get one together. I was still nervous as it was usually me who was asking the questions or me who was looking through the other side of the two-way mirror in the F. B. I. interview room. The agents all assured me that anything said in the interview would be held in the strictest confidence. Even the fact that I had been there would be kept secret. It was then that I pointed out a security lapse that surprised them. "Well, if that's true, how is it that I know you just had two couriers from the Rose Law Firm in here before me?" I asked to their amazement. "How did you know that?" they asked as they looked at one another. I then informed them of a sign-in book at the front desk of their offices. When I signed in, I simply looked at the last names that had gone in before me. Right there for anyone to see were the names and where they worked. They assured me that would be changed right away.

I did have a valid excuse for wanting to get out of there early. It was Valentine's Day and I had to pick up Becky for lunch at the school where she worked. But before I left, there were the perfunctory questions about whether or not Bill had slept with Susan McDougal and if Vince and Hillary were really as close as they had heard. Now, some have been outraged that investigators would ask such questions. For the record, it is done all the time and it is quite appropriate. 'Pillow talk' is sometimes the source of the most damaging information that a person or, in this case, a target of an investigation reveals. But you have to know whom to ask. In time I would reveal the names of all the individuals I have named in this book to the Office of Independent Counsel. I would have to tell all I knew about the McDougals, of Dan Lasater and the cocaine, all of it. But first I took Becky to lunch.

My escape from Fiske's office was only a reprieve and I knew it. The pressure from Danny Wattenberg at the *American Spectator* was increasing. Bill Rempel and the *L. A. Times* had the essentials of my story and told me they were ready to run with it. I had to make a quick decision on whether or not to co-operate. There was one last thing I needed to consider before I would either agree to go public with this story or decide to keep my mouth shut. I could have decided to lie for Clinton but that was not a possibility unless... well, let me relate a series of extraordinary events that unfolded in 1994.

I had a contact in the Clinton administration at that time. I have never disclosed who that was and will call him George for now. George had asked me if I might want to try and get that C. I. A. operations job I had wanted years ago. I thought it really strange that I would have a sure shot at the job now, when I had to go through all the trouble of flying on those airplanes way back when to even have a chance. Now that Bill was president, it would be a done deal. It also, as in the earlier days, would be for the wrong reasons.

I had to talk it over with Becky and I knew what her answer would be. Our son had already started kindergarten in Little Rock. We were settled in our lifestyle there and she did not want to make the move that would be inevitable with a job in the Agency. I knew, however, that with the story coming out I would eventually lose my job at the state police, and I was right. I decided to give it a little time and let her think about it. But time was running out.

I stayed in contact with George and with his contact who could arrange the job. Everyone was obviously uneasy about dealing with the parties involved and understandably so. No one trusted anyone else. It would have suited me fine to be able to move out of Little Rock and never come back, and that's exactly what the Clintons wanted. If I was out of Little Rock, better yet out of the country, I would be out of the media spotlight and unavailable to be assailed for comments (or subpoena) from the people the Clintons feared the most.

It was a curious arrangement for me to be in contact with these people on such an issue. It didn't surprise me that one more effort was being made to keep me quiet, but Becky was holding fast on her determination to stay in Little Rock. "It'll turn out all right," she would say as she assured me that if we stayed in Little Rock we could survive the storms to come. She reminded me how tumultuous the times were when I was involved with the Agency in years past.

I finally relented, and told George I wasn't interested. George responded that it was probably for the best since they were having second thoughts on the arrangement anyway. I know they had expected that I would jump at the chance; they probably interpreted my procrastination as a sign that I was telling what was going on to the Independent Counsel or to Congress. An assumption that was not true then or now. I never told the Office of the Special Counsel about the contacts and that was one reason I left the room when talking with D'Amato's people in an episode I will relate later in this book. I am revealing the C.I.A. job offer now for the first time. I am sure I will be subpoenaed again to talk about it.

The incident with Skip Rutherford was what pushed me over the edge. The way I looked at it, Bill's people just didn't know when to leave someone alone. I would sign on to the article written by Danny Wattenberg within limits. The conversations I had with him were limited to mainly the things he had been able to substantiate on his own.

The *American Spectator* magazine had missed one month of its production because of my not giving them the green light to run my story. When they did finally run it, my telephone rang off the wall. I gave only one interview to my local newspaper, the *Arkansas Democrat-Gazette*. In that interview, I stated the reasons for my going on the record. I was through with the media since I had more pressing matters at hand. The Office of the Special Counsel had subpoenaed all documents in my possession regarding Bill Clinton and I obviously needed a lawyer. I would really need one as the machine politics in Arkansas was still at work.

Bill Clinton's successor in the governor's office was Jim Guy Tucker, the man whom Larry Patterson and I had met with when Tucker opposed Clinton in the 1990 gubernatorial primary. The same man who, according to Patterson, backed out of the governor's race and ran instead for lieutenant governor from where he would walk into the governor's office after Clinton's supposed election to the presidency.

I mentioned at the beginning of this book that I was working a criminal investigation concerning the way state money had been allocated to the state's school districts. Jim Guy had inherited the mess from Clinton's previous administration. The focus of the investigation, which had been requested by Attorney General Winston Bryant, was to determine whether or not anyone in state government had benefited from the way the money had been allocated. Tucker had already called a special legislative session and the defective law had been fixed. The machinations through which the money had been spent and who knew about it had already been disclosed during that session and had been written up in the media. It was at this point that I got a call from my boss Tommy Goodwin, director of the state police. He wanted me to do what I considered an extraordinary thing. He wanted me to meet with Governor Tucker about the case.

It wasn't a good idea to politicize investigations in the state police. I had been investigating and interviewing all the former directors of the state education department during the course of the investigation. This included Jim Guy Tucker's appointee to the department, Gene Wilhoit. There was evidence that Wilhoit knew of the defective application of the law in distributing the state money. My partner Danny Harkins eventually showed that Wilhoit indeed did know of it.

I immediately conferred with the prosecuting attorney in Little Rock, Mark Stodola who told me not to give the file to Tucker. It was an obvious conflict of interest for Tucker to intervene in the case since one of his own political appointees was a subject of the investigation. Again, as in the Betsey Wright meeting, I met with Tucker to save Tommy Goodwin any retribution from the governor.

Tucker had at least one familiar face in the room, Jim Pledger, Clinton's former senior aide who was there at the Mansion the day when Clinton caught himself blowing up on me because I had stood up to him and called him a liar. Dent Gitchell, Tucker's lawyer, was also in the governor's office at the Capitol where we met. Tucker entered the room and sat down with paper and pen in hand. He flipped over a page and told me, "Now, I want to know who, what, when, where and why about this case." Wow, the five w's, I remember thinking to myself. This guy's really sharp, almost as sharp as when he was groveling over the salacious aspects of Clinton's life just a few short years ago. I proceeded to explain what I had done in the case, how I had interviewed the witnesses, talked with the prosecutor. I also reminded him that this was a criminal investigation and that since any violations would be misdemeanors, there was a one year statute of limitations on any crimes that had been committed. The time frame of the investigation stretched back some eleven years. I also told him the matter had been fully discussed through a legislative session and had been in the media, a story essentially the same as mine.

Tucker was livid. He slammed his pen down on his paper and shouted, "You can't tell me these goddam Clinton people didn't know anything about all this!" There I was, in the strangely unfamiliar situation of defending Bill Clinton! I told Tucker that indeed some of Clinton's appointees to the education department did know, some did not. Clearly not satisfied, he asked me if I was going to write a report on this. I stopped short of telling him that no, I might just write up something on a Kroger sack and turn it in. I said that yes, indeed I would. He commanded that I deliver the report to him before the prosecutor saw it. That set the stage for my next encounter with a corrupt Arkansas governor.

It was not long before Tommy Goodwin was asking if the report was done. I told him it was not. He told me to get together what I had and deliver it to the Capitol. I told him I would copy what I had at the time and deliver it to him. If he wanted to give it to Tucker, he could. He did.

The next week Tommy Goodwin paged me to call him at his home in Little Rock. Over the telephone he said he had been told by Jim Guy Tucker that Tucker wanted me transferred from my position in the special investigation's unit to the highway patrol—writing tickets and working accidents! I told Tommy I would be right over to his house; I wanted to hear this from him in person. When I arrived at Tommy's house, I was incensed. Here was a governor who had intervened in a criminal investigation that involved one of his own political appointees. An investigation that was called for by the Attorney General. A criminal case file that the governor demanded to see against the wishes and advice of the prosecuting attorney who had jurisdiction in the case.

Tommy told me that I knew what the reason was. I took this to mean that because I had confirmed to Danny Wattenberg at the *Spectator* that Jim Guy had solicited all the information on Clinton described in the piece Wattenberg had written, Tucker was retaliating. Tommy told me he was sick and tired of being pressured, first by Clinton and now by Tucker to fire me and get me out of the way. He said he was turning in his retirement papers the next day.

Tommy did turn in his retirement papers. He explained to me that if he didn't transfer me to the highway patrol, that Tucker would appoint the next director who most certainly would do it with no questions asked. My natural instinct was to fight the transfer by going public. I ultimately did so to an extent, but Tommy promised me he would give a sworn statement as to what had transpired with Tucker. I could then use it in a civil suit which I ultimately filed against Tucker .

Tucker wasn't done with me.  He made comments to the *Arkansas Democrat-Gazette* that I was an incompetent investigator.  He stated that I had mishandled the state school funding formula investigation, a fact clearly refuted by Tommy Goodwin and proven out by the case being finished by my now ex-partner Danny Harkins.  He again showed that Tucker's head of the state education department did in fact know of the misapplication of the state money.

But there was to be another caveat to this story.  It would later be revealed that Tucker had private meetings with Bill Clinton in the Oval Office.  Another was to take place in Seattle, Washington during an Asian Economic Conference.  Now, Bill Clinton and Jim Guy Tucker were not friends.  Even though they had made the deal to secure the holding of the Arkansas governor's office by corrupt politicians like themselves, they did it only because of the mutual benefit.  There is no doubt the two would have met only to get their stories straight on Whitewater and to talk about how they would get rid of me.

There is equally no doubt that what Jim Guy Tucker, now a twice-convicted federal felon, did to me was wrong, illegal.  If this is not a clear-cut case of obstruction of justice and witness tampering, I don't know what is.  In addition, I have never heard of a better case of criminal violation of someone's civil rights than this incident.  With the attendant outrage, I immediately telephoned Special Agent Steve Irons of the F. B. I. with whom I had met earlier and told him what had happened.  He couldn't believe it.  I demanded to know what they were going to do about it.

What the Office of Independent Counsel did about it was nothing.  What a way to treat your witnesses.  I learned a long time ago that if you wanted to get the truth out of someone you had to treat them with respect and dignity, but above all take care of them.  I wasn't being taken care of and felt I had been betrayed.  I had one meeting with an attorney from the Office of Independent Counsel.  The guy acted like he was literally going to fall asleep on me. I was disgusted and although I knew I had to cooperate, I vowed to watch both sides like a hawk for the rest of this convoluted investigation. I would have to.

Danny Wattenberg had assured me he would assist me in at least getting in touch with a lawyer who would represent my interests in this unique investigation. I now needed one in the worst way. I had been taken off a job that was an elite position in the Arkansas State Police, if there is such a thing. I previously worked straight days with weekends off and now was reduced to working shift work, 3pm till 12 midnight or 7am till 4pm and having Tuesday and Wednesday off. I had cooperated with the attorneys in Whitewater and had been pushed into working highway patrol by a governor who was every bit as corrupt as the last one, who was now our corrupt president. I was up to the job but it was hell on my family. That is something all the parties in these cases have seemingly stepped right over; the realization there are innocent parties in this affair who have been damaged irreparably. My family is just one of many. It was one heck of an endorsement for Arkansas.

I talked with several lawyers in Washington, DC and in Little Rock. Many had conflicts. Others were obviously not wanting to get involved in such a high profile investigation. Eventually, and more or less on my own, I talked with an attorney named Justin Thornton in Washington, DC. It was clear Justin was not the run-of-the-mill D. C. lawyer. He had extensive experience with grand juries like the one I would be facing soon. He had served as a senior trial attorney in the United States Department of Justice and would know many of the people who were running this investigation. Not to be overlooked, Justin was a Southerner from North Carolina and his personality matched his legal acumen. To this day, I have yet to meet an attorney with these attributes and an impeccable honor to match.  He has been a guiding light through the darkness of the 'Whitewater' affair.

I was to set up a legal fund to pay the bills, a fund still active today (address in the appendix).  Justin was setting up a procedure for the Independent Counsel's Office to contact me through him when they needed to talk with me.  In the years to come, Justin and I would interact with the OIC many times.  Congress would be knocking on our door (and still is) with calls for testimony and other evidence.  Round two with Bill Clinton would be deception and lies from both sides of the aisle, Republicans and Democrats.  As I write this, there is still an ongoing tornadic controversy with Whitewater.  And I am still caught in the middle of it.

I had met several times with the agents of the F.B.I. and lawyers for the first special prosecutor Robert Fiske.  I detailed much of the information contained in this book, the philandering, the money being passed out to black preachers and the McDougals.  I didn't dare tell them about Mena or the Bahamas since this was 1994 and the statute of limitations for conspiracy had not run in Arkansas.  If they had wanted to, or if someone else found out about it and it got back to a state prosecutor who might be a friend of Bill's, I would certainly be in jeopardy.

This first thing I had to do was respond to the subpoena *duces tecum*.  This meant I'd been ordered to produce any document which bore a relationship to Bill and Hillary Clinton, Madison Guaranty Savings and Loan, basically any document considered relevant to the Whitewater investigation.  They also wanted my day books from the period when I worked at the Governor's Mansion.  This would present a problem.

I kept a day book ever since I'd been in law enforcement.  I kept notes of trips Bill and I took, the Boca Raton trip, for instance.  I also made notations of the C. I. A. activity I had been involved in.  I would do my best to make the entries as cryptic as possible. Depending on the degree of sensitivity, I would either make the entries in Spanish or Russian. For really sensitive entries I would use the Russian alphabet which is phonetic, but when you read the word it would be sounding out a Spanish word. This would provide added security so the casual observer would not be able to easily decipher what I had written. It also presented a problem with the OIC. How did we turn over relevant materials in my day books while at the same time keeping these entries about Mena and the C. I. A. confidential?

Justin Thornton's experience in these matters provided the answer. I simply sat down and photocopied the entire day books and then redacted or blacked out the entries that were not relevant to any Whitewater concern. I then copied the day books again and the entries were effectively gone. Justin put them on notice that the subpoenaed day books had been redacted to omit the irrelevant items. I held my breath that the OIC would balk at the procedure but they didn't.

I also had in my possession the briefing notes and schedule from the Campobello function at the Excelsior. That was the one Susan McDougal had telephoned the governor's office about Bill attending. It was also the night Bill told me he was to have a liaison with Susan. This was important to the Office of the Independent Counsel in that it showed there was a connection between Bill and the Campobello operation which was and is being investigated by the OIC. It also gave them a reason to interview Susan to learn what Bill had told her. It ultimately resulted in Susan spending time in a federal lockup for contempt in refusing to answer questions before the Whitewater grand jury.

I never met Robert Fiske. It wasn't until Kenneth Starr was named Independent Counsel that Justin and I were up and running in making preparations to meet with the F. B. I. agents and lawyers working for Starr. The media frenzy was going full force and they were staked out at the OIC offices on Financial Parkway in west Little Rock. The OIC had an idea to hold the meeting at the AmeriSuites hotel located across the street from the OIC headquarters. This would provide us the security and privacy we would not have at their offices.

Justin and I arrived to find a host of F. B. I. agents and deputy counsels for Kenneth Starr. After the introductions were made, I again reiterated my concern for my job and personal security if it were known I was cooperating with the investigation. In fact, I had not totally cooperated with the investigators and they were about to try to influence me to do just that. They announced that Mr. Starr himself would stop by, he wanted to meet me.

We began the interview with a discussion of the encounter with David Hale and Bill at the state capitol. This was the instance when Bill told Hale he would have to "help them out" and "raise some money" for what prosecutors alleged was an illegal loan to Susan McDougal. It was clear the lawyers wanted to make sure I was sure of my story, judging for themselves whether they believed me or not. In the middle of the interview, Kenneth Starr stepped into the room. A very cordial and polite man, he began an almost rehearsed sounding statement of the purpose and intent of the investigation he was conducting. Indeed, I would hear the same verbiage over and over again as he would address the media in years to come. As he talked, I sensed that he really believed what he was saying. This was a man who would go out of his way to be fair to everyone involved, witness or suspect. I was relieved to a certain extent that he had made an appearance, but it would not be Mr. Starr who would cause me consternation in the future. It would be some of his underlings who were the transient lawyers who passed through the Office of Independent Counsel through the years.

My attorney would have many conversations in person and over the telephone with these numerous lawyers and F. B. I. agents. One meeting in Washington, DC was particularly eventful. It occurred on January 31, 1995 and was conducted by Tim Mayopoulos, a meek lawyer working for Starr.

Mayopoulos had plenty of help in the room and he would need it. Jackie Bennett, a career Justice Department attorney with the Division of Public Integrity had come on board with Starr and was in the meeting. Bennett is a competent attorney, the kind which Starr could have used more of. A number of agents from the F. B. I. were there and even a special agent with the criminal division of the Internal Revenue Service.

But Mayopoulos would be in charge. I was seated at the end of the table, sort of in the barrel of the gun with everyone looking at me. Mayopoulos who sat next to me, spoke in what was a barely audible level, so low that I continually had to ask him to repeat almost everything he said. After about an hour of that, my attorney Justin Thornton, who is much more diplomatic than me, even joined in making the request that Mayopoulos turn it up a bit. It became so annoying that I had to make an announcement I couldn't hear a word he was saying. The others at the end of the table couldn't hear either so I couldn't see how we were getting anywhere with the interview.

Justin and I were concerned about my liability in what I was telling the Office of the Independent Counsel in this and other interviews. Justin, a former career prosecutor with the United States Department of Justice, suggested we ask for an immunity deal. Justin had already broached the subject with the OIC and we had a draft of the proposed agreement to look over before the meeting. I looked at the document which basically gave me immunity from prosecution as a result of anything I told the OIC that day and that day alone. This is the so-called 'king for a day' agreement where you get one chance to tell all and not have what you say be used against you. The problem with that lies in the fact the government can use what you say to develop leads independent from what you have said and then prosecute you with that new evidence. It's not a cinch that you won't be prosecuted by any stretch of the imagination and I knew that.

I was afraid they might think I wasn't telling them everything I knew. It takes a seasoned prosecutor or investigator to know when a witness is not being forthcoming with them. I told the group of how we would carry cash around Arkansas to pay off people. I related what had happened with David Hale and Clinton, and the story of Dan Lasater and the state police radio system. The acts of picking up cash at Lasater's office and at the Little Rock Airport were discussed. The relationship between Susan McDougal and Bill seemed of particular interest to them. I elaborated on how Bill felt that Jim McDougal was a 'cash cow' and that he berated him behind his back.

I told them pretty much everything. But it was that last question that hit me. "Is there anything you haven't told us regarding anything we may be investigating?" was the catch-all question that Mayopoulos asked. I told him I didn't know everything they were investigating and thus it really wasn't clear how I should respond. Justin and I had talked about telling the OIC about Mena and I was on the verge of doing so. As I looked around the room I asked the question of what they were going to do to protect me and to rectify the problem of Jim Guy Tucker interfering in my job situation. Mayopoulos told me the OIC couldn't right all the wrongs committed in Arkansas, that wasn't their job. That made up my mind. I told the group the OIC should be protecting their witnesses and got up from the table. For my part, the interview was over.

Many of the meetings having focused on the incident I had witnessed with David Hale and Bill, Justin and I both knew this meant I would be soon called before the grand jury to tell what I knew. I have included a copy of my grand jury statement in this book. We were to deal with a deputy of Kenneth Starr who was one of the best prosecutors I would meet in this never-ending investigation. Brad Lerman was a lawyer from Chicago who had joined Starr's staff and apparently been assigned the task of dealing with me. I realized I wasn't the easiest witness in this case since I had already lost a lot. Brad was easy to deal with and obviously a sharp lawyer. He wasn't biased in any respect and wanted to get to the truth in the investigation. He left the independent counsel's office much too early, but he was great while he was there.

The OIC would accommodate me by flying me up to Washington, DC since I did not have the money to fly my attorney down to Arkansas. I crafted my statement in Justin's office on L Street Northwest as Brad and Justin looked on. Most of the statement to the grand jury would focus on the David Hale encounter after laying out a brief background on who I was and how I came to know the Clintons. Brad told me I would testify to the grand jury in Little Rock. The OIC would fly Justin down to be with me outside the grand jury room.

When you go before a federal grand jury, you go in by yourself. That is, unless of course you're Bill Clinton who got to have David Kendall by his side and was to testify by videotape. I had been before grand juries before as a result of my many criminal investigations, and knew that your lawyer doesn't get to go in with you. He can wait outside the door and you can speak with him there if there is a question you need to ask during your examination. Above all, I knew I had to tell the truth when I testified or I would go to jail for perjury. That is a fundamental concept of the American judicial system, I have believed in for twenty-three years. That has changed forever with the advent of the American people and Congress seemingly giving Bill Clinton a pass to commit felony perjury.

The makeup of this grand jury in Little Rock was a big secret. They would possibly determine the fate of the president and his wife. Their identities were being withheld in order to prevent possible witness tampering, a really good idea given Clinton's track record in that area.

Justin and I were placed in a secure area of the federal court house in downtown Little Rock to await my turn before the grand jury. There was another witness who was taking the impending examination a bit more casually than I was. He said he was an accountant from Dallas and I never really knew whether or not he was a government employee or not.

With statement in hand, I was called to come inside the grand jury room. As I entered the nondescript room, I was greeted by a familiar face in Brad Lerman. Amy St. Eve, another of Kenneth Starr's deputies, was there as well. I didn't even scan the room. My attention was focused on the foreman of the grand jury who asked me to raise my right hand and be sworn. I remember my adrenaline was pumping as I immediately thought this guy looked like a retired military drill sergeant. I later remarked to Justin that if the foreman was any indication of how the Clintons may fare in this, they may need to hire a couple more lawyers.

I took my seat at the front of the room and made eye contact with the grand jurors for the first time. They were a middle class looking group for the most part. Mostly white, and I believe I even caught the sight of a couple of pairs of bib overalls in the group, a sure sign of a conservative Arkansas juror. Brad Lerman went through the perfunctory questions and then asked me if I had a statement I wanted to read. I had a quick thought of saying no and then asking to leave but I knew I wouldn't get off that easily so I began to read the seven page statement.

I began by telling many of the things I have related so far in this book. Who I was, where I was from and what I had done in my career that led up to my involvement with the Clintons. I told the grand jurors of how the Clintons and I had become close, how I had married the Clintons' baby-sitter Becky. I then gave an outline of how the governor's security force operated. I talked of the meeting after I left the Governor's Security Unit of the state police where I was asked by Betsey Wright whether or not I was going to 'talk about' Bill and Hillary. The fact that Bill had lied about the job he had promised me, as well as the legislative pay bill he reneged on, were mentioned as well.

The focus of the statement was the incident concerning David Hale. I could see the grand jurors were interested, some of them even leaning forward in their seats. I detailed how I was at the Capitol on other business when Clinton uttered his famous lines to Hale, "We need to raise some money, you're going to have to help us out."

There was one area the Independent Counsel wanted me to speak to. It was the frequent 'jogging' trips Bill would take. These were the ones where he would jog to the Excelsior or to Madison Guaranty where Jim McDougal's offices were.

I was sure they would use these statements later against Clinton. The grand jury ultimately indicted the sitting governor, Jim Guy Tucker and the McDougals, Jim and Susan. The trial strategy eventually would not allow my testimony in evidence since it was considered hearsay. Bill testified by videotape and denied using any pressure on Hale to make the loan. Prosecutors told us the only way my testimony could have been used was if Clinton had been named as an unindicted co-conspirator, an omission that I and others believe was a serious mistake.

We were borne out in that belief when before his death Jim McDougal began to cooperate with the Office of Independent Counsel. He confirmed what I had told them early on in my interviews about the fact that Bill had told me in the 1980's he was having an affair with Susan. Jim had in fact known about it. He later stated Bill had indeed known about the loan which was at the crux of the prosecution's case.

The news media had been after me to tell my story regarding what I knew about Whitewater. Word had gotten out that I had witnessed the encounter with Hale and Clinton. An ABC News producer by the name of Chris Vlasto had approached me to tell the story on national television. I declined the offer for a long time. There came a point, however, where we agreed to do an on-camera interview if the piece was to include the current predicament of my transfer to highway patrol by Governor Tucker. I was upset that the independent counsel had not indicted Tucker over what had happened and I needed to get the story out in an effort to raise some money to pay the legal bills and continue to pursue the case. I called producer Vlasto and took him up on the standing offer.

Going on national television was something I had never done before. I had been on television many times concerning trooper association business but never anything that would be seen by millions of people. It didn't much bother me, however, because I knew that all I had to do was tell the truth, just like in this book. Chris Vlasto, the ABC producer, is a professional, ethical journalist who worked hard to get to the truth of the Whitewater matter. He still does. He had secured the services of Jim Wooten, a veteran political reporter from ABC whose work I also respected. Jim was to do the interview with me in the Capital Hotel, a venerable landmark in downtown Little Rock across from the Excelsior Hotel.

Vlasto was trying to keep me apprised of the time line of the taping and when it would appear on the ABC Evening News with Peter Jennings. Wooten arrived in Little Rock and the taping was set.

I first met Wooten on the day of the taping, in fact just a few minutes before we were set to start the interview. We began to chat about Bill Clinton and he told me of an interview he had conducted with Bill and of his impressions of the new president. It was interesting to talk with a seasoned journalist who had seen it all in American politics, to get his take on what was going on with the man I knew so well. We saved my comments for the camera.

We talked on-camera for about two hours. All the while, I knew the final product that would appear on the evening news would be distilled into maybe four minutes, the content of which I would have no control over. I did have the assurance of Vlasto that my current problems in Arkansas would get into the piece. Wooten and I talked of the encounter between Bill and Hale. I also told of some of the many occurrences at the Mansion and stories Bill and I would share.

Jim was particularly interested in a story Bill told me once involving courage and moral leadership. It revolved around Charles DeGaulle and his heroism after the liberation of Paris during World War II. As hundreds of people stood at a service giving thanks for the expulsion of the German army, a shot rang out. Everyone hit the floor save for DeGaulle who stood ramrod straight refusing to cower down during the special moment. Bill thought that was a great example of courage and I made it clear that I thought Bill, to say the least, was no DeGaulle. The cowering down he is doing today, in the face of what are obviously truthful accusations, proves out my statements during that interview.

There came a point in the interview when Wooten asked me if I had been pressured by anyone with Clinton connections not to tell the truth about what I knew. I paused. Wooten asked again and I turned to a lawyer I had present at the taping and told him I didn't want to answer that. Wooten stopped the taping abruptly and said that if the Clintons were attempting to intimidate witnesses, he wanted to follow up. I maintained my silence, refusing to talk about what had happened to me with Skip Rutherford, the man my brother Dwayne had put me in touch with to see if there was a way around talking to the media. The same Skip who made the intimidating comments.

Dwayne still worked at ARKLA Gas Company and I knew he would suffer severe retribution if I revealed to Wooten the details of that incident.

But there was another reason why I had not answered the question. Once, while in Washington, DC, I had telephoned my mother-in-law Ann McCoy at the White House for reasons that were purely innocent. In the call that I now clearly regret ever making, she became defensive about what Becky and I had said in the Spectator interview—the truth about Bill and Hillary. She urged me not to 'say anything else about Bill and

Hillary.' I did not want to involve her in the ABC news story because I felt it was a private conversation and also very embarrassing that my wife's mother had abandoned her daughter and grandchildren in deference to the Clintons.

I continued to maintain silence on the issue as ABC began to run the revelations of the interview by the White House for comment. Bill obviously thought I had told everything— Mena, C. I. A., Whitewater, all of it. Bill knew I was telling the truth but in his typical fashion of attacking the messenger instead of the message he cooked up a batch of lies like none other I have seen to date. He also did it through his personal lawyer, David Kendall. He came back with what amounted to criminal slander in Arkansas.

Bill armed David Kendall with a pack of lies designed to embarrass and destroy me once and for all. It backfired. As the ABC film crew prepared to set up lighting in our home to shoot some video of my family in Little Rock, producer Chris Vlasto called me outside and shared what Kendall was doing. "L. D. what's this about you *murdering your mother!*" I was in a state of disbelief. Bill had dredged up an event that had happened when I was a child, an event of which he knew full well what the story was, and used it to kill a story which he knew to be true. This was the lowest of the low. I had seen him do some rotten things to save himself, but this was a perfect example of how desperate people do desperate things to save themselves.

Kendall would later tell the lie to print journalists. In an August 4, 1997 *Weekly Standard* article the writers quoted additional reporters who had been told by Kendall as well. More stories began to appear and I sought a lawyer who would assist me in suing to bring the liars into court. As yet I have not been able to find one who would take the case on a contingency basis.

But Vlasto had more. "What's this about you flunking a C. I. A. psychological test?" he asked, totally puzzled now. "Does that have something to do with Mena?" he added. Bill Clinton had declared total war now. He knew I had passed the psychological and written test and had seen my letter of nomination to the agency. What was even more incredulous to me was that he had opened the door to the discussion of Mena airport in which he had gotten me involved. I knew then Bill thought I was talking about C. I. A. in the interview.

I immediately told Vlasto the story of how my mother had died and that Bill and I had talked about it before. "My God L. D., these people will stop at nothing," Vlasto observed, quite correctly. A fact that anyone who knows the Clintons can testify to. But Bill had no idea I had kept all the documentation on C. I. A. contemporaneous with the events at Mena airport. I was not ready to delve into a complete explanation of Mena just yet. I still had a real and justified concern that a state prosecutor may come after me if I admitted to some of the activities that had occurred there. I instead took Chris to my office in my house and showed him a letter I had kept from the C. I. A. The letter stated I had been nominated for a position with the agency. This was sent to me after I had completed all of my testing and interviews. Vlasto sensed he was on to something and wanted more but I was holding within the scope of the interview I had given.

Instead I told Chris he could talk with my former boss, the director of the Arkansas State Police Tommy Goodwin. Goodwin could and would confirm I had been administered a psychological test at about the time of the C. I. A. employment issue. Chris subsequently did contact Goodwin and confirmed I had been examined as had all Arkansas State Police personnel. The occasion was due because the state police had hired several employees without the proper examinations. To avoid singling out these new hires, the department tested everyone. Indeed, some employees were found to need counseling and received it. Goodwin emphatically confirmed I had passed the exam. Since I worked directly for him, he would have known if I had failed the exam and furthermore, he had been informed of the names of every person who had failed the test.

There was still the issue of my mother's death. The tragic death of my mother has been brought up ever since the ABC News interview. It has been reexamined and found to be in every case a tragic accident. What has not been examined enough is the fact that Bill Clinton criminally slandered me and my family. How someone can defend this man is beyond me. I would like to see the Louisiana donkey James Carville, who clearly should have been more active in the era of Hee Haw where he could have been the star, defend Bill on this one.

The real tragedy of the ABC News interview is that it never ran. I kept asking Chris Vlasto when the piece would be aired. He kept telling me that Peter Jennings, the news anchor of the *ABC Evening News* wanted more information before they ran with the story. Jennings reportedly felt it was a major story and needed more investigation. Chris also said that Ted Koppel would want to do a piece on *Nightline* as well. The White House, however, was in full damage control mode.

Chris broke the news to me over the telephone. ABC had buckled under pressure from the Clinton White House. He seemed almost as disgusted as I was. It seems that Clinton's lawyer had the awful displeasure of 'missing his Washington Redskin's game' and instead flew to the ABC News headquarters on Sunday before the segment was to air on the nightly news. He had garnered a private audience with the top ABC News executives in New York and had persuaded them not to run the story or, in news parlance, 'spike' it. I have seen the evidence of the ABC coziness with the Clintons every time I look at the guest list for White House functions and see Roone Arledge's name at the top. As head of ABC News it's obvious that taking dives in reporting the news the 'Clinton' way has its advantages.

I did not take the Kendall matter lying down. My children had begun to ask me why I had not taken any action against a lawyer who spreads lies about a person who has done nothing but give truthful testimony regarding his client. How could I as their father sit back and allow the President of the United States and his lawyer slander their father and grandmother? I took action by filing a complaint with the District of Columbia Bar Counsel's Office, the agency that polices the Washington, DC legal community. I had no other recourse since I couldn't afford the costs to hire an attorney to file a civil action.

The original complaint filed on September 30, 1998 included copies of all the news articles in which the lie had been spread by Kendall. I poked and prodded at the Bar Counsel's office for weeks with no results. On November 18, 1998 I received a letter from John T. Rooney of the Bar Counsel's office stating that "we do not find allegations of disciplinary misconduct warranting a formal investigation." It didn't surprise me that I would not get any more justice in the puzzle palaces of our nation's capital than I had received here in Little Rock. Adding insult to injury, the Bar Counsel's Office continued with, "If a court of competent jurisdiction finds that Mr. Kendall acted improperly, please write to us again, enclosing a copy of the court's decision and referring to the above-referenced undocketed number." Yeah, you bet. The letter's in the mail.

* * *

The media attention one receives in the frenzy that is the Whitewater matter cannot be controlled, even if you just tell the truth and try to stay out of the fray. I had made up my mind that if you couldn't trust ABC, who could you trust? That was my level of naiveté at the time. I was determined to remain behind the scenes and provide information to the news sources I trusted to present the facts. I wasn't going on record as it was obviously counterproductive to my career and since the Office of Independent Counsel was clearly going to do nothing to protect their witnesses. One instance of even that methodology proving to be ruinous, came in the form of published reports of exactly what I had said regarding the David Hale/Bill Clinton encounter at the state Capitol.

One day I got a call from my attorney Justin Thornton in Washington. He told me the *Washington Times* newspaper had a story on the front page that detailed what the writer, Jerry Seper, said was my recollection of what had happened when I overheard Bill talking with David Hale that fateful day. The story was wrong.

Seper, a writer who specialized on Whitewater related stories, had written that I had overheard Clinton specifically ask Hale for $300,000 and that the money was for Susan McDougal. I had never said I had overheard that to the Office of Independent Counsel or to ABC News, or to anyone else. There was yet another important point. Seper had never talked to me about the story. This is the same person who, at an American Spectator dinner I had attended, had been awarded the 'Journalist of the Year' award.

To compound matters, the story took on a life of its own. Sue Schmidt, a well known writer with the *Washington Post* was in Little Rock and staying at the University Hilton. Sue has followed the Whitewater story since its beginnings and has taken hits from the White House for her intelligent and hard-hitting accounts of the developments of the Clinton scandal. I was visiting with her at the hotel when she showed me the article she had written that unfortunately was based on the Seper story. She, too, had the facts wrong about the $300,000 loan and about the Susan McDougal name being mentioned. She also had never called me about the story. Her editors were livid. As I listened to her telephone them back in Washington, I could tell they would have to take the not often used step of printing a retraction to the story. Sue stepped up to the plate and did the right thing by correcting the erroneous story.

Hillary and her minions have orchestrated a move to get Sue. Presidential Press Secretary Mike McCurry found out about the conspiracy and wisely put a stop to it before the smear campaign could be implemented[9].

But the debacle over the mucked up story was not over. Mary Hargrove, an *Arkansas Democrat-Gazette* newspaper reporter whom I had told the correct account regarding what had happened long before this, wrote a story giving the true account in the Little Rock paper. The Clintons had a field day over the confusion among the media and used the opportunity to take a swipe at me personally. John Podesta, one of the White House stooges who has never met me, sent a letter to the editor of the Little Rock paper saying that no one could believe L. D. Brown because even he couldn't get his story straight. It seemed to him I had told so many lies I couldn't keep them clear in my own head.

All of this happened even though I had never spoken with Jerry Seper or Sue Schmidt once about the Hale/Clinton meeting.

Perhaps an even better example of how the media and Kenneth Starr can get it all wrong sometimes was the incident when *The National Enquirer* apparently hired a firm in Michigan to investigate the alleged love life of Starr. Starr apparently got wind of the plan and heard that two friends of mine had done the dirty work here in Little Rock—and that Bill Clinton was behind it. Then-retired Arkansas State Police Colonel Tommy Goodwin, my old boss, had been subpoenaed by Starr to appear before the Whitewater grand jury in Little Rock to tell what he knew about the investigation of Starr in February, 1998. His former business partner, Bill Mullenax, who was also a state police retiree, was called as well. The two had been named by some source as the culprits and they were going to answer to Starr.

I saw the story on the front page of the Little Rock newspaper and immediately started laughing. The incident in reality was one that *I* had worked for Mullenax, who at the time had a private investigator business with Goodwin. Mullenax had telephoned me regarding a civil case and asked me to take some video and photos of a car at a woman's home. He said the client was very cryptic about the nature of the case and I didn't even know what the case was about. All I knew was that Mullenax wanted some video shot and I needed the work.

I took the video and gave it to Mullenax and never heard another word about it until the subpoenas were issued for Goodwin and Mullenax almost a year and a half later. I telephoned Goodwin and asked him what the commotion was about and he told me it was about that video I had taken for Mullenax. I laughed at the thought the Clintons would hire me to take video of Starr, even in a round about way.

I immediately called Steve Irons of the F. B. I. in Starr's office and told him they were barking up the wrong tree on this one. He laughed and the subpoenas were withdrawn. It just shows how sometimes the Whitewater investigation looks like a dog chasing its tail.

✹    ✹    ✹

All during the time I was giving testimony to the grand jury and talking with the independent counsel, I was working the highway patrol job Jim Guy Tucker had sentenced me to. I was looking for a lawyer who would file a lawsuit for me on a contingency basis. I couldn't afford to pay an attorney on an hourly basis, and still can't. I did finally get the suit filed through the help of an attorney in Little Rock, Tona DeMers, and am awaiting the outcome of a trial as I write this.

In the interim I was seeing my family less than usual. Becky and I had three children and they knew something was wrong since their daddy wasn't around as much as before. It was obvious I wasn't wearing a coat and tie anymore and had traded in my plain car for one with blue lights on top. I was miserable in the job and Becky knew it. I had written all the tickets and worked all the accidents I ever wanted to work years ago. But I had one more accident to work before my career would be over.

I had been assigned to patrol the west Little Rock area on the day shift on January 16, 1995. Our job in the morning rush hour was to park somewhere and wait for the inevitable call to work one of the many accidents that would occur. I received such a call at about 8 a.m. to respond to an accident on Interstate 430. It was a typical fender bender rear-end accident. I had worked dozens of them.

I hated to write the poor guy who had caused the accident a ticket. Unless there were extenuating circumstances, if a driver was clearly at fault that driver received a citation. I gave the guy one and started to walk away from his car. I had moved the cars out off the road from where the accident had occurred, standard practice in these minor accidents. The young man was starting to get into his car, which was parked in front of mine, when we heard a loud crash. It was the familiar sound of another rear-end accident but this one was close, only thirty feet away. I looked up to see a car coming directly at me. I rolled violently out of the way to avoid being hit directly. The young man I had just ticketed froze. Standing beside his car door, he was hit at the knees by the car that had been rear-ended and driven into us. He was pinned between the onrushing car and his own, pushed down an embankment and trapped. I got up with a shooting pain down my back and made it over to him. He was screaming, obviously in intense pain. "Get it off me!" he screamed repeatedly as the driver of the careening car that had careened into us had frozen at the wheel. I kept yelling to her until she finally backed the car off the injured man. He immediately fell to the ground and was bleeding from a leg crushed almost in two.

I made it to the radio in my car and called for help. I needed an ambulance and another trooper to work the accident. The trooper who arrived complained that he was to be off for the next few days and asked me to work the accident myself. I reluctantly agreed even though I had been injured as a result of the accident. After the man was taken to the hospital and the scene cleared of the cars, I went to the hospital to see how he was doing. He was not well. The doctors were not sure they could save his leg but in the end they did. I would visit him several more times as he tried to recover, but he was crippled for life.

I immediately went to state police headquarters to prepare my report and try to get to a doctor for my back. I tried for two days with my shift sergeant telling me he needed me to stay on duty since we were short-handed. I finally told the state police I was going to a doctor as I was getting worse. I had severe pain radiating down my back and it wasn't going away.

January 18, 1995 would be the last day I would work for the state police in the field. My neurosurgeon eventually operated on the three herniated disks in my lower back. After extensive physical therapy, I was, as they say, 'as good as I was going to get.' I wrote a letter to Jim Guy Tucker's appointee to the state police directorship, John Bailey, asking to come back to work. He wrote a short letter in response saying they had no 'permanent light duty assignments' and that if I couldn't perform as well as all the other troopers, I didn't have a job. That's the Arkansas State Police. There are people who have been hurt in the line of duty who have been accommodated with suitable jobs. Not me. I filed a complaint with the federal Equal Employment Opportunity Commission. I have yet to have a hearing even though it's been over four years since the incident.

The ruination was total. I had children from college to kindergarten and no job, and this nightmare wasn't nearly over.

I needed a job desperately. I turned to the people who had prodded me to tell everything I knew about the Clintons, the Republicans and other conservatives that were agenda-oriented and wanted to see Clinton fall. My family was living off Becky's salary and, for a while, the worker's compensation check I would receive. After that ran out, the best I could do was to get my private investigator license and try to solicit case work from the legal community in Arkansas. I tried direct mail, personal telephone calls, essentially every marketing technique known to man. I didn't have much success. I was branded as a Clinton enemy and the legal establishment in Arkansas was by and large a Clinton-sympathetic one.

I'm sure it didn't help that Jim Guy Tucker had slandered me in the newspaper stating I was an incompetent investigator. I couldn't get enough work to live on. It was clear I had to develop another career outside the legal system. My brother Dwayne and I had already received a license from the Arkansas Board of Private Career Education to conduct business information seminars and to train individuals through independent study in research, my biggest strength. I had to broaden my educational base in order to do so and set my sights on obtaining my master's degree and ultimately my doctorate in politics and business by pouring myself into a program. I have just now finished that program conducted here in Arkansas and in England through intense study and research that has drained every penny Becky and I made. All this while still trying to maintain a full-time work load. I even took on clients for genealogical research, a hobby of mine I thoroughly enjoyed. It was time consuming but not very profitable.

I applied to foundations for scholarships to fund my education. I finally received a favorable response from a conservative foundation that would fund my Ph.D. education effort in England. The liberal end of the media spectrum has looked for financial connections between witnesses in the Clinton investigation and financiers on the right—the 'vast right wing conspiracy.' I didn't see receiving a scholarship as a payoff, bribe or any other nefarious effort to get me to do anything I wasn't already predisposed to do. Indeed I had already given all the testimony before the grand jury I would ever give. It was all truthful, complete and not coerced by anyone.

Even though I obtained a scholarship to fund the tuition, the time away from home took its toll. The somewhat unconventional route I took, however, would lead to further opportunities for the Clinton camp to try to intimidate me even then. It would happen outside the United States.

Through contacts I had made earlier, I applied at a British University to enter a Master of Philosophy/Doctor of

Philosophy program that would expedite the process leading me to the Ph.D.. I would have to spend six weeks per year there and be a full time, year-round student. I received credit for my previous writing to an extent, but had to enroll in research methodology courses that were intensive to say the least. I immediately started compiling my literature review on my topic of criminal law enactments in Arkansas, a subject with which I could conduct research based in the states while having a public policy application worldwide. It was hard to leave my family in the States but I hoped that in the end it would be worth it. While in the States I would have to deal with the Independent Counsel and Congress and still keep up my research. It worked well for the literature review, a significant segment of the dissertation, since the Library of Congress in Washington, DC was a primary source for material. When I wasn't meeting with my attorney or members of Congress, I would be at the library until it closed.

Becky and I saved enough money so that she could visit me in England on one of the longer stays. But it would be the high school graduation trip my daughter would take to England to see me that would demonstrate just how far the tentacles of Bill Clinton's intimidation machine really reached.

My family, friends, and I have been the targets of enough abuse at the hands of the Clintonites, so I have chosen to withhold the name of the city and university I attended from this book. Many there have already been unduly bothered by media inquiries due to my attendance and the friendships I forged . They are not intended to be the focus of this book. The city was not far from London, nothing really is in England as compared to the vast expanse of the United States and its remoteness from the puzzle palaces of Washington, DC. Life in England is vastly different from that in the United States. Space is at a premium. The cities are crowded, the cars are small, but the people are overly nice, always in the mood to talk to an American.

I soon found that most of them think all Americans are rich. It seemed that as much as I enjoyed being there, they very much more wish they were in America. "America, that's the place to be," was a statement I heard all too often. When I became friendly enough with someone to tell them I was from Arkansas, the first thing out of their mouth was the name Bill Clinton. Almost universally no one seemed to discount the stories that Bill was a philanderer, and almost to a number no one cared.

I soon learned not to talk politics as I was encountering a much more liberal and socialistic tone almost everywhere I went. But all that aside, the education was superb. The professors and students seemed more interested in providing and obtaining an education. They were more deliberate and universally serious about it than what I had seen and experienced in the states. The research methodology training was excellent and the faculty was comprised of from all ranges of disciplines. Many of the professors were scholars from foreign countries that brought with them the knowledge from their research on the great thinkers of their countries to share with their students. England and its educational system is that way. Multicultural by way of the many races and cultures of the old empire, it is as much a melting pot as America.

Throughout my time in England I remembered how much Bill had loved the time he spent there at Oxford. Although, unlike Bill, I would remain to finish my degree, I did not have the leisure of making the side trips to the continent and on to Russia as he did. From the discussions Bill and I would have of England, he was more interested in the political education of Bill Clinton than of learning. His ability to retain and cram for tests to get him through classes where others might need to actually be hands-on students, allowed him to freely range the continent. I am better for the experience, but I soon found I couldn't get away from all the Whitewater chaos even an ocean away.

*       *       *

My daughter, Jan, had just graduated from high school at Little Rock and had saved enough money to make a trip to England. Her plane would be arriving at Heathrow airport in London at 6:30 a.m. and it was a daunting prospect to get there that early by public transportation. I didn't have a car there and the only economical way of transportation was by bus.

I had to take a 2 a.m. bus to get there, and would have to wait a couple of hours at the airport until she arrived. I knew well in advance she was coming over and had purchased the ticket at substantial savings. I got to the bus station early and was sitting on a bench reading one of my required university texts by myself. The ticket agent had already closed the office and it was eerily quiet. About ten minutes had passed after the office had closed when a taxi came flying up. As many people know, British taxis are the best in the world, but they waste no time getting where they are going. The taxi stopped about twenty feet from me and a man got out the curb side near where I was sitting on the bench. He had a brief conversation with the driver and walked over to me briskly. "Waiting on the bus?" he asked, surely knowing the answer. What else would I be doing there at 2 a.m. "Right," I said, "It'll be here at 2 o'clock." Just then it dawned on me. The guy had an American accent. I say American, but it was more like that of a Brit trying to talk like an American.

This guy was a chatterbox. He extended his hand and in-troduced himself as T. John McBrearty, formerly of Houston, Texas. Now, I have known lots of Texans, but I have never known one with an accent (or lack of one) like this guy. Just then, the same taxi that had brought him pulled up to where he was standing, now close to my bench. John, as he called himself, lunged back toward the taxi and produced some cash and gave it to the driver. The cabbie handed over a sack which John immediately began rummaging through. He walked back to me and pulled a sandwich from the bag and offered it to me.

"You hungry?" he asked with a mouthful of another sandwich he had already began to attack. This guy was not only chatty but vociferously hungry. I declined. I didn't eat that late, ever.

John acted like he knew where he was. But he obviously didn't know where he was going. "Where can I buy a ticket?" he asked me over the munching of the sandwich. I told him the ticket agent had already left but I thought he could buy a ticket on the bus. "Well where does it go?" he continued, as I became further confused about who or what this man was. I shared with him that I was going to Heathrow airport in London but that the bus made many intermediate stops along the way.

Just then the bus arrived and let off all the passengers. John was already tiring me by asking stupid questions and offering me sandwiches he kept producing from that bag like so many clowns from a car in a circus act. John walked to the bus driver-cum-ticket-agent and began fumbling for more cash. He eventually paid for a ticket while I picked a seat near the front on the empty bus. I let out what must have been an audible moan when John took the seat directly across from me, dropped the tray table and dove in the bag for more food. "You sure you don't want a sandwich?" he asked. It was going to be a long ride.

The commuter buses in England are rather nice. Not anything like a city bus you might catch across town, or even a Greyhound. During normal hours they have an attendant who serves soft drinks and even beer, along with snacks and sandwiches. Since this was an odd hour, we had no food or beverage service, it was just us and the driver. John, apparently seeing I was determined to get some sleep on the two-hour ride, abruptly changed the content and direction of his chatter. "I'm over here flying airplanes into Russia," he said. This perked me up a little bit. He went on to explain he would fly in food to the former Soviet states and in return he would receive airplane parts. At times, he said, he would receive entire airplanes like an intact Sukhoi-29 fighter which he said he had flown to Ireland where he maintained an office.

If he was trying to get my attention he had succeeded. He thought it a good idea then to exchange business cards. I only carried my personal card that had my home address and telephone number. It also had the name L. Douglass Brown on it. John didn't have a card so he took one of mine and jotted down his name and telephone numbers including a Dublin, Ireland address.

I thought maybe this would satisfy the man and this time I told him that I was going to get some sleep. He immediately changed tactics and lowered the boom on me. "Well L. D.," he said, "when did you and Clinton actually break up?" I'm sure I visibly shot up in the seat as I knew I had never told him I was called 'L. D.' I certainly never mentioned I had been close to Bill Clinton. He really had my attention now and any hope of sleep had vanished. They had reached me even in England.

"You know L. D., we could use a man like you in this operation," he said, as I was now leaning toward him to catch every word. Going deeper, he asked me, "You know what a proprietary is don't you?" I knew that after I had flown on the airplane trips with Seal and the subsequent Iran-Contra hearings that proprietaries were the cutout fake airline companies C. I. A. set up to facilitate their business. I was waiting for the other shoe to drop, or maybe the gun to go off. Here I was in the middle of the English countryside, alone with a guy who had obviously been sent by the C. I. A. to get me involved in another operation—and Bill Clinton was involved in some way.

I didn't have any choice but to play along. If they were out to get me then and there, I could do nothing anyway. I decided to do a little probing of my own. "How much would this pay?" I asked. "Well, how about $300,000?" he threw out, like we were trading for an old '75 Dodge at the car lot. The figure sounded nice. "Exactly what would I have to do?" I asked, as I thought there would be a real kicker attached to his answer. There was.

John then began to lay out the plan for my involvement which was really bizarre and telling at the same time. "You know who James Carville is, don't you?" he asked, as if knowing the answer. "I want you to call James Carville and work with him to get the intelligence agencies off our ass." Me working with James Carville on a project would be like Bill Clinton hiring me to be the director of the F. B. I. But I wasn't thinking of the absurdity of the offer at the time John made it. I knew that it was a payoff, or at least an attempt to keep me quiet.

I would soon learn that it would also be an attempt to keep me out of the country. John said I would accompany him on airplane trips out of the country as well. He told me he would soon be flying to Brazzaville, Congo with a load of food for example. "You've heard of Southern Air Transport?" he asked, again knowing my answer. "Sure, in Florida," I answered, familiar with SAT having been a C. I. A. proprietary. "Well, I fly some of these airplane parts to Florida. You know, Jack Stephens buys some of them, and we go on from there." He was referring to Jackson Stephens the billionaire Clinton supporter at whose house I had met John Glenn. But there was more.

"L. D., a lady by the name of Nancy Soderberg is involved in this. She works for Clinton as an adviser on Northern Ireland," he explained, as the machinations of how the operation worked began to unfold. John told me of a plant that makes electronic equipment in Ireland near the border with Northern Ireland. Being familiar with the 'troubles' between the Northern Protestants and the Catholic Irish Republicans, I realized what he was saying. The goal was to provide employment to the Irish near the border who were sympathetic to the Irish Republicans. The money made from the airplane trips would fund these activities. He told me Soderberg would soon be leaving her position and would be focusing on the operation. I did not know Soderberg and asked what that had to do with me.

We finally arrived at the Heathrow airport and I was not about to allow this guy to follow me to the gate where I would be meeting my daughter. We both got off the bus but he was clearly lost. He didn't even know we were at Heathrow. He asked me where I was going and I told him nowhere. I was intent on letting him leave first. I still had two hours until Jan would arrive anyway, and I wasn't about to even give an indication as to which terminal I was going. John took the opportunity to reiterate all the key points he had made on the bus trip. He made sure I had the business card with all his numbers on it. He wouldn't leave until I had assured him I would telephone him when I returned to the states. I finally had to show him the way to the taxis and watched him leave. But I wasn't done with T. John McBrearty.

My daughter Jan arrived safe and sound but I looked over my shoulder the entire trip. I have always known anyone can be taken out if someone wants to get you badly enough, is smart, and is willing to suffer the consequences. But it's a different story when it comes to my family. I was determined to get to the bottom of this fast. When I arrived back in the States I made contact with a friend in England who had worked with MI-6, the British intelligence agency. Brian Crozier is a world-renowned journalist who has had acknowledged ties with the intelligence community for five decades. Brian is a brilliant man, a scholar who has fought Communism from many different fronts. He was once known internationally as the journalist who had interviewed more heads of state than anyone else. He is a good friend who has entertained my wife and children at his flat in downtown London and a patriot I have been privileged to know.

Brian would also be a great aid to me in trying to sort out what was happening with McBrearty, Clinton and the many other assorted characters who would enter the picture as I struggled to 'do the right thing.' Brian, of course, smelled a rat as I did—an Arkansas rat with size 13 shoes. I decided to play along and find out as much as I could by telephoning McBrearty in Dublin. In almost every case I would get an answering service that would take a number for McBrearty to call me back. This would be the pattern of our communications which took place for several weeks to come. The first time McBrearty called I was worried since he talked to Jan, my daughter who had visited me in England. My first word of it came as I returned home one night to hear Jan talking about the 'real nice guy from Ireland' who called looking for me. Jan said she had talked for nearly half an hour with him and talked of her trip and how she enjoyed the English countryside. It scared the heck out of me and I worried that it was a subtle reminder in the vein of 'I know who you are and where you live.'

John finally caught me at home and began what would be a much more clear and concise dialogue with me. There would be no more doubts as to the associations he had forged and what he knew about me. "L. D. you come highly recommended. You know we're just a bunch of old 'air thugs' tired of just hanging around our pools now that the cold war is over," he assured me, as if including me in the group. In a way I guess I was. He again wanted me to call James Carville and set up a liaison immediately. I stalled for time and asked when he would be flying me over to check out the operation in Ireland. He told me he would send me a ticket when I decided how much money I wanted. John also began sharing with me information on Clinton. He told me Bill would be giving an audience to a liberal member of Parliament who was an ardent supporter of the Irish Republican Army.

At this point I hadn't even told my wife Becky about the incident. She had questions when John called and talked to Jan, but I played it off as being some guy I had met on the airplane. But I needed further information on McBrearty before I made a move either way. I couldn't ask anyone in the media for fear that it would make it to the newspapers, an event I wanted to avoid at all costs. I knew that if McBrearty found out I had talked with journalists, especially conservative ones, the deal would be blown. Since I was still considering taking the offer, leaking it to the press would blow the prospects of it going through. If I wanted to maintain contact for purposes of joining in the operation to prove Clinton's attempts of witness intimidation, that too would be compromised by a printing in the press.

I would receive many more calls from McBrearty. He told me the operation was opening an office near the Capitol in Washington, DC and gave me a name that would be my contact there. "We need to get the intelligence agencies off our ass," he told me once. Knowing of the rift between Bill Clinton and me, it was obvious this would be a 'make work' payoff since I would be working with Clinton apologist James Carville as my contact. When I pressed him on what I would do on the airplane trips, I heard the familiar line first offered by Barry Seal ten years earlier, "Just sit back and enjoy the ride." I guess they figured if I was stupid enough to fly under those rules back then, I would surely do it for a lot more money now. I was at a point where I had to do something. Becky didn't want me to take it. I saw the utility of it in that I could be in England the required amount of time I had to be for the Ph.D. program and our financial problems would be solved at the same time.

Brian Crozier, my friend in London, had made inquiries and had come to the same conclusions that I had. Ever the adventurer, he thought I should go for it and sign on. It would certainly be an experience and, after all, it paid well. But I needed more information and I decided to turn to someone who had the resources to investigate further.

Yes Hillary, there is a vast right wing conspiracy out there, well sort of. The problem is that it sometimes comes back to bite the people who are perceived to be a part of it in the... well you get the point.    Becky **and** I had been invited once to an American Spectator dinner in Washington, DC earlier and had met Bob Dole and Fred Thompson there among others active in the Republican party. The keynote speaker was Phil Graham, who was running for President, and Bob Dole had crashed the party by coming to the reception beforehand and shaking hands at the reception.    I later telephoned a trusted contact I had come to know after that dinner.    I still trust that contact who deserves no grief from me or the readers of this book and shall remain unnamed.

I knew the contact was connected to the 'vast right wing conspiracy' that Hillary says exists out there.    I also knew they had the time and money to investigate the operation I was considering entering.    My contact assured me of confidentiality and realized the prospects of nailing the Clinton machine for witness intimidation if I could make a case by documenting my every move.    They also knew I needed a job and I didn't want to screw this up.    I was not prepared for what would happen next.

It didn't take two days for me to get a call from an acknowledged cog in the wheel of the 'vast conspiracy' machine. David Henderson, a board member at the *American Spectator* magazine and liaison to the magazine for Richard Mellon Scaife, the millionaire conservative activist, telephoned me at home.    To my shock he told me, "I hear you've had some problems at a bus station in England."    I was outraged that Henderson had the information.    I knew if Henderson knew the facts he would tell all assorted conservative journalists. Journalists who never had understood or cared that there was real danger and consequences in it becoming public that I had talked about operations such as the Mena activity and the incidents in England.    I immediately told Henderson I did *not* want Bob Tyrrell at the *American Spectator* or anyone else to write about the incident.    I impressed upon him the need of secrecy for the reasons that I may take the job whether to develop evidence or to make money for my family.    He agreed not to say anything and I continued my telephone contacts with McBrearty in Dublin.

I was on the verge of taking the job.    I had again contacted my friend in London, Brian Crozier, and confirmed additional facts regarding the member of Parliament but I was concerned about the legality of being a liaison to the United States government for a corporation headquartered in Ireland. I needed a legal opinion and this was out of the field in which my personal attorney practiced.

Enter Ted Olsen, a noted conservative attorney in Washington, DC and a good one. Henderson offered to have Olsen talk with me and give me advice on whether or not to take the job. I traveled to Washington and met with Henderson and Olsen at Ted's office. I laid out the extensive story as Ted listened with interest. Ted is an exceptional lawyer and I trusted his advice explicitly. It was with his opinion that I took what he had to say to heart. "I would stay away from it L. D.," he said flatly. He saw that it may be a setup to get me out of the country and have something 'happen' to me. Also it could be a ruse to get me to perform work without being a registered agent for a foreign corporation. Henderson was clearly surprised and dismayed. But I still was undecided.

I returned to Little Rock still needing a job desperately. I was spending more and more time on my research, but unfortunately that didn't pay anything and my business in Little Rock was not growing. I decided I still may take McBrearty up on the offer. Not too long after the trip I received another call from David Henderson. "Are you sure Bob (Tyrrell) can't write about this incident in England?" he asked, with the high-pitched tone of a man asking a question to which he already knew the answer. I emphatically replied, "Hell no, Dave!" I proceeded to reiterate how much trouble I would be in if it was found out I was talking to the media. Not only would I lose the opportunity, I also reminded him, as I had in the Mena affair, but these people don't play by the rules. I could end up dead. My point was if he didn't care about me he should consider my family. He said he understood.

I never talked to Bob Tyrrell about my desire to keep the story under wraps. Only two days after I had admonished Henderson not to allow Bob to print the story, one of Tyrrell's columns appeared in the Creators Syndicate.   In the column, Bob alluded to witness tampering of state troopers.   I can only assume he took his cue from Henderson, since I knew Dave was working at the *Spectator* offices and was close to Bob. The column which ran on July 18, 1997 spoke of an unnamed trooper who was approached 'while abroad' at '2 a.m.' and offered to engage in a 'very dubious foreign endeavor.'   I found out about the story through browsing on the Internet.   I was incensed, shaken about the consequences, and felt betrayed.   I immediately telephoned Bob who said he knew nothing of the secrecy and I believed him.   I still do.   Bob Tyrrell is an honorable man and he knew where the problem was.

I next called David Henderson and demanded to know why he had told Tyrrell he could write the story.   "Well I didn't think you were going to take the job after what Ted (Olsen) had told you," he offered.   I was done with Henderson.   He had placed my family and me in jeopardy and I knew all chances of the operation were blown.   I learned later that Mr. Richard Scaife had cut all ties to the *Spectator.*   I hope Henderson was at least in part the reason Mr. Scaife did so because of what had happened to me.

If there is one thing Bill Clinton's people do it's following the press stories.   Even when he was Governor of Arkansas, we would have people clip stories that had even remotely anything to do with him or his policy initiatives.   Considering Bob Tyrrell and the *American Spectator* were on the hit list since the first Troopergate story, I knew this story would not go unnoticed.   It would be obvious to them who the unnamed trooper was since I didn't believe Patterson or Perry would fit the description of the trooper in the article.   I was proven right.   McBrearty from that day on did not return my telephone calls and he never called me again.   I had been burned.   See Hillary, it doesn't always happen the way you think.   Overzealous and agenda-oriented people are in it for one thing, to destroy Bill Clinton, whoever has to be used or sacrificed in the process.

I was afraid for my family. I told Justin Thornton, my attorney, what had happened and we both decided I had better contact the Independent Counsel in an effort to provide myself a measure of protection. I subsequently met with F. B. I. Agent Steve Irons and Deputy Counsel Jackie Bennett at the OIC's office in west Little Rock. Justin was on the speaker phone for the meeting that lasted several hours.

I explained what had happened in great detail. I told them I was concerned about the safety of my family since the people at the heart of all this clearly knew I had talked. I didn't know there was hardly anything they could do to protect my family and me. Telling the story in this book is probably the best solution to that problem. They assured me a detailed report would be made of the incident and told me they were concerned. That was all they could do for now. I still don't know if they have investigated the incident to this day.

I was particularly apprehensive about taking my entire family to England on what would be the last trip before I would finish my studies. Becky and I had worked hard to save the money and had found a good off-season ticket price. With help from some of my friends in England, I was able to find cheap accommodations but I was concerned about what had happened. I was also bothered that I still had not heard from McBrearty. I had not received an overt backlash from Tyrrell's story—yet.

So it was with some apprehension I took my family to London and to an academic conference in another part of England where I was to present a paper. Everything went without incident until we arrived at the university. We checked into our hotel and were to stay for two days. We did our own linen changes as the room we all shared was quite crowded. This meant there was no hotel personnel entering the room. That's the way I wanted it since my last experience while in town. I didn't want to take any chances.

The day we were to check out I reached for my case in which I kept my day-timer, receipts and notes for this book. It was gone. We turned the room upside down but to no avail. Whoever took it undoubtedly puzzled at the Cyrillic notes made in Russian. The Spanish they may have been able to translate. I looked over my shoulder the rest of the trip.

When we returned from the trip I again contacted the OIC to tell them of the event. They had told me to keep them posted if anything else happened, so I did. I knew that again there was not much they could do, but as I write this I am still waiting for the proverbial 'other shoe' to drop. I telephoned F. B. I. Agent Steve Irons and told him what had happened. He sincerely asked how I was doing otherwise; I said my family and I were okay, but we were tired of being dogged by the media and the Clintons. But there was another incident that would cause me to be disenfranchised with the right, the vast 'right wing conspiracy.'

# CHAPTER THIRTEEN

## Congressional Inaction

At the height of the Senate Banking Committee hearings, it was public knowledge I had given testimony to the grand jury in Little Rock concerning the incident that occurred at the state Capitol between Bill Clinton and David Hale. My attorney Justin Thornton knew the Committee would be interested in my testimony; we should expect a call. It came in the person of David Bossie, a political operative that had worked for Floyd Brown, who had orchestrated the Willie Horton/Michael Dukakis episode in the 1988 presidential campaign. Bossie wanted to talk with us about my potential testimony at the hearings taking place on Capitol Hill. The leader of the hearings was New York Senator Alfonse D'Amato. D'Amato was the Senator who blew the chance to catch Betsey Wright in a lie. She was testifying about me in the same hearings.

Bossie talked with Justin many times. Justin and I both made the determination that we needed to be dealing with an attorney who was involved in the investigation instead of

Bossie. Dave clearly was biased in his dislike of the Clintons and I wanted to, if possible, stay out of the hearing process all together. I soon found this would be impossible.

Mike Chertoff reminded me of the Starr Deputy Counsel Bradley Lerman. He was himself a former U. S. Attorney in New Jersey, and possessed the legal acumen to be on the team investigating the president. He had an able assistant in Alice Fisher, with whom he would alternate questioning of witnesses during the hearings. Both were personable and wanted to get at the truth of the Whitewater investigation. Bob Guiffera was another matter. Guiffera was an attorney who worked with the committee and was a friend of its chairman, Senator D'Amato. He acted as if he needed to prove something to someone and treated us as if we were part of some sort of agenda-oriented effort. He reminded me of a sort of Richard Dreyfuss on speed. Especially during the scene in Jaws where they say they're 'going to need a bigger boat.'

Justin related to all the parties involved in the Senate Whitewater Committee hearings that I had lost a lot already by cooperating in the ongoing investigations. I had been removed from a prestigious position in the state police and assigned to a highway patrol job where I had been hurt and lost my job. I was not making nearly the amount of money I once was and I couldn't find a job. I didn't need any more exposure. That is what initially got me into my predicament.

This committee had subpoena power. Justin and I knew they would use it to get me before them for an interview, so we decided to make it easy on ourselves. We agreed to a meeting with the group at the offices of Senator Lauch Faircloth of North Carolina. It would prove to be one heck of a night.

Justin and I arrived at the Hart Senate Office Building after the Senate had recessed for the day. We were told to come to the offices of Senator Faircloth where we'd be met by David Bossie, Alice Fisher and Bob Guiffera. Apparently the Whitewater Committee had not recessed for the day, so Justin and I were led up a flight of stairs, in the rear of the offices, to a small room which looked like a break room of sorts. Chertoff, Fisher, Bossie and Guiffera joined us after a while, and we began to talk about the David Hale incident. I told them, as I had told the grand jury, what I had seen. I also related what had happened to me in Arkansas concerning the threats and intimidation. I also mentioned I was out of a job due to my involvement in Whitewater. As I related the incident that Skip Rutherford was involved in, Chertoff remarked, "That's obstruction of justice." I agreed, and asked them what they were going to do about it. I never got an answer. They seemed more interested in what the Office of Independent Counsel had been asking us about than in anything else. I quickly found out there was not a conspiracy between D'Amato's committee and Kenneth Starr since I clearly knew more than they did.

They told me of a piece of evidence that had been produced by Bill Clinton's lawyer David Kendall. The paper was regarding the Arkansas Development Finance Authority, an entity rumored to have been a source of illegal financial transactions. The agency was headed at one point by current White House personnel chief Bob Nash. The words 'the L. D. Brown problem' were written on it and they wondered why. I thought it had something to do with the money I had carried around in the paper bag and/or Mena.

An assistant to Senator Faircloth came into the room and sat down to listen to what was going on in the interview. The daughter of a federal judge in North Carolina, she clearly enjoyed listening to the conversations we were having. The talk turned to Bill and Hillary and their personal lives, Bill's womanizing and Vince Foster and Hillary. We were talking casually as I was being more open with them by now.

I suddenly heard someone stomping up the stairs that led to the room. I knew from seeing him on television that the man entering the room was Senator Lauch Faircloth from North Carolina. Justin introduced himself. The Senator was glad to learn my attorney was a native North Carolinian. Faircloth turned to me, plopped down in a chair which he had pulled up

next to me and blurted, "L. D. that Hillary Clinton is a lying
overbearing bitch isn't she?" I was, needless to say, a little
surprised. I said I felt Mrs. Clinton had not told the truth on
several issues. As I spoke, I noticed the remark had not
startled anyone else but Justin and me. The Senator knew
who I was and pretty much had his mind made up that he
liked me, I think. He didn't stay long but the time he spent
with us sure had an impact. It didn't much surprise or bother
me that he lost his bid for reelection in November 1998
either.

I was growing weary. The night of questioning had been
tough on me since I don't travel well anymore due to my back
surgery. We all went downstairs to a conference room on the
first floor of the Senator's office. As we walked into the room
Justin and I were greeted by Chertoff and Fisher who had
already set up shop there after they had left Justin and me.
The table was an absolute mess with peanut shells all over the
place. Chertoff offered me and Justin some but we declined. I
could tell Justin considered the spectacle of a United State
Senator's office being strewn with peanut shells about as
weird as I did. They were hungry too. Peanut shells were
flying as Chertoff, Fisher and Bossie were tearing into a bag of
nuts that had come from Faircloth's North Carolina. Whoever
the lobby was that sent them, should know they were put to
good use.

We continued to talk about the Clintons until we got to the
point where Guiffera asked if anyone had approached me to
try and influence my testimony. In a retake of the ABC News
interview, where I refused to answer the same question, I told
them I couldn't answer. That's when Guiffera popped off,
"You need to be on the right side L. D." That remark didn't
set well with me. I swiftly told Guiffera I was on the side of
telling the truth and protecting my family from any more
harm. I wasn't on one side or the other. Justin stepped in at
just the right time and we walked outside the peanut gallery to
talk. Justin reminded me the committee had subpoena power

and we needed to cooperate to a point. There was one other person who had become involved that I refused to name, I still do, and Guiffera was not about to get that name either.

Guiffera asked if we had eaten yet. I felt like saying we had, since we had turned down those nuts, but we admitted we hadn't. The 'Senator' wanted to meet me for dinner and Guiffera asked if we would hang around. I assumed he was talking about Senator Faircloth whom I had vividly remembered meeting. No, the *Senator* wanted to meet me. He meant Senator Alfonse D'Amato of New York, the Chairman of the Senate Banking Committee which was conducting the Whitewater hearings. Justin and I agreed and said we would stick around for dinner. We thought the Senator wanted to talk to me about my potential testimony. I didn't know if Guiffera had talked with the Senator about my reluctance to be more forthcoming or not but it was obvious they wanted to put the schmooze on me that night.

We were told to come to Senator D'Amato's office in the same Hart Senate Office Building to meet the Senator. His office was not far from the one from which we had just come. It looked as if the hearings had just broken up as there was a flurry of activity. We were met inside by a receptionist who told us the Senator would be right with us. Before long we were being led into the spacious office of Senator Al D'Amato. It didn't take long to pick him out from the few aides who were in the room as well. "L. D., how ya doin?" he asked, as if we had known each other for years. He strode to me and grabbed my hand as if I was a New York voter. A smallish exuberant man, he was far from the person I had seen on television where he was reserved and deliberate in the hearings. He nearly tugged my arm off as he reached back immediately to a bookcase behind his desk and grabbed a book off the shelf.

"Here L. D., have a book," he said as he opened it and scribbled something inside the cover. He closed the cover and handed it to me. I saw it was his *Power, Pasta and Politics: The World According to Senator Al D'Amato.* That's exactly what I was to hear that night. He had dated the book '1-25-96' and signed it, 'To L. D., hope you enjoy the book'. I must confess I haven't read it yet.

The affable hyper-Senator asked me if I smoked cigars. I sure did. He opened a humidor and handed Justin and me one while again giving me a good back slap. I could see several people in a back room peeking around the door. D'Amato, clearly wound up now, yelled to a man about 30 years old, "Hey Frankie, get your ass in here. I want you to meet someone!" D'Amato dragged me over to the door and said, "L. D., I want you to meet Frank Sinatra." I thought it was a joke and I was about ready to join in the fun so I didn't miss a beat and shot back, "Hello Frank, I'm Tony Bennett." I was clearly now in the Senator's good graces. He thought that line was a good one. He assured me, however, that Frank Sinatra really was the guy's name, I guess it was. I felt a little embarrassed, but the atmosphere was so loose that I quickly got over it.

"L. D., you hungry?", he asked, as if Justin wasn't there. We said "sure" and were led out through the door from where the crooner had come. I saw there was a large contingent of people in the room and it was apparent we were all going to dinner together.

The Senator, Justin and I were led to a black Lincoln in a back lot of the office building. He had a driver who let us into the car with the Senator riding up front. We weren't in the car for five minutes before we had arrived at the upscale La Colline restaurant on Capitol Hill. The Senator was clearly at home in the restaurant. Bob Guiffera was there to meet us, but Mike Chertoff and Alice Fisher couldn't make it. There were a few people who saw our grand entrance as the Senator swaggered in and said hello to the proprietor, who obviously knew the Senator well. I thought we were going to get a table in the somewhat small but elegant restaurant but we were all directed around to the back.

A hallway opened up to a small banquet room where there were about forty people seated at a table too small for the group. D'Amato was clearly among friends and supporters. They all cheered at his arrival; Justin and I looked for a seat. The Senator had his sights set on me sitting right next to him. He told someone to get out of the seat next to where he would sit at the head of the table. I squeezed into the spot beside the Senator as he grabbed me in a hug again and announced to the attentive group, "Gentlemen, this is L. D. Brown from Arkansas. He's my guest tonight." There was a little applause, I guess, but I know no one knew who I was. They were obviously not all there to greet me. I never did figure out who these people were, but they were all from New York and there to see their Senator.

A good red wine was served as everyone ordered their entrée, while the Senator was on an even better roll now. He was clearly revved up and in his own element. I've never been around a New York politician but have read quite a bit about Tammany Hall, Boss Tweed, and Thomas Dewey and I wasn't quite sure where the esteemed Senator fit in with the historical New York politicians. I sensed he was one of those 'one-of-a-kind' politicians you don't run into every day. The closest comparison I could make to him was to a South Arkansas Clinton coordinator who you couldn't run off with a gun. The kind who would almost smother you with hugs and glad-handing whenever he saw you with the governor.

D'Amato then turned his attention to the guests at the table with whom he was clearly familiar. Probably only three of the forty people were women and D'Amato had no words for them. His remarks were reserved for the guys whom he would alternatively address. "Now this son-of-a-bitch," he blurted out as he pointed to a man on his right who clearly enjoyed being singled out, "I've known him for twenty years." He would point to another and command, "Get your ass down here, I want to give you a hug." The two would embrace and then the guy would go back to his seat. I never did figure out who that guy was.

But the Senator saved his real cuss-loving for Guiffera. Bob Guiffera had apparently come to D'Amato's rescue when the Senator's brother was being accused of crimes in New York. D'Amato gave me the 'New York headlock' again and drew me close to tell me the story. As everyone in the room listened, he told me of how Guiffera telephoned him after the allegations of his brother's misconduct had become public. He did not know Guiffera then, but after accepting his help, they have been good friends ever since.

"This son-of-a-bitch," he said, now with a tear welling in his eye, "he stood by me all the way as these bastards tried to get him." Guiffera just smiled and basked in the warm light that was being shined down upon him from the Senator. D'Amato, now fighting back the tears, hugged me closer as it was obvious he felt he and his brother had been targeted wrongfully for political purposes.

The Senator then switched gears and asked me softly, "L. D., that Mena thing, that was just a drug deal gone bad wasn't it?" I was startled by the question and told him I didn't have all the answers. I followed up by telling him it could have been all of that and more. I just didn't know for sure. I didn't know and still don't what his specific interest was in Mena, but like a lot of other occasions in the past, I wish I had pressed the matter. I came away from that conversation thinking *he* was trying to convince *me* Mena was nothing but a drug operation. It reminded me of the strange Bush and Clinton connection all over again.

Everyone at the table had by now received their food and we all started to eat. Conversations ran over each other as people would stop at the Senator's seat to pay their respects. The wine was flowing but no one was sufficiently drunk to explain the evening's more bizarre moments. D'Amato kept me close at hand. Justin was sitting by me and David Bossie had arrived and was sitting near Justin.

As we finished our meal, the cigars came out. We fired up, as did many others around the table. The small room was clearly not equipped for the smoke and a haze hovered over the room.

"C'mon, L. D., let's go take a leak," the Senator commanded as Justin and I got up from the table. An aide of the Senator also got up. He apparently never went anywhere without a staff person. We walked to the rest room while the Senator had his arm around my neck. I was beginning to think that he liked me a little too much and was wondering if I might have to tell him that I peed alone when we got inside. What happened next I have never told for the public record before this.    I am glad my lawyer was there as I'm sure he'll be by my side when I tell it again.

There were a couple of people in the rest room. While they finished their business, we also did what we ostensibly came there to do. But there was more business to do. The Senator's aide checked the stalls in the rest room to make sure they were vacant and then walked to the only door leading into the room. The Senator now grabbed me in the familiar headlock, which had me in a perpetual lean since D'Amato is about six inches shorter than me. Justin looked around to see what was going on as the aide put his foot at the bottom of the door, thus placing an improvised locking mechanism on it. Then the Senator went for the kill.

While putting an extra squeeze on the headlock he said, "L. D., we got to have your help. We need you to cooperate with us." I could hear by now that people were banging on the door to get in the rest room. "We're fucking in here!" the aide yelled. D'Amato continued on, oblivious to the commotion as the aide struggled to keep the door shut. "Now L. D., we'll take care of you, we'll get you a job." With the cigar in his mouth and his arm around my neck, the Senator looked more like a character from a Mario Puzo novel making me 'an offer I couldn't refuse' than a United States Senator conducting an investigation on the President of the United States. I was shocked and I could tell Justin didn't want to be there either.

People outside obviously were about to wet their pants while this seemed to drag on forever. The aide was now vigorously struggling to keep the door shut while I had 'the arm' put on me. The Senator finally released his grip and I mumbled something about being concerned for my family as we finally walked out of the bathroom. The aide, clearly exhausted from his bathroom chores went back to the table with Justin and me while being led by the Senator. The party was about to break up and I was wishing I had never come. Justin and I rolled our eyes at each other at what had just happened. We knew it was improper at best to offer jobs to potential witnesses. It also disappointed me to no end to find yet another person in this entire Whitewater fiasco who wanted to use me.

We were to get a ride back to the Hart Building with the Senator. But before we left La Colline, the Senator had another surprise. He departed from his hard-edged brusque style long enough to stop at the piano located in the main dining area of the restaurant. To the interest of the patrons who were by now whispering that the man was Senator Al D'Amato, the Senator sat down and played a tune for the us, cigar in his mouth, while he swayed gently with the music. This had been an interesting night indeed.

I would meet several members of Congress that are conducting investigations into the scandals of the Clinton administration. I received a telephone call one day from the office of Congressman Bob Barr of Georgia. I was in Washington for a meeting with my attorney on the various Whitewater matters in which I was involved. The Congressman was in the middle of a Judiciary Committee hearing at the committee's offices. An aide met me at his office and walked me to the meeting room to await the Congressman.

Bob Barr is an interesting man. He obviously has the courage of his convictions in taking on corruption in government. A former federal prosecutor from near Atlanta, he is clearly learned in the law and has a very good idea where he is going, a prospect I think eludes most of the people in that town. He is committed to the principles for which he stands, unlike some others I have met who talk one way and act another. In my view, he gets a high rating when scoring politicians on matters of leadership and integrity, much the same way Jim Leach does, although Barr is more outspoken.

The Congressman was on a break from the committee meeting and gave me a warm welcome. We looked for a place to talk and settled for a 'quiet room' where other members were taking a break. He wanted to assure me that he needed my testimony at some point in time and just wanted to meet me and say hello. We chatted about Georgia and I told him my Revolutionary ancestor Robert Brown was buried there and that one my relatives, Joseph Brown had been Governor of the state during the Civil War. He listened intently as I told him how rough all this had been on my family. I could sense he really cared and I pledged to cooperate with him every way I could. In October of 1998, Congressman Barr would speak ahead of me at a rally in Washington, DC.

I left that meeting feeling I had found an honest man trying to do right. A man with a conscience and a sense of duty. I would meet a couple more.

Dan Burton has held hearings on the campaign finance scandals that have been a part of the Clinton administration ever since I carried paper bags of money around the back roads of Arkansas. The Indiana Congressman was at a dinner I attended in mid-1997 in Washington. There was a cocktail reception before the event which was held a La Brazzerie, a trendy eatery near the Capitol. When he was introduced to me, he had his staff member get my telephone numbers so he could contact me and get more information for use later in the investigation. He was very likable and at the time was the target of a

Clinton counter punch directed at the Congressman's fund raising activities. He seemed clearly upset the media was paying as much attention to the attack as they were the issues he was bringing forward in his investigation.

At the private dinner he spoke on conditions of his remarks being off the record, and so shall they remain. He was an eloquent, forceful speaker and I came away thinking he too was a good man. He convinced me he believed in what he says and in what he told me. I'll take that any day in that town.

At the same restaurant in February of 1998, I met a man whom really impressed me. I had stopped in for only a few minutes but ended up staying for the entire dinner. I hadn't realized that Steve Forbes was to be the speaker until it was too late to rearrange my schedule. I wish I had. I arrived early and there were only two or three people at the restaurant. Forbes arrived early with a couple of aides and started shaking hands. He got to me last and I told him my name which clearly took him by surprise. I didn't know what that meant exactly, but I had his attention and he wanted to talk. An extremely polite and engaging person, I had only seen him on television and was impressed with his self-effacing appearance on Saturday Night Live which demonstrated his ability to poke fun at himself, a quality I think is severely lacking in politics today. I quickly sensed he took his policy positions much more seriously. I decided to be late for an appointment and stick around for some of his talk.

I took the opportunity, while we were talking one on one, to tell him I would never forget a line he used while he was running for President in 1996. The incident on which he was commenting concerned allegations of impropriety by one of his top aides in years past. When asked by a reporter if he would fire the aide, Forbes stood his ground and responded, "Every saint has a past and every sinner has a future." I told him I had used that line and I hoped he didn't mind. He just laughed and clearly knew what I had meant.

I knew there would be pressure as the congressional hearings picked up steam. I would come under pressure not only from people like D'Amato but somehow from the Clinton camp as well. I didn't know from where or when but I knew that it was brewing. Bill and his minions could not leave people alone and it was clear no one was protecting the witnesses they were trying to intimidate, particularly not the Office of Independent Counsel.

One of the most startling instances of intimidation occurred when my friend Tommy Mitchum came to tell me of an incident that he thought I should know about. Mitchum was one of the state representatives who had changed his vote in the state legislative session when Bill lied about keeping his end of a deal with me. Tommy had been a very close friend for many years. I had even confided in Tommy about some of the C. I. A. activities at Mena, particularly after things had gone wrong. I also took him to Grand Bahama island and showed him around the spots where I had earlier protected the gun shipments.

Tommy had bad news for me. Clinton was going to 'sick the Internal Revenue Service on me.' It seems that one of Tommy's friends, a former lobbyist named Bill Lawson, had met with Senator David Pryor from Arkansas. Pryor was a liberal Democrat who later would meet with the federal judge overseeing the Paula Jones case to try and get Susan McDougal out of jail[10]. Pryor, who has now retired from the United States Senate, is spearheading a Clinton legal defense fund to pay Bill's legal bills.

Lawson had told my friend Mitchum that Pryor had confided in Lawson about a meeting Pryor had with Bill Clinton. In that meeting they had talked of me and my future congressional appearance. Mitchum quoted Lawson as saying Pryor heard Clinton using the "sick the I. R. S. on me" line and that the Democrats in Congress were "ready for me" when I came to Capitol Hill to tell the truth.

I first telephoned my attorney Justin Thornton in Washington and then the Office of Independent Counsel. It didn't surprise me Bill had said that and I knew the account was plausible since I realized Lawson had access to Senator Pryor as a lobbyist in Washington as well as having been a long-time Arkansas based lobbyist.

Tommy Mitchum swore to me he quoted Lawson verbatim and I was not going to sit back and take this sort of abuse. To me it was an obvious criminal conspiracy to violate my civil rights. I wanted to confront Lawson but Tommy told me Lawson would never admit what had happened since he was a Clinton fan. I persuaded Tommy to set up a meeting with Lawson and we indeed met at the Capital Bar. Bill, a man I had known since my lobbying days at the Capitol, admitted that Pryor did say the Democrats would be 'ready' for me and had talked with Clinton about me. He 'didn't recall' the I. R. S. comment. It was clear that was all he was about to admit to, and I was grateful for that. He too knows how the Clinton machine can still mete out retribution if you cross them in Arkansas, even by telling the truth.

I did tell the Office of Independent Counsel what happened. They took a report and I suppose when the reams of volumes are released on Whitewater next century, there will be a note that one of the witnesses they called before the grand jury did telephone one day to say he had evidence a United States Senator and the President of the United States had threatened him. Unfortunately there will be no report of prosecution to go along with it.

# EPILOGUE
## Where We Stand Today

As 1998 began, I was in high hopes of at least seeing Jim Guy Tucker go to jail. My day in court had yet to come with my civil trial against him for intervening in my criminal case and for transferring me to the highway patrol where I would be injured for life. But Jim Guy had already been tried along with Jim and Susan McDougal of fraud in the management of federally insured funds. All three were convicted with Jim and Susan getting jail time. Jim died in jail and Susan served time for contempt which she had begun to serve after the federal judge held her in contempt for refusing to answer questions before the federal grand jury.

I was there on sentencing day for Jim Guy. He didn't have the guts to look me in the eye. He grinned like nothing was happening, and maybe he knew nothing would. Federal Judge George Howard (the same judge that presided in the Reed vs. Young case) listened as the tearful Tucker wailed about how he had been a good public servant and how the 'Court' knew this. He choked up as he related how the conviction had damaged his family and reputation. Neither then or now has the man expressed any remorse or guilt for his felonious wrongdoing. Judge Howard recessed to consider the punishment.

The spectators barely had time to shift in their chairs as Judge Howard quickly returned, obviously having his mind already made up. I was flabbergasted when Judge Howard declared that Jim Guy would have home detention and would be required to write papers on ethics in government for delivery in person to high school students around the state. I saw almost a smile come across Jim Guy's face as he stood at the podium and wrote down his sentence. Study hall and term papers for this felon who ruined my career while Jim and Susan McDougal sat in jail. That's Arkansas justice.

Jim Guy Tucker, now a convicted felon and ex-Arkansas governor, was succeeded by the Republican Lieutenant Governor Mike Huckabee, a Baptist preacher who had been elected to the post after making a name for himself in a run for the United States Senate post held by Dale Bumpers. Mike is a nice guy who now has himself embroiled in the throes of an ethics investigation of his own in Arkansas. He has been widely criticized for keeping on many Democrat appointees on boards and commissions.

One day, during the time Governor Jim Guy Tucker was under investigation, but before he was actually indicted, I had occasion to meet with Bob Tyrrell, editor of the *American Spectator*, in Little Rock. I had scheduled a meeting with Huckabee to talk of my situation with the state police, hoping that the Republican would help me when he assumed the office of governor when and if Tucker was removed after a possible conviction.

Bob and I met with Huckabee alone in his office at the state capitol. Mike was all but a declared candidate for the United States Senate as he was convinced Tucker would remain in office for an indefinite period of time. I told the lieutenant governor I strongly believed Tucker would be indicted and convicted soon enough. Mike leaned forward in his chair and was clearly interested in what I had to say. I was right, of course, and the point of the meeting was to let him know of the upcoming indictment. I needed help when he walked into the governor's office just as Tucker had assumed the post after Clinton was elected president.

Bob Tyrrell and Huckabee made conversation about the politics of Arkansas, a topic Bob is well familiar with and has written so eloquently about since Bill's ascension to the presidency. But Mike Huckabee was not to help me one bit when my prophecy proved true. Huckabee has even kept some of the same people from the state police as the Governor's security force. People who worked for Clinton and Tucker and were slandering me for years.

Huckabee has been a major disappointment to many people who saw him as a breath of fresh air in the corrupt political climate that is Arkansas. Unfortunately the air remains polluted as Huckabee fought the state ethics commission on charges filed against him regarding disclosure of the sources of money paid to him by entities from outside government. I am about to agree with what many journalists have observed in Arkansas over the past few years. There must be something in the air down here.

And what of Pasta Power D'Amato? I did try to get help in finding a job from the Senator from New York. After the hearings were over, I telephoned Senator D'Amato's office many times. My attorney, Justin Thornton, who had witnessed the entire cigar smoking, foul-mouthed bathroom episode at La Colline restaurant that night, tried too. The Senator never called Justin or me back but one of his minions did. Bob Guiffera, one of the attorneys who worked on D'Amato's committee, the one who had come to his rescue in D'Amato's brother's criminal case in New York, did call one day. After talking to me as if we had never met, Guiffera finally rudely asked, "L. D. what is it that you want?" I answered with what I realize now is an almost impossible request for a Washington politician, "Bob, just tell the Senator I just want him to do what he said he would do. That's all." I never heard from them again.

I seriously considered going public before the November elections with the jobs-for-testimony dinner encounter with the Senator at La Colline that night. However, I did not want to be responsible in any way for another Democrat sitting in the Senate when a possible impeachment conviction came up for a vote. It didn't matter, as Representative Charles Schumer defeated D'Amato in the general election anyway.

As the country lurched toward impeachment, I followed the campaigns in the heartland of America with an eye toward seeing what would really happen to Republican fortunes in the wake of the Clinton misfortunes. I didn't believe that Republicans would indeed make considerable gains in the House or Senate, but I was hopeful.

In Arkansas I had a friend who was challenging our liberal Democrat congressman in Little Rock. A smart and competent state senator, Phil Wyrick did not have much of a chance according to the polls. Considering the fact that the incumbent Vic Snyder was a Clinton apologist, I again hoped for the best.

There were two other congressmen I knew well who were facing only token opposition in their district races. Jay Dickey, who represented my old home town of Pine Bluff as well as Clinton's birthplace of Hope, Arkansas, was well on his way to a landslide victory on election night as I stopped by his headquarters at Little Rock's Embassy Suites Hotel. Wyrick had already been declared defeated in his race and Jay's victory was the only high note of the evening.

Jay Dickey is a very unassuming man, easygoing and frank in his conversations. He is a lawyer who returns to his district every weekend for constituent services. Even though his district is a traditional Democratic stronghold which Clinton carried every election, Jay has been elected four terms as a Republican.

I arrived late, and saw Jay finishing up the congratulatory reception. As he saw me approaching, he stood and greeted me with a most ominous salutation. "L. D. Brown, I'm surprised you're still alive," he said quite glumly. The remark took me aback to say the least. I simply responded by saying I was proud of him in Congress and that I hoped he did the right thing if he ever had the opportunity to vote on impeachment.

Weeks later I would send Jay a two page e-mail urging him to consider what Bill and Hillary have done to the reputation of this state. Jay was then undecided on whether or not to vote yes on impeachment. I reminded him also of what he had said to me on election night, a clear indication that he knew very well the cost to my family and me from the Clinton presidency.

It wasn't a week later that a White House official threatened Jay that if he voted for impeachment, Jay would be the target of White House attacks in his next election. They would 'make sure' that he would lose[11]. That made up Jay's mind. He did the right thing. It didn't matter. While the House impeached Clinton, the Senate failed to muster the necessary two-thirds vote to convict. Clinton was acquitted.

My family has been changed forever as a result of my involvement with the Clintons. My wife and I have had our lives turned upside down. But it is our children who have been most affected in ways that are sometimes hard to quantify. They listen closely even when you guard your conversations, making sure not to ever mention the names Bill and Hillary Clinton. But you can't keep the newspapers or magazines out of their hands. My oldest son, Benjamin, who is eleven years old, was looking through the March 23, 1998 issue of *Time* magazine when he ran across my photograph in an article about the Clintons. I took the issue from him but hours later I noticed he was not playing in the yard. I found him in the bedroom with the door closed. He had read every word of the article.

Benjamin is a smart little boy who takes in everything. An avid reader, I have tried to explain to him in ways that an eleven year old would understand why his daddy all of a sudden didn't work at the state police anymore, why there were politicians who weren't accountable for their actions. He knows that things have been very tight for us, and he realizes it had its genesis in the problems with Bill Clinton. I have never made one adverse comment about Bill and Hillary in front of him. I want him to respect the office, if not the man, but as he gets older it is becoming increasingly hard to do so.

The best example of this was the occasion when he was asked to write an essay in his fourth grade class. He obviously took out his anxiety on Bill with a story which I'll excerpt. In his strained handwriting, which is not his best subject, he started with, "It was a very dark night when Bill Clinton got reelected. That night James Bond came in with James Dean (his hero) and fought Bill Clinton. And then they took Bill Clinton down to the police station and put Bill in jail."

I asked Benjamin what the story meant. He told me that he knew Bill Clinton "had hurt you and Mommy." He was right about that.

The breakup of my wife's family and Becky has not gone unnoticed by my children either. Becky's mother Ann has worked a total of 14 years for Bill and Hillary. First at the Governor's Mansion and then on to Washington as deputy social secretary, Ann was profiled on the cover of a Little Rock paper's 'Style' section one week. She talked in the article about how she loved her grandchildren, when in reality she has never even held two of them. Her husband has never touched any one of them. All in deference to their great leader, Bill Clinton. This does not go unnoticed by our children.

One day Ann came to my youngest son's school to give a talk. Nicholas, a precocious boy of eight, listened intently to the speaker who talked about her job in the White House. Nicholas remembers that she was a pretty lady and very nice. He did not even know that the woman was his grandmother— and she didn't bother to tell him.

My oldest daughter, Jan, who is now in college, has known for many years who the Clintons really are and how they have treated her parents. After we left the Mansion where Jan played dress-up with Chelsea, Jan would run into Chelsea at parties. Chelsea, understandably taking her dad's line, said, quoting her gubernatorial father, "My dad says your dad is crazy." Jan, who is tough and resilient, just felt sorry for Chelsea and didn't say a word. Jan has better insight into Clinton's policy making methodology, or I should say the lack of it, than most professors of political science because of her life in which she has shared the Clinton experience.

My youngest daughter Caroline has been the only one to truly escape the direct effects of the Clinton experience. She is her mother made over, tough and beautiful. I know when she is old enough, which will be very soon, she too will see how corrupt politicians can ruin people's lives.

But for my wife's part she is the better person for the ordeals we have suffered at the hands of the Clintons due to our speaking out. The best Christian mother to our children, she sees the good in everything and never misses a chance to point out that we would never have met if it weren't for that time in our lives when we both thought the Clinton Governor's Mansion was the place to be.

Before deciding to self publish this manuscript I signed a contract with Regnery Publishing of Washington, DC. I negotiated with Alfred Regnery in the best of faith hoping to become part of their stable of books. It made sense for me to offer the manuscript to them first, since they had what I considered a built-in market having published many Clinton-related books. After I presented the outline of the book's chapters, which did not reveal the details of the manuscript, I told Regnery that this book would cut both ways. The truth about my experiences would be damaging to both conservatives and to the Clintonites. I was told that this made no difference. I would later believe that my revelations about

Alfonse D'Amato and Kenneth Starr, among others, would kill the chances for the book to actually make the book stores. I was right.

After months of work on fine tuning the manuscript I was told that, as stated in the contract I had signed, Regnery had the right to decline publishing the book. They invoked this right. At first I was disappointed, but after thinking through the matter, I decided that it was best that I go this alone by self-publishing. I had no idea what would happen between the Regnery experience in early 1998 and now.

Almost immediately word leaked out that my contract with Regnery was no longer in existence. E-mails and questions on Internet forums began to surface as to why the book had been canceled. Conspiracy theories (some of which may have been true) sprang up. The media was clearly interested in what had happened to my story. I eventually told anyone interested that the book would see the light of day, sooner or later. I never dreamed that Regnery would become part of the story instead of being the vehicle through which the story got out.

Since my wife and I decided to  publish this story on our own I have made a choice few public appearances. One was a sort of coming-out party for thousands of the Internet-based 'Free Republic' forum. A rally was held on the Capitol Mall October 31, 1998 at which I spoke to approximately 5,000 conservatives who had traveled from coast to coast for the event. The rally was broadcast live on the C-SPAN television network and I made up for lost time and opportunities to set the record straight on the Clinton's before the November elections.

Later that day, I appeared on the Fox News television 'Drudge Report' show. Hosted by the Internet king, I was asked about Vince Foster and Hillary Clinton's relationship. I reiterated my point that until whoever investigates the death of Vince acknowledges he and Hillary had a torrid affair, the investigation will never really come to a valid conclusion.

✳    ✳    ✳

How could Bill and Hillary ascend to the highest office in the nation? By remaining silent about the truth at the time of their first election in 1992, I know we did not live up to our patriotic responsibility. The 'mainstream media' gave them a pass as we sat in Little Rock and watched in disbelief.

The successful impeachment and failed conviction effort in the Senate dismayed me in that the real crimes of the Clintons have never been addressed. I will go so far as to predict that this is not the last move that will be made to effect their removal from the White House. The Clintons don't know when to leave well enough alone. I know after this book is published they will redouble their efforts to destroy my family and me.

Only time will tell if Bill and Hillary Clinton are products of the American people's apathy toward politicians. I believe, from having been close to these people, that they are much more. Bill is an intensely personal man. He likes to get up close to people even on television. I believe he has gotten very close to the American people and sold himself to them. I think he is symptomatic of what is wrong with America. I firmly believe the American people, at least the fraction that voted, deserve everything they get from this man. As Robert Bork pointed out recently, Clinton is like a rock star. He may fade away as most eventually do. But I fear there are another Bill and Hillary Clinton out there waiting to take their places.

# NOTES

¹ "Clinton had blood connections, some claim," *Arkansas Democrat Gazette*, October 18, 1998

² "There were distinguishing characteristics in Clinton's genital area that were obvious to Jones." From Civil Action no. LR-C-94-290, Jones vs. Clinton filed in United States District Court for the Eastern District of Arkansas, May 6, 1994. ·

³ This flight took place in October 1994, after the third Boland Amendment to the appropriations bill that included the C.I.A. took effect, specifically prohibiting the C.I.A. from spending any money to support "directly or indirectly, military or paramilitary operations in Nicaragua by any nation, group, organization, movement or individual." A C-123 cargo airplane was shot down over Nicaragua two years later, in October 1986, carrying a load of arms to the Contras. Copilot Wallace "Buzz" Sawyer, a native of Arkansas, was found dead in the wreckage. The account of the surviving Eugene Hasenfus blew the lid on what became known as Iran-Contra, the CIA's violation of the Boland amendments. Reportedly, that C-123 had previously been owned by Barry Seal.

⁴ Reed vs. Young and Baker, case no. LR-C-91-414 filed in the United States District Court for the Eastern District of Arkansas.

⁵ Order of March 8, 1996 on motion in limine by defendants in case no. LR-C-91-414.

[6] Trooper Patterson repeated this allegation under oath in his testimony for the Reed vs. Young lawsuit.

[7] "Love and Hate in Arkansas, L.D. Brown's story," Daniel Wattenberg, *The American Spectator* April/May 1994.

[8] "The Lonely Crusade of Linda Ives," Micah Morrison, *The Wall Street Journal*, April 18, 1996.

[9] "First Lady Ordered 1996 Critique of Coverage; After Heated Debate, Lawyer's Analysis of a Post Reporter's Work Was Kept Confidential," Howard Kurtz, *Washington Post*, February 14, 1998.

[10] "Pryor Visit Puts Judge in a Pickle," *Arkansas Democrat-Gazette*, January 7, 1998.

[11] "Pressure mounts on fence-sitting Dickey," Jane Fullerton, *Arkansas Democrat-Gazette*, December 12, 1998.

# SUPPORTING
# DOCUMENTS

SPEECH HONORING HARRY TRUMAN

BY

GOVERNOR BILL CLINTON

Harry Truman. The very mention of his name
evokes feelings of pride and nostalgia, especially
among Democrats. It is so easy to turn away from our
present problems and think of him.

We live in a time which rewards glamour and
charisma. He thought it was more important to be a
good citizen, and my people in Arkansas thought of him
as one of them, a friend.

We live in a time when politicians often hedge
their bets in language that leaves their options open.
He spoke plainly and he meant what he said.

We live in a time when politicians mouth words
written by others, that reflect the ideas and learning
of others. Harry Truman spoke for himself, thought for
himself and prepared himself for his work through a lifetime of reading and study.

We live in a time when politicians too often
fear decisions, especially if they break new ground,
alienate entrenched groups or carry the possibility of
error. Harry Truman could make a decision.

**Speech honoring Harry Truman**
Bill gave this speech at the 1984 Democratic National Convention in San
Francisco. I'm sure his hero Truman would be very disappointed in Bill's
record as president.

**Copy of signed Ben Franklin autobiography**
Bill was always a fan of history. It is sad that while he consumed every book he came across, he would be unable to follow the advice of learned men in history such as Ben Franklin. This is one of many signed books Bill gave me as gifts while at the mansion.

Bill Clinton
fayettville 1975

BENJAMIN FRANKLIN, states
philosopher, and man of le
was born in Boston in 1706 of Protestant parents. He
tered Boston Grammar School when he was eight and
attended George Brownell's school. When he was tw
his father apprenticed him to his half-brother James
printer. James was later the publisher of the *New Eng
Courant*, where Franklin's first articles, *The Dogwood
pers*, were published before he was seventeen. He wer
Philadelphia in 1723 and pursued his trade of printer.
was befriended by William Keith, Governor of Penr
vania, who offered to help the young man get starter
business. Franklin left for England, where he hoped te
range for the purchase of printing equipment. Arrivin
London in 1724, he was soon deserted by Keith, and a
turned to printing for a livelihood. His privately prir
*Dissertation on Liberty and Necessity, Pleasure and I*
(1725) introduced him to leading Deists and other intel
tuals in London. A year later he returned to Philadelp
and by 1730 he had been appointed public printer for Pe
sylvania. In 1731 he established the first circulating libr
in the United States; in 1743-44, The American Philosoj
cal Society. In 1748 he retired from the trade of printer
continued to advise and back his partner and to draw pr
from the business. *Poor Richard's Almanack* was his n
spectacular success as a publisher, having gone through
merous editions and been translated into many langua;
During the next 35 years he devoted himself largely
politics and diplomacy, but still wrote and engaged in sci
tific ventures. He resigned as Minister to France in 17
returned to America, and was elected President of the Co
monwealth of Pennsylvania. Still concerned with the rig
of the individual, he published papers encouraging the al
lition of slavery. He died in Philadelphia in 1790.

NJ Clinton Yale

# POLITICAL AND CIVIL RIGHTS IN THE UNITED STATES

Third Edition (1967)

*by*

*Thomas I. Emerson    David Haber    Norman Dorsen*

## 1969 SUPPLEMENT TO VOLUME II

### NORMAN DORSEN
PROFESSOR OF LAW AND DIRECTOR OF THE
ARTHUR GARFIELD HAYS CIVIL LIBERTIES PROGRAM,
NEW YORK UNIVERSITY

### KENT GREENAWALT
PROFESSOR OF LAW, COLUMBIA UNIVERSITY

LITTLE, BROWN AND COMPANY
*Boston*    1969    *Toronto*

**Political and Civil Rights book**
Bill has obviously violated just about every political and civil right I know of during his career.  The list of women and political enemies he has destroyed is still being expanded.

**Nacrelli Bar School book**

Bill and Hillary studied hard before their bar examinations to practice
law. The highlighted entries they made are telling more of the laws
they would choose to violate.

# CRIMINAL LAW

A crime is an act of commission or omission which the law forbids or demands under pain of punishment to be imposed by a sovereign in a proceeding brought in its own name.

## DIFFERENCES BETWEEN A CRIME AND A TORT

| Crime | Tort |
|---|---|
| 1. Action is instituted by the state. | 1. Action is instituted by the injured party. |
| 2. Agreement not to prosecute is a crime. | 2. Agreement not to sue is valid. |
| 3. Object is to punish. | 3. Object is to compensate. |
| 4. Infancy, in certain cases, and insanity are defenses. | 4. Infancy and insanity, generally, are not defenses. |
| 5. Contributory negligence is not a defense. | 5. Contributory negligence is a defense. |
| 6. Consent is not a defense, except | 6. Consent is a defense. |

    (1) when the state permits it,

    (2) when lack of consent is an essential element of a crime, and
    (3) in assault and battery when it does not amount to a breach of the peace.

## KINDS OF CRIMES

Crimes are divided into three general classifications: treason, felony, and misdemeanor.

Treason is waging war against the United States or adhering to the enemy or giving aid and comfort. There must be an overt act in the presence of at least two witnesses or a voluntary confession in open court. An alien residing in the United States and subject to its jurisdiction can be convicted of treason because he owes temporary allegiance to the United States as long as he remains in this country. 16 Wall. 147.

Criminal intent is divided into three classifications: general intent, specific intent and constructive intent.

General intent is inferred from the doing of a wrongful act without justification or excuse. A person is presumed to intend the natural and probable consequences of his wrongful act.

Specific intent is doing the act contemplated. Specific intent cannot be inferred from the mere doing of the act. It must be proved by either actual or circumstantial evidence. *premeditation?* When specific intent is an essential element of a crime, general or constructive intent is not sufficient.

Constructive intent takes place when a person does an act malum in se with intent to produce a certain result and instead produces another result. *X*

    Example -  A shoots and kills B while trying to kill C.

In some instances when there is culpable or gross negligence, mens rea is presumed and proof of criminal intent is not required.

    Example - Killing a pedestrian while driving an automobile under the influence of liquor.

    Intent is not an essential element of a crime malum prohibitum; the mere doing of the act is sufficient.

## CAPACITY TO COMMIT A CRIME

### Infant

An infant under seven years of age is conclusively presumed incapable of committing a crime. Between the ages of seven and fourteen, he is presumed incapable of committing a crime, but this presumption may be rebutted. Over the age of fourteen, an infant is presumed capable of committing a crime.

### Married woman

A married woman is responsible for her own crimes. If a married woman commits a crime in the presence of her husband, it is presumed that he coerced her. But this presumption can be rebutted by very slight evidence. 14 Am. Jur.811.

### Corporation

As a general rule, a corporation cannot be held liable

## CRIMES AT COMMON LAW

### Adultery

Adultery was _not_ a crime at common law.  This crime is
the voluntary sexual intercourse of a married person with
another married person who is not his spouse.  If one of the
parties is unmarried, the latter is guilty of fornication.

### Arson

*degrees by statute*

Arson at common law was the malicious burning of the
dwelling house of another.  It was not arson to burn one's
own dwelling or the personal property of another.  Such malicious burning was a high misdemeanor.  Arson both at common
law and by statute is a felony.  The changes by statute are

  (1)  attempt to burn is arson;

  (2)  arson includes the malicious burning of an
       unoccupied building, railroad car, boat, goods,
       wares and merchandise; and

  (3)  arson includes the malicious burning of one's
       own property when it is done to defraud, such
       as an insurance company.

### Assault

Assault is an attempt or offer of force or violence to
do bodily harm to another.  It was a misdemeanor at common
law.  By statute, simple assault is a misdemeanor, but aggra-
vated assault, such as assault with intent to kill, is a
felony.

### Attempt

Attempt at common law was an act done with intent to
commit a crime and tending toward its consummation but falling short of the crime itself.  The essential elements of the
crime are

  (1)  a specific intent to commit a particular crime,

  (2)  an apparent possibility to commit the act, and

  (3)  a direct ineffectual act toward its consum-
       mation.

The act must be more than mere preparation.

Personal deductions
① Non Itemized deductions
  (a) personal & dependency - 750    TAKE REGARDLESS
  (b) moving expenses
? ② standardized deduction - 15% of adjusted gross y or 2000 whichever is less
  ③ Itemized Non-Business Expenses (rather than standard)
    (a) interest pd on indebtedness - home mtge loan
    (b) non-fed taxes, sale & gas
    (c) medical expenses - ded only to extent they exceed 3% of
       TP's adj.g.y + not reimbursed by insurance.
       Payment must be for care of dependent n spouse. A funeral ver sonal support
    (d) casualty losses - π lost prop. must be sudden
    (e) non-bus bad debts
    (f) alimony
    (g) charitable contribs - cash n prop, services π ded
       to qualifying org
          Max allowable deductn - 50% adj.g.y; Excess may be
          carried over
       gifts of prop deductible only to extent of TP's adj. basis in prop
       Capital prop fully ded if to put charity; but 30% if to
       private hldten

    (h) Expenses for care of dependents
       TP > dep 14 or under n for spouse n day incapacitated
       expense must be incurred to allow TP to be employed
       π more than 400; ded reduced $1 for every $2 by wh
       TP's adjusted gross y exceeds 18000
  ? (g) financing polit campaigns - credit of 25 if jt; 12.50
         n deductn of 50/100 jt.
_____
Trust - sep taxable entity, if prop trans/earned irrev to it,
income taxed to trust n beneficiaries. If grantor retains
interest in n use of y, taxed to him.
_____
5. interest on all govtal obligation is exempt
Deductible - 1) medical expense - 1% floor on drugs & medicines π app. 5%
floor, π 3%, i.e. med expense ded only if exceed 5% of TP's agy - MAX
allowable del is $1250 (2500 jt)
           2) charitable - 15% agy if ng acts subst n oc
           3) moving expenses ded to reimbursement by emplyr
           4) No other taxes del; but credit to resident buy to domicile's
  y tax     5) No del for alimony unless ct decree
           6) No del for any dep. whose gross y > 499
           7) standard ded - 10% agy n 1000 whichever smaller

The Presidential Inaugural Committee
Washington, DC 20533-0001

L. D. Brown

Little Rock, AR 72207

HANDLE WITH CARE

1993

The Presidential Inaugural Committee
requests the honor of your presence
to attend and participate
in the
Inauguration of
William Jefferson Clinton
as
President of the United States of America
and
Albert Gore, Jr.
as
Vice President of the United States of America
on Wednesday, the twentieth of January
one thousand nine hundred and ninety-three
in the City of Washington

**Invitation to President Inaugural**

Becky and I were still on the mailing list in 1993 as I had kept my mouth shut about the Clintons. All that would change in 1994. This would be the only inaugural we would be invited to after the interview with the *American Spectator*.

JERRY JONES
SHEFFIELD NELSON
LARRY WALLACE

REQUEST THE PLEASURE OF YOUR COMPANY FOR
COCKTAILS ON THE OCCASION OF THE FORMATION OF THE
CAMPOBELLO ISLAND CLUB.

FIVE-THIRTY
THURSDAY EVENING, THE THIRTEENTH OF SEPTEMBER
GRAND BALLROOM, EXCELSIOR HOTEL

## Campobello Island Club Reception

Bill always denied any knowledge of this Jim McDougal boondoggle involving a Canadian real estate deal. As this document shows, he not only was very interested but was taking calls from Susan McDougal about the event.

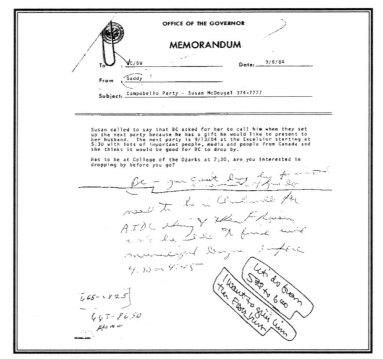

## Memorandum Regarding Campobello

The calls from Susan McDougal made sure Bill knew of the event. Bill told me he would be seeing Susan that night - after the public activities were over.

THURSDAY
SEPTEMBER 13, 1984

*Buddy you*

(GOVERNOR DON'T FORGET TO FAST)

| | |
|---|---|
| 8:15 a.m. | Trooper will take Governor to the North Little Rock Hilton. Rasco will meet Gov. at Mansion. |
| 8:30 a.m. | Speaking at the Health Care Conference, NLR Hilton |
| 9:45 a.m. | Tooper will take Governor to Food-4-Less Store, 4135 JFK Boulevard, NLR |
| 10:00 a.m. | Dedication of a "Mart Cart"/RASCO |
| 10:45 a.m. | Trooper will take Governor to 1100 N. University 664-1540 |
| 11:00 a.m. | Dr. Jim Metrailer, (FASTING) Blood & Urine Test |
| 11:30 a.m. | Trooper will take Governor to Camelot-JOAN will meet Governor in Lobby for CBS interview. |
| 12:30 p.m. | State Chamber of Commerce Community Development Awards - NASH |
| 1:30 p.m. | Trooper will take Governor to Capitol |

*Call Betsey before going back to Capitol*

(PHONE CALL TIME)

| | |
|---|---|
| 3:15 p.m. | Trooper will take Governor to 2nd & Willow in NLR |
| 3:30 p.m. | Meet with Arkansas Municipal League Officers & Executive Committee - GOSS/BRATTON |
| 4:30 p.m. | Trooper will take Governor to Capitol |

(PHONE CALL TIME)

| | |
|---|---|
| 5:15 p.m. | Trooper will take Governor to Excelsior - Grand Ballroom |
| 5:30 p.m. | Campobello Party, Excelsior |
| 5:45 p.m. | Trooper will take Governor to Central Service - Plane |

## Governor's Schedule regarding the party

I saved this schedule that shows where Bill and I would be the day of the Campobello party.

**CIA ad in New York Times**

On April 1, 1984 I showed Bill this ad to which he encouraged me to respond. 'I've always told you you'd make a great spy', he would say at the time.

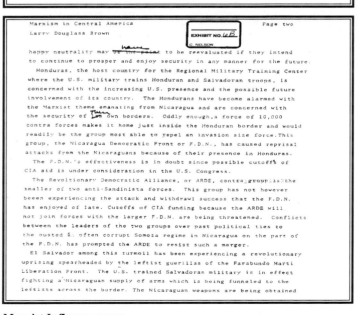

Larry Douglass Brown.                                    July 17,1984
4723 Fairlee Dr.
Little Rock, Ar. 72209
501-562-6933

Marxist Influence in Central America

Until recently the words, 'south of the border', brought thoughts
of vacation in Acapulco, and devalued peso bargains to the minds of
Americans.  In present day reality the growing threat of spreading
Marxism south of this country's borders particularly in Central
America is the current afterthought experienced by many upon hearing
those words.

The Marxist regime in Nicaragua headed by Junta Coordinator Daniel
Ortega Saavedra is celebrating its fifth anniversary of the Sandinista
takeover of that country.  Promising November 4 elections Ortega is
being challenged by an Opposition Party whose leaders must take re-
fuge in the United States.  The United States meanwhile is funding
anti-Sandinista guerilla activities through covert CIA operations
from staging bases in neigboring Honduras, Costa Rica and El Salvador.
This funding, currently a controversial issue on Capitol Hill, is
in danger of serious cutbacks or termination.

Capitalizing on this sentiment in Washington the Sandinistas have
begun attacking border villages in Costa Rica, an avowed neutral
country, causing the Costa Ricans to reevaluate allowing the anti-
Sandinista, or contra, groups and their training facilities to exist
there.  Costa Rica however is the recipient of more per capita aid *from the U.S.*
than any other country except Israel and has used the aid to build
the strongest economy in Central America with it. The Costa Ricans

Marxism in Central America                              Page two
Larry Douglass Brown

happy neutrality may ~~be the point~~ *have* to be reevaluated if they intend
to continue to prosper and enjoy security in any manner for the future.

Honduras, the host country for the Regional Military Training Center
where the U.S. military trains Honduran and Salvadoran troops, is
concerned with the increasing U.S. presence and the possible future
involvement of its country.  The Hondurans have become alarmed with
the Marxist theme emanating from Nicaragua and are concerned with
the security of *their* ~~its~~ own borders.  Oddly enough, a force of 10,000
contra forces makes it home just inside the Honduran border and would
readily be the group most able to repel an invasion size force.This
group, the Nicaragua Democratic Front or F.D.N., has caused reprisal
attacks from the Nicaraguans because of their presence in Honduras.

The F.D.N.'s effectiveness is in doubt since possible cutoffs of
CIA aid is under consideration in the U.S. Congress.

The Revolutionary Democratic Alliance, or ARDE, contra group is the
smaller of two anti-Sandinista forces.  This group has not however
beeen experiencing the attack and withdrawl success that the F.D.N.
has enjoyed of late. Cutoffs of CIA funding because the ARDE will
not join forces with the larger F.D.N. are being threatened.  Conflicts
between the leaders of the two groups over past political ties to
the ousted & often corrupt Somoza regime in Nicaragua on the part of
the F.D.N. has prompted the ARDE to resist such a merger.

El Salvador among this turmoil has been experiencing a revolutionary
uprising spearheaded by the leftist guerillas of the Farabundo Marti
Liberation Front.  The U.S. trained Salvadoran military is in effect
fighting a Nicaraguan supply of arms which is being funneled to the
leftists across the border. The Nicaraguan weapons are being obtained

## Marxist Influence essay

Bill suggested I write about a topic the agency would approve of.  I didn't
realize the significance of the subject at the time. The reader can see some
of the handwritten changes he made.

from Cuba and ultimately the Soviet Union.  Newly elected Salvadoran
President Jose Napoleon Duarte brings new hope for the country's
human rights problems and for unity within the country as well.  Convictions and sentencing of four former Salvadoran Guardsmen for the
deaths of U.S. churchworkers in 1980 has given the U.S. hopes also
that the government is stabilizing.  The area of human rights  reform
tied to continues aid for the country has been stressed by some U.S.
leaders.

In the United States the current administration fears the worst
for the region's future.  The Sandinistas are reportedly setting the
stage for an anti-Reagan foreign policy initiative designed to effect
public sentiment in the U.S. toward the region.  The Nicaraguans would
like for the effect to be the same as the Vietnamese Tet offensive
had just before the 1968 presidential elections.  To do this, a major
offensive would be planned for September of this year designed to
turn the tide of the war in El Salvador and convince the U.S. that the
Salvadorans are doomed to failure.  Stepped up arms shipments and leftist
recruiting drives are also planned.  Among these subversive activities
the Nicaraguans are denying some recent charges that they have offered
and are engaging in supporting drug traffickers from South America by
financial means as well as providing strategic help in importation of
drugs into the U.S..

The critical implication from this information is that a vital part
of the world, not only in its politically strategic sense, but to the
halting of the spread of Communism in the world free waiting in the
balance of U.S. support and attention it receives.  The burden lies upon

the United States to provide for security in the region which in the
strictest sense will be for its own national security.  To do this
an understanding by the American people as to that security and
how it best can be maintained is essential.  The region itself must
cooperate with each other and for the U.S. effort to
succeed.  Without this cooperation and effort, 'south of the border'
will surely be redefined only as Marxist.

                                        Larry Douglass Brown

*The obvious conclusion is that the U.S
must maintain a presence in Central America,
not only for the strategic importance,
but also to ensure relationships with
friendly nations in this hemisphere which
has been a policy since the Monroe
Doctrine was conceived.*

**CENTRAL INTELLIGENCE AGENCY**
SOUTHWEST PERSONNEL REPRESENTATIVE
PO BOX 30611   DALLAS, TEXAS 75250
214-767-8550

19 April 1984

Mr. Larry D. Brown
4724 Fairlee Drive
Little Rock, Arkansas   72209

Dear Mr. Brown:

Thank you for your recent expression of interest in the employment opportunities of the Central Intelligence Agency.

Your personal data has been reviewed and it appears appropriate to begin the next step in our application process.   Please find enclosed an admission ticket for our Professional Applicant Test Battery (PAT-B), to be administered on 5 May 1984 at the University of Arkansas at Little Rock.

I would appreciate a collect call from you to confirm the above test date.

Again, thank you for your interest in our organization.   I look forward to receiving your call.

Sincerely yours,

Personnel Representative /sc
Central Intelligence Agency

Enclosure

## Letters from Kent Cargile

I kept a few of the letters I received from the agency.  They would always have me call collect.

**CENTRAL INTELLIGENCE AGENCY**
SOUTHWEST PERSONNEL REPRESENTATIVE
PO BOX 30611   DALLAS, TEXAS 75250
214-767-8550

28 June 1984

Mr. Larry D. Brown
4724 Fairlee Drive
Little Rock, Arkansas   72209

Dear Mr. Brown:

I would appreciate a collect call from you, at your earliest convenience, to discuss the status of your application.

Sincerely yours,

Kent M. Cargile
Southwest Personnel Representative

**CENTRAL INTELLIGENCE AGENCY**
SOUTHWEST PERSONNEL REPRESENTATIVE
PO BOX 50411   DALLAS, TEXAS 75250
214-747-6850

5 September 1984

Mr. Larry D. Brown
4724 Fairlee Drive
Little Rock, Arkansas   72209

Dear Mr. Brown:

Your application papers for employment with the Central Intelligence
Agency have been forwarded to our Headquarters in Washington, D.C. for
consideration.

After adequate time for review, you will receive definitive word from
Headquarters as to whether or not there are presently any employment
opportunities fitting your background and qualifications.

If you receive a tentative job offer, you may expect a lengthy period of
processing before a firm offer will be made.  During this period, you will be
invited to visit our Washington Headquarters, at government expense, where you
will be interviewed by officials of the component interested in employing
you.  You will also complete the remainder of your processing.

I am pleased to nominate you for employment with the Central Intelligence
Agency.  Whether we have an opening at this time or not, I enjoyed talking
with you and wish you only the best in the future.

Sincerely yours,

*Kent Caigl*

Southwest Personnel Representative
Central Intelligence Agency

EXHIBIT NO. 8A

C. NELSON

# PROFESSIONAL APPLICANT TEST BATTERY

*Instructions to Candidate*

1. Submit your application forms as soon as possible. The submission of these forms is not contingent on the outcome of this examination. You will not receive a report of your test results. The test is not graded as such but rather is designed to assist in determining your suitability for a long-range career with our organization.

2. <u>Sign and detach the examination admission ticket below. Present this ticket for admission.</u>

3. Bring 2 or 3 sharp No. 2 pencils with erasers to the test room.

4. Report to the test center at 8:20 a.m. and be prepared to stay until 5:00 p.m. If you are late, you will not be admitted. A lunch break will be given.

5. This ticket is not transferable.

EXHIBIT NO. 3B

C. NELSON

## Professional Applicant Test

The agency sent me a ticket to get in the testing facility for my entrance examination.

---

PROFESSIONAL APPLICANT TEST BATTERY

*Examination Admission Ticket*

EXAMINATION DATE    5 May 1984

TEST CENTER    Room A101, Student Services Building, University of
Arkansas at Little Rock, 33rd and University Streets

Ms. Fanye Porter, Test Administrator

KENT M. CARGILE    317

THIS TICKET MUST BE PRESENTED FOR ADMISSION    CANDIDATE'S SIGNATURE

EXHIBIT NO. 3C

C. NELSON

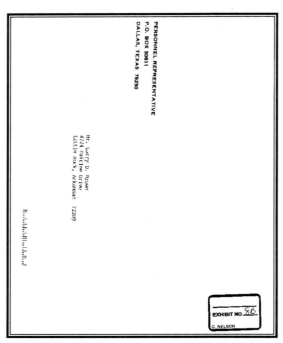

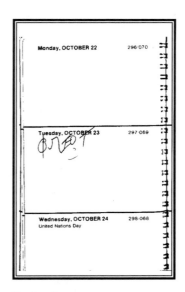

| | |
|---|---|
| **Monday, OCTOBER 22** | 296·070 |
| **Tuesday, OCTOBER 23** | 297·069 |
| **Wednesday, OCTOBER 24**<br>United Nations Day | 298·068 |

| | |
|---|---|
| **Monday, DECEMBER 24** | 359·007 |
| **Tuesday, DECEMBER 25**<br>Christmas Day | 360·006 |
| **Wednesday, DECEMBER 26** | 361·005 |

## Daybook

I made several entries in my daybook regarding the CIA activities. Trips to Dallas and important dates given me to me by Seal are some of the notes I took. Many were in the Cyrillic or Russian alphabet.

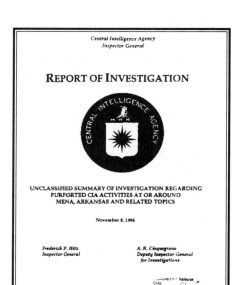

otherwise brief discussions with Seal. During the course of these discussions, Seal was escorted by DEA personnel. No evidence has been found to indicate that CIA knew Seal's true identity prior to the operation or that its personnel had any other contact with Seal before or after this 1984 operation.

*DID CIA REQUEST DIRECTLY OR INDIRECTLY THAT THE DEPARTMENT OF JUSTICE (DOJ) OR OTHER FEDERAL AGENCIES TERMINATE OR ALTER ANY INVESTIGATIONS OR PROSECUTIONS RELATING TO MONEY LAUNDERING ACTIVITIES AT OR AROUND MENA, ARKANSAS?*

11. No evidence has been found to indicate that CIA or its personnel requested directly or indirectly that DoJ or other federal agencies terminate or alter any investigations or prosecutions relating to money laundering activities at or around Mena, Arkansas.

*WHAT WAS THE NATURE AND EXTENT OF ANY CIA CONTACT OR RELATIONSHIP WITH LARRY DOUGLASS "L.D." BROWN?*

12. Agency records indicate that Larry Douglass Brown was an applicant for employment with CIA in 1984 and that he did have contact with one or, possibly, two CIA recruitment personnel in that context. Those records also indicate that a decision was made on December 4, 1984 not to offer him such employment. No evidence has been found to indicate that he was employed or otherwise associated with CIA.

*WHAT WAS THE NATURE AND EXTENT OF ANY CIA CONTACT OR RELATIONSHIP FROM 1980 TO THE PRESENT WITH CERTAIN INDIVIDUALS OR BUSINESSES BASED AT, OR OPERATING THROUGH, THE AIRPORT AT MENA, ARKANSAS?*

13. No evidence has been found that CIA had contact with any individuals or businesses based at, or operating through, the airport at Mena, Arkansas, except for the joint training operation and maintenance activities addressed elsewhere in this summary.

## CIA report on Mena, Arkansas

The CIA Inspector General issued a report that skirted the real questions being asked by Congress about the Mena airport. In the report, CIA acknowledged having a relationship with me. Incredibly, they stated that it was their decision to terminate that contact. In reality, I had made the call after returning from my second flight with Barry Seal.

# GEOSYS

Computer Generated

Fax Transmission

to the attention of:

C. Douglas Brown

Little Rock, Arkansas 72207
United States of America

Origin:

T. John McBrearty

CEO

**McBrearty documents**
These are a few of the documents that show the contact I had with T. John McBrearty in Ireland. Shown here are a facsimile transmission and telephone records. McBrearty also wrote his address and telephone number for me on the back of one of my business cards.

## IN THE UNITED STATES DISTRICT COURT FOR THE
## EASTERN DISTRICT OF ARKANSAS

PAULA CORBIN JONES,                    CASE NUMBER: LR-C-94-290

    PLAINTIFF,

    V.

WILLIAM JEFFERSON CLINTON

    and

DANNY FERGUSON,

        DEFENDANTS

### MOTION TO QUASH SUBPOENA

L. D. Brown moves the Court to Quash the Subpoena for Deposition issued to him at the request of Plaintiff Paula Corbin Jones, a copy of which is attached, upon the following grounds:

#### Section I:

1. L. D. Brown left the service of Defendant, William Jefferson Clinton, in a security capacity in June, 1985, approximately six years before the activity alleged in the complaint filed by the Plaintiff, Paula Corbin Jones took place and thereby has no relevant information in this case.

1

## Motion to Quash

I prepared my own motion to avoid being deposed in the Paula Jones case. I knew that the Clinton camp would only intensify their desire to see me ruined if I cooperated with the Jones attorneys.

IN THE UNITED STATES DISTRICT COURT
FOR THE EASTERN DISTRICT OF ARKANSAS
WESTERN DIVISION

PAULA CORBIN JONES,                 :
                                    :
              Plaintiff,            :      CIVIL ACTION
                                    :      NO. LR-C-94-290
     v.                             :
                                    :
WILLIAM JEFFERSON CLINTON           :      Judge Susan Webber Wright
                                    :
       and                          :      (UNDER SEAL)
                                    :
DANNY FERGUSON,                     :
                                    :
              Defendants.           :

**PRESIDENT CLINTON'S RESPONSE TO PLAINTIFF'S OPPOSITION
TO L.D. BROWN'S MOTION TO QUASH SUBPOENA**

President Clinton, through counsel, hereby submits this
response to plaintiff's Opposition to L.D. Brown's Motion to
Quash Subpoena.

As a threshold matter, plaintiff's Opposition over-
states the Court's ruling with respect to the deposition of Mr.
Brown. We understood that the Court's order permitting Mr.
Brown's deposition, and certain other third party depositions, to
proceed was based, in part, on the fact that the third parties
themselves had not moved to quash or for a protective order. The
Court made its ruling solely on the general relevance objections
of counsel and did not have before it the specific information
presented by Mr. Brown.

Furthermore, plaintiff should not be surprised that
third parties such as Mr. Brown will seek the advice of counsel

**Clinton's response**
Clinton's attorneys answered my motion quickly and favorably.

```
        IN THE UNITED STATES DISTRICT COURT
          WESTERN DISTRICT OF ARKANSAS
              LITTLE ROCK DIVISION

LARRY DOUGLASS BROWN                          PLAINTIFF

V.                    NO. _____

JIM GUY TUCKER, personally                    DEFENDANT
and in his official capacity as
Governor of the State of Arkansas

                      COMPLAINT

      Comes the plaintiff, Larry Douglass Brown, by his attorney,

Tona M. DeMers, and for his complaint states:

      1. This is a civil action against the defendant, Jim Guy

Tucker, brought pursuant to 42 U.S.C. s. 1983, seeking redress

for violation, under color of state law, of plaintiff's civil

rights guaranteed by the United States Constitution.

      2. Jurisdiction is properly in this Court pursuant to 28

U.S.C. s. 1343 in that this case is a civil action commenced to

redress violation of plaintiff's rights guaranteed by the United

States Constitution.

      3. Venue properly lies in this Court pursuant to 28 U.S.C.

s. 1391.

      4. Plaintiff resides in Little Rock, Arkansas, and is a

United States citizen. At all times material to this action,

plaintiff was employed by the Arkansas State Police and had been

since 1980.

      5. Defendant Jim Guy Tucker is a resident of Little Rock,

Arkansas and is a United States citizen. At all times material

to this action, defendant Tucker served as Governor of the State

of Arkansas.
```

## Complaint against Jim Guy Tucker

I still am fighting to get my day in court with another of our corrupt
Arkansas governors.

# United States District Court

EASTERN ——————————— DISTRICT OF ___ARKANSAS

TO:

L.D. Brown

## SUBPOENA TO TESTIFY
## BEFORE GRAND JURY

SUBPOENA FOR:

☐ PERSON  ☒ DOCUMENTS OR OBJECT(S)

**YOU ARE HEREBY COMMANDED** to appear and testify before the Grand Jury of the United States District Court at the place, date. and time specified below.

| PLACE | ROOM |
|---|---|
| Federal Grand Jury<br>U.S. Post Office, 4th Floor<br>600 West Capitol<br>Little Rock, Arkansas | |
| | DATE AND TIME<br>February 16, 1994<br>10:00 A.M. |

**YOU ARE ALSO COMMANDED** to bring with you the following document(s) or object(s):

See Attachment to the Federal Grand Jury Subpoena

_ Please see additional information on reverse

This subpoena shall remain in effect until you are granted leave to depart by the court or by an officer acting on behalf of the court.

| CLERK | DATE |
|---|---|
| JAMES W. McCORMACK | February 14, 1994 |
| (BY) DEPUTY CLERK | |
| _Cecelia Y. Norward_ | #120 |

| This subpoena is issued upon application of the United States of America | NAME, ADDRESS AND PHONE NUMBER OF ASSISTANT U.S. ATTORNEY<br>Independent Counsel<br>Robert B. Fiske, Jr.<br>Julie R. O'Sullivan<br>10825 Financial Centre Parkway<br>Two Financial Centre, Suite 134 |
|---|---|
| *If not applicable, enter "none. | To be used in lieu of Little Rock, AR  72211     FORM OBD-???|

## Subpoena from Robert Fiske

The subpoena that formally sealed my involvement with the government's case against Bill Clinton.

# United States District Court

EASTERN ——————— DISTRICT OF ——————— ARKANSAS

TO L. D. Brown

## SUBPOENA TO TESTIFY
## BEFORE GRAND JURY

SUBPOENA FOR:
[X] PERSON  [ ] DOCUMENTS OR OBJECT(S)

YOU ARE HEREBY COMMANDED to appear and testify before the Grand Jury of the United States District Court at the place, date, and time specified below.

| PLACE | ROOM |
|---|---|
| Federal Grand Jury U.S. Post Office & Courts Bldg., 4th Floor 600 West Capitol Little Rock, Arkansas | DATE AND TIME December 12, 1994 9:00 A.M. |

YOU ARE ALSO COMMANDED to bring with you the following document(s) or object(s):*

[ ] Please see additional information on reverse

This subpoena shall remain in effect until you are granted leave to depart by the court or by an officer acting on behalf of the court.

| CLERK | DATE |
|---|---|
| JAMES W. McCORMACK | December 01, 1994 |
| (BY) DEPUTY CLERK | #720 |

This subpoena is issued upon application of the United States of America

NAME, ADDRESS AND PHONE NUMBER OF ASSISTANT U.S. ATTORNEY
Independent Counsel
Kenneth W. Starr
Bradley E. Lerman
2 Financial Centre, Suite 134
10825 Financial Centre Parkway
Little Rock, Arkansas  72211  (501) 221-8700

*If not applicable, enter "none"

## Subpoena from Kenneth Starr

I received another subpoena from the new prosecutor Kenneth Star when it came time to visit the grand jury.

<u>AGREEMENT</u>

With respect to the meeting of L.D. Brown ("Client") and his attorney, Justin A. Thornton, Esq., with the Office of the Independent Counsel, Kenneth W. Starr, and representatives of the Federal Bureau of Investigation and Internal Revenue Service to be held at the Office of the Independent Counsel in Washington, D.C. on January 31, 1995 ("the meeting"), the following understandings exist:

(1) Should any prosecution be brought against Client ~~by this Office~~, the Government will not offer in evidence in its case-in-chief, or in connection with any sentencing proceeding for the purpose of determining an appropriate sentence, any statements made by Client at the meeting, except in a prosecution for false statements, obstruction of justice or perjury.

(2) Notwithstanding item (1) above: (a) the Government may use information derived directly or indirectly from the meeting for the purpose of obtaining leads to other evidence, which evidence may be used in any prosecution of Client by the Government; and (b) the Government may use statements made by Client at the meeting and all evidence obtained directly or indirectly therefrom for the purpose of cross-examination should Client testify, or to rebut any evidence offered by or on behalf of Client in connection with the trial and/or sentencing, should any prosecution of Client be undertaken.

(3) It is further understood that this Agreement is limited to the statements made by Client at the meeting and does not apply to any oral, written or recorded statements made by Client at any other time. No understandings, promises, agreements and/or conditions have been entered into with respect to the meeting other than those set forth in this Agreement and none will be entered into unless in writing and signed by all parties.

Dated: Washington, D.C.
       January 31, 1995

KENNETH W. STARR
Independent Counsel

_____
L.D. BROWN

By: Timothy J. Mayopoulos

_____
JUSTIN A. THORNTON, Esq.

_____
WITNESS

## Immunity agreement

My attorney negotiated a 'use immunity' agreement with the Office of Independent Counsel. On the day this was signed, my attorney Justin Thornton and I were in Washington, DC to meet with lawyers and agents of the special prosecutor.

I, MICHAEL G. DOWD, an attorney representing Terry K. and Janis Reed in a civil action filed against Buddy Young and others in the U.S. District Court in Little Rock, Arkansas, do hereby represent and affirm to Larry D. Brown on behalf of Terry K. and Janis Reed that no legal action or proceedings shall ever be instituted against Larry D. Brown as a result of any information or documents provided to me or representatives of Terry and Janis Reed by Larry D. Brown.

MICHAEL G. DOWD

8/25/95
Date

WITNESS          8/25/95

## Immunity in Reed case

I needed protection in the Terry Reed civil suit due to my activities in Mexico. This agreement was signed by Reed's attorney, Michael Dowd of New York City.

AO 88 (Rev. 1/94) Subpoena in a Civil Case

**Issued by the**
**UNITED STATES DISTRICT COURT**
EASTERN —————— DISTRICT OF —————— ARKANSAS

PAULA CORBIN JONES,
　　　　PLAINTIFF,

V.

WILLIAM JEFFERSON CLINTON
and DANNY FERGUSON,
　　　　DEFENDANTS.

**SUBPOENA IN A CIVIL CASE**

CASE NUMBER:

LR-C-94-290

TO:　L.D. Brown
　　　209 W. Capitol Avenue, Hall Bldg., #401
　　　Little Rock, Arkansas 72201

☐ YOU ARE COMMANDED to appear in the United States District Court at the place, date, and time specified below to testify in the above case.

PLACE OF TESTIMONY | COURTROOM
 | DATE AND TIME

☐ YOU ARE COMMANDED to appear at the place, date, and time specified below to testify at the taking of a deposition in the above case.

PLACE OF DEPOSITION | DATE AND TIME

☒ YOU ARE COMMANDED to produce and permit inspection and copying of the following documents or objects at the place, date, and time specified below (list documents or objects):　See Schedule A hereto

PLACE　Wright, Lindsey & Jennings
　　　200 West Capitol Avenue, Suite 2200
　　　Little Rock, Arkansas 72201

DATE AND TIME
November 10, 1997
9:00 A.M.

☐ YOU ARE COMMANDED to permit inspection of the following premises at the date and time specified below.

PREMISES | DATE AND TIME

Any organization not a party to this suit that is subpoenaed for the taking of a deposition shall designate one or more officers, directors, or managing agents, or other persons who consent to testify on its behalf, and may set forth, for each person designated, the matters on which the person will testify. Federal Rules of Civil Procedure, 30(b)(6).

ISSUING OFFICER SIGNATURE AND TITLE (INDICATE IF ATTORNEY FOR PLAINTIFF OR DEFENDANT)
_Katharine S. Sexton_　Attorney for Defendant | DATE 11/3/97

ISSUING OFFICER'S NAME, ADDRESS AND PHONE NUMBER
Katharine S. Sexton, Esquire　(202/371-7000)
Skadden, Arps, Slate, Meagher & Flom LLP
1440 New York Avenue, N.W., Washington, D.C. 20005

(See Rule 45, Federal Rules of Civil Procedure, Parts C & D on Reverse)

## Subpoena in Jones vs. Clinton

I had tried to avoid testifying in the Paula Jones case by talking with her lawyers before being subpoenaed. My efforts proved hopeless as I received a subpoena anyway on November 10, 1997. I would eventually spend hours being questioned by lawyers from both sides.

IN THE UNITED STATES DISTRICT COURT
FOR THE EASTERN DISTRICT OF ARKANSAS
WESTERN DIVISION

PAULA CORBIN JONES,           :
                              :
            Plaintiff,        :       CIVIL ACTION
                              :       NO. LR-C-94-290
      v.                      :
                              :
WILLIAM JEFFERSON CLINTON     :       Judge Susan Webber Wright
                              :
      and                     :
                              :
DANNY FERGUSON,               :
                              :
            Defendants.       :

### SCHEDULE A

President Clinton, through counsel, requests, pursuant
to Rules 26, 34 and 45 of the Federal Rules of Civil Procedure,
that L. D. Brown produce for inspection and copying at Wright,
Lindsey & Jennings, 200 West Capitol Avenue, Suite 2200, Little
Rock, Arkansas 72201, on November 10, 1997, at 9:00 A.M., any and
all of the following documents in accordance with the definitions
and instructions set forth herein.

### INSTRUCTIONS

A.   All documents are to be produced that are in your
custody, control, or possession or within your right of custody,
control, or possession.

B.   Objections to specific requests, if any, shall be
signed by the attorney making them. If an objection is made to
part of a document request, the part objected to shall be specified and the document(s) shall be otherwise produced. All objec-

## L.D. BROWN GRAND JURY STATEMENT

My name is Larry Douglass "L.D." Brown. I was born in 1955 in Greenville, Mississippi. When I was very young, my family moved to Pine Bluff, Arkansas, where I grew up. I attended the University of Arkansas for one year, and later, I attended the University of Arkansas, at Pine Bluff and at Little Rock.

My first law enforcement job was at the Tucker State Prison. I worked there as a field sergeant for approximately three years. In about 1977, I was hired as a police officer with the Pine Bluff Police Department.

In 1980, I was hired as an Arkansas State Trooper. I have been an Arkansas State Trooper since that time. My present rank is Corporal. I currently am assigned to the highway patrol.

Back in 1980, when I first started as an Arkansas State Trooper, I worked on narcotics cases in St. Francis County. Later, I was transferred to Little Rock, where I continued to work narcotics cases.

In approximately August 1982, I began working on the Governor's security detail. At that time, the Governor was Frank White.

In 1982, the Governor's security detail consisted of about 11 Arkansas State Troopers whose job it was (1) to provide security to the Governor at the Mansion; (2) drive or otherwise provide transportation to the Governor when he traveled outside the Mansion; (3) provide security to the Governor when he appeared in public; and (4) provide other appropriate services to the Governor's immediate family, such as security and transportation.

## Grand Jury Statement

I had a statement prepared before I went to the grand jury. It detailed my answers to the questions relevant to the Whitewater matters at hand.

Troopers on the security detail might also be responsible for
answering phones on occasion at the Mansion, or performing routine
errands for the Governor and/or his family, like delivering a
speech or picking up packages and things like that.

Members of the Governor's security detail were assigned in
shifts. There were always two troopers working during each shift,
except for the midnight shift, which involved only one trooper.
The Governor's security detail would travel with the Governor,
and/or his family, outside of Little Rock, or even outside of the
state.

I worked for Frank White's security detail until he lost his
bid for re-election to Bill Clinton. In about December 1982, the
Clintons began the process of moving into the Governor's Mansion.
I believe that this was the first time that I met Governor Clinton
and his family. Governor Clinton decided that he would like me to
stay on his security detail, and I agreed.

In January 1983, I drove Governor Clinton to his inauguration.
Many of the troopers on the security detail did not like to travel.
I did. As a result, I volunteered frequently to accompany Governor
Clinton whenever he traveled outside Little Rock. I soon developed
a close relationship with Governor Clinton and Mrs. Clinton too.

When Frank White was Governor, he usually had a trooper with
him whenever he left the Governor's Mansion. Bill Clinton was not
like that. Governor Clinton often would leave the Mansion without
an escort.

I worked on Governor Clinton's Security detail until June

1985. During that time, I became very close to the Governor and
his family. No other trooper on the detail was as close to the
Clintons as I was during that time.

I do not intend to discuss here the personal matters of the
Clintons. Because of my relationship with Governor and Mrs.
Clinton, I saw and learned of various private matters.

I met my wife while working on Governor Clinton's security
detail. She was employed in the Mansion as Chelsea Clinton's nanny
when I met her. Later, I was able to help my wife's mother get a
job at the Governor's Mansion as well.

During the time I worked for Governor Clinton's security
detail, I observed Governor Clinton leave the Mansion and go
jogging. Governor Clinton frequently went for a run without any
troopers accompanying him. Sometimes, he would finish his run at
some other location in Little Rock and call back to the detail to
pick him up.

In June 1985, my relationship with Governor Clinton changed.
At that time, I had had conversations with Governor and Mrs.
Clinton about being appointed to the position of Assistant Director
at the state crime lab. During a series of conversations with
Governor and Mrs. Clinton, they promised me an appointment to that
post, which had just become vacant. As it turned out, however, I
was not appointed to the position of Assistant Director. I talked
to Governor Clinton about the situation and was not satisfied with
his explanation as to why I did not get the position. I felt
deeply hurt and disappointed with the way things had worked out

regarding the Assistant Director position and the way the Clintons had dealt with me concerning it.

On June 21, 1985, I asked to be transferred off of the Governor's security detail. I decided that it would be best not to work for the Clinton's anymore. I was then assigned to the auto theft unit of the Arkansas State police.

Shortly after I left the detail, around the end of June 1985, Colonel Goodwin, the then director of the Arkansas State police, asked me if I would meet with Betsey Wright and Jim Clark. Betsey Wright was a political aide to Governor Clinton, and Jim Clark had just been appointed to be the Director of the state crime lab. I met Betsey Wright and Jim Clark at Betsey Wright's home on Hill Road.

At the meeting, Betsey Wright told me that she was concerned that I was "mad" at Governor and Mrs. Clinton. At one point in the conversation, Betsey Wright said to me words to the affect of: "Well, you're not going to say anything." By that, I understood that she was concerned with the possibility that I might make public statements regarding the Clintons that could embarrass them, which she knew that I could do. I told Wright and Clark that I just wanted to be left alone.

Following that meeting with Wright and Clark, I came to feel that Governor Clinton and his aides viewed me as a possible threat to them.

For the next several years, I had a distant, but cordial, relationship with Governor Clinton. I became the President of the

4

Arkansas State Police Association in approximately late 1985. In that capacity, I had occasion to be involved in legislative efforts, lobbying and the like. From time to time, I would be at the State Capitol working on matters concerning the Arkansas State Troopers.

In 1989, Governor Clinton and I had a political dispute concerning a piece of legislation. Governor Clinton had asked for my support, and the support of the Arkansas State Police Association, for his controversial tax increase proposal. The tax bill was in trouble in the Arkansas House, and Governor Clinton needed our organization's support to help pass the bill.

During the legislative effort to pass the tax bill, I met with the Governor. He asked for my support of the bill. He promised me that if our organization helped pass the bill, he would introduce legislation in a special session of the legislature providing for a pay raise for troopers. I agreed to support his tax bill, and our organization's efforts helped the bill pass. The bill passed by one vote in the Arkansas House.

Later that fall, Governor Clinton called a special session of the Arkansas legislature. The Governor did not place a trooper pay raise bill on the legislature's call, as he had promised repeatedly that he would. The special session never considered a trooper pay raise bill. This was contrary to the Governor's promise to me.

Throughout 1989, I had been telling my organization that the Governor had promised us a pay raise bill in the special session. Our organization had spent considerable effort and resources in

5

trying to win support for the expected pay raise bill. When I realized that the Governor was reneging on his promise to the Arkansas State troopers and me, I made a statement to the press indicating that I felt the Governor had broken a promise to the troopers. This was in late October 1989.

When Governor Clinton became aware of my public statements regarding a trooper pay raise bill, he became extremely upset with me. Later, we had a meeting with Governor Clinton at the Mansion. I think this meeting was a couple months after the late October statements. At the meeting, Governor Clinton was indignant that I had gone to the press and suggested that he had broken a promise. At the conclusion of the meeting, the Governor asked that we put our differences behind us and that we work together for a pay raise bill in the next regular session of the legislature. I agreed, and a pay raise bill did pass in 1991.

I recall seeing an encounter between Governor Clinton and David Hale at the state Capitol. I was in an area that I call "the tunnel," which is a drive-through, pick-up point under the steps of the east side of the state capitol building. I was talking to Governor Clinton alone. There were other people in the general area, as there usually are when the Capitol is open for business. We had been talking for a few minutes. During our conversation, Clinton saw David Hale in the area. He turned away from me to talk to Hale. The Governor's back was to me as he spoke to Hale. I heard Governor Clinton say to David Hale words to the affect of: "We need to raise some money. You're going to have to help us

out." I do not recall if Hale said anything in response, but I could see his facial expression. He appeared surprised and taken aback. Governor Clinton turned back to me and finished our conversation shortly. I left. I do not recall if David Hale remained in the area to continue talking to Clinton or not.

I remember the encounter between Clinton and Hale, because of the timing and location of the exchange, and because I felt Governor Clinton had put Hale on the spot in a way that was unusual. I also felt that Hale was visibly uncomfortable with Clinton's remarks.

I have tried to remember when this encounter between Governor Clinton and David Hale occurred. I do not have an exact date or month that I can be 100% certain of. I believe that the encounter occurred in the time period of 1985-1986. I don't think I was in the Governor's security detail at the time. I do recall that I was at the Capitol frequently during the month of January 1986, because there were matters concerning the troopers that I was working on and that I recall discussing with Governor Clinton personally.

**ARKANSAS STATE POLICE ASSOCIATION**
Post Office Box 15835
Little Rock, Arkansas 72231

*L. D. Brown, President*

State of the State

Our Governor, Bill Clinton, has just recently reneged on a promised upgrade pay raise for all Arkansas State Police Officers. Our Association has been working for two years on this legislation which should have culminated in a November Special Legislative Session giving our troopers an additional 2 percent pay raise. Having promised me and our ASPA to place pay raise legislation on the agenda, Governor Clinton ultimately went back on his word and did not do so. Also money for new state police vehicles was not provided since the Governor predicated purchase of the vehicles on raising new taxes instead of shifting revenue spending priorities. The entire session was a flop and we are still driving vehicles with over 120,000 miles on them. A battle has ensued between the Governor and the ASPA with me at the forefront attacking each other in the media. All the while there is a heated Governor's race going on. We desperately need help and our Governor is only lying to us. Since he has and always will have Presidential ambitions, please take what I say to heart. He does not care for state police!

I will keep you posted so if and when you encounter him on the national political scene, you will know his record of dealing with the ASPA and troopers. We are continuing to work toward a January 1991 Legislative Session; perhaps with new leadership.

Sincerely,

L. D. Brown
President
Arkansas State Police Association

LDB/dmw

Attachment

## A National Troopers Coalition Letter

I addressed a National Troopers meeting in Atlanta, Georgia while Vice Chairman of the national organization. Bill soon learned that I had put the entire United States organized state police forces on alert that he was a liar and enemy of the police and that he wanted to be President of the United States. He would exact his revenge through starting a revolt within my own organization against me.

**Chelsea artifacts**

My wife Becky taught Chelsea to read at the mansion when she served as her nanny. These are just a couple of the mementos we have from those days.

Bill Clinton
Governor

Col. Tommy Goodwin
Director

## L. D. Brown
### Arkansas State Police
### Governor's Security

Governor's Mansion
1800 S. Center
Little Rock, AR 72206

Mansion 501/371-1580
Capitol 501/371-8001

**Business card**

It was through a school teacher keeping one of my state police business cards that *American Spectator* reporter Danny Wattenberg got on my trail as a source for reporting on Bill.

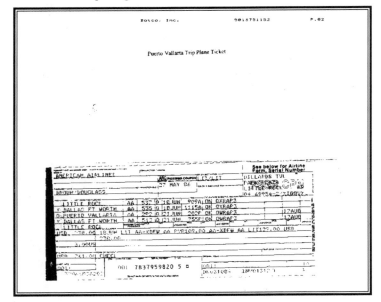

**Airline Ticket**

I kept many things from my association with CIA. Fortunately (or perhaps not) I kept a copy of the plane ticket to Puerto Vallarta, Mexico. This was the trip I told Bill about. The one where I would 'take care' of the problem with the other guy flying the airplane with Seal. Terry Reed also kept receipts from his trip to Puerto Vallarta which placed him there with me.

Bill and I had a stormy relationship at the state capital as this photo clearly shows. Bill had just lied to me about a pay raise bill in the legislature.

We put on a good face for the cameras when it was mutually beneficial. This bill signing ceremony for legislation sponsored by State Representative Bobby Tullis, left, was a good example.

Bill and I would meet occasionally in his state capitol office concerning legislation. Even though he and I had split socially, we both knew that we had to get along in public.

I accompanied Bill and Hillary on their inaugural day activities only days after first meeting them at the Governor's Mansion.

Marvin Bush, George and Barbara's son, came to Little Rock during the 1988 campaign. Even though Bill was Michael Dukakis's co-chairman, I was allowed to escort the Bush siblings and others around the state.

Even George Bush's brother Bucky came down from Missouri to campaign.

Years before when I worked for Frank and Gay White, the previous Republican governor and First Lady of Arkansas, I had contact with the Bush family. Barbara Bush was a pleasure to meet.

'George Junior' as we called George Bush's eldest son, George W. Bush, is now the governor of Texas. Considered a likely presidential candidate in the year 2000, George is a more folksy version of his father.

George Bush made several trips to Arkansas during the 1988 campaign. To this day I have yet to understand the relationship between Bush and Clinton.

Neil Bush, George's son who was implicated in the Silverado Savings and loan scandal, was the most personable of the Bush siblings.

This photo, taken on Jack Stephens's jet, captures one of the most enjoyable moments of the 1988 presidential campaign. Senator Strom Thurmond of South Carolina was a joy to meet. Then a still-spry 85 years old, he could still bring a crowd to its feet while stumping for Bush.

Celebrities flocked to Bill, they still do. I enjoyed the parties with celebrities like Leslie Nielsen, right. With Becky to my right, I share a laugh with Bill's cousin, Marie Clinton. Leslie had just pulled his 'whoopie cushion' trick on the group. He was one of the funniest people I met through my work at the mansion.

My daughter Jan and Chelsea Clinton would sometimes play dress up at the mansion. Hillary thought it would be good for Chelsea to play with Jan because I was teaching her Spanish. Hillary always 'carefully selected' Chelsea's playmates.

Bill adored Chelsea and it's obvious he still does. Becky took this shot at Disney-World.

Hillary and Chelsea at Boca Raton, Florida. Hillary could indeed relax from time to time. Invariably it would be when we were out of Arkansas.

Chelsea and Goofy while at DisneyWorld.

As President of the State Troopers Association in Arkansas and Vice-chairman of the National Troopers Union, I had a platfrom to be an advocate for issues in law enforcement. Bill had always despised the police, indeed anyone in uniform. We would battle constantly over pay and benefit legislation at the state and national level.

My brother Dwayne Brown, left, and my white-collar crime partner Danny Harkins, would be witness to many of the incidents recounted in this book. Life in Arkansas will never quite be the same for them due to their friendships with me.

Justin Thornton, my attorney in Washington, DC, guided me through the maze of investigations conducted by the Office of Independent Counsel and Congress.

Many times I've wondered just how miserable I would be if I had stayed on with the Clintons. I worked (far right) with the Presidential Protection Detail many times, such as this time when Nancy Reagan was in Little Rock. Here she is greeted by Governor and Mrs. Frank White at the Little Rock Airport.

# INDEX

*American Spectator*, 33; 36; 90; 131; 160; 165; 166; 186; 201; 203; 222
AmeriSuites, 174
Angel Fire, New Mexico, 74
Aramony, Bill, 39
Arkansas Razorback, 46; 56-57; 82
ARKLA, 160; 181
Arledge, Roone, 184
Ashley, Liza, 45
Asian Economic Conference, 170

bag man, role as Clinton's, 76; 87-88
Bailey, John, 190
Barling, Arkansas, 72
Barr, Robert, 216-217
Bennett, Bob, 34-35; 37; 38; 40-41
Bennett, Jackie, 175; 204
black money campaign financing, 75; 86-87
Boca Raton Hotel Resort and Yacht Club, 50
Boca Raton, Florida, 39; 49- 58; 147; 172
Bork, Robert, 229
Bossie, David, 207-208; 210; 214
Bristow, Bill, 35; 39; 41
Brown, Becky, 27; 32; 43; 49-51; 55; 64; 70-71; 73; 79; 80; 97; 110; 114-
          116; 123-130; 133; 137-147; 153; 158-159; 164-166; 178;
          182; 188; 190-192; 199; 200; 204; 226
Brown, Benjamin, 225; 226
Brown, Bobby, 1
Brown, Caroline, 227
Brown, Dwayne, 1-3; 34; 115; 128; 160; 181; 191
Brown, Jan, 14; 194; 198-199; 226
Brown, Joann, 2
Brown, Nicholas, 226
Brown, Robert, 217
Bryant, Louis, 73-74; 145
Bryant, Winston, 167
Bumpers, Dale, 22; 136; 222
Burks, Liz, 45

## Excerpts from Crossfire:

"The Boca Raton Resort had several bars which were first class and full of patrons. With the conference being over, Bill felt a little more at ease in the hotel, not fearing being seen drunk or womanizing by any of the other governors. We met a couple of people in the bar and Bill stepped out for a few minutes, long enough for me to become concerned. As I went to look for him, I first checked the bathroom. I called his name but got no answer. Just as I was about to leave, I saw his number 13s protruding from under one of the stalls. 'Bill, are you okay?' I asked, knowing there couldn't be another foot that big in Boca Raton. 'Yeah, yeah L. D., these damned sinuses are killing me!' As I retreated to the bar, I realized what was going on. Bill knew that with my prior experiences in drug enforcement I didn't tolerate illicit drug use—particularly 'nose candy.'"

✳   ✳   ✳

"'C'mon, L. D., let's go take a leak,' the Senator commanded as Justin and I got up from the table. An aide of the Senator also got up. He apparently never went anywhere without a staff person. We walked to the rest room while the Senator had his arm around my neck. I was beginning to think that he liked me a little too much and was wondering if I might have to tell him that I peed alone when we got inside. What happened next I have never told for the public record before this. I am glad my lawyer was there as I'm sure he'll be by my side when I tell it again."